REMNANTS OF EMPIRE

Memory and Northern Rhodesia's White Diaspora

Pamela Shurmer-Smith

On 24th October 1964 (in this Act referred to as "the appointed day") the territories which immediately before the appointed day are comprised in Northern Rhodesia shall cease to be a protectorate and shall together become an independent republic under the name of Zambia; and on and after that day Her Majesty shall have no jurisdiction over those territories.

Zambia Independence Act, 1964

Gadsden Publishers

P O Box 32581, Lusaka, Zambia

Copyright © Pamela Shurmer-Smith, 2015

ISBN 978 9982 24 0932

Printed by Lightning Source UK

To Louis with love

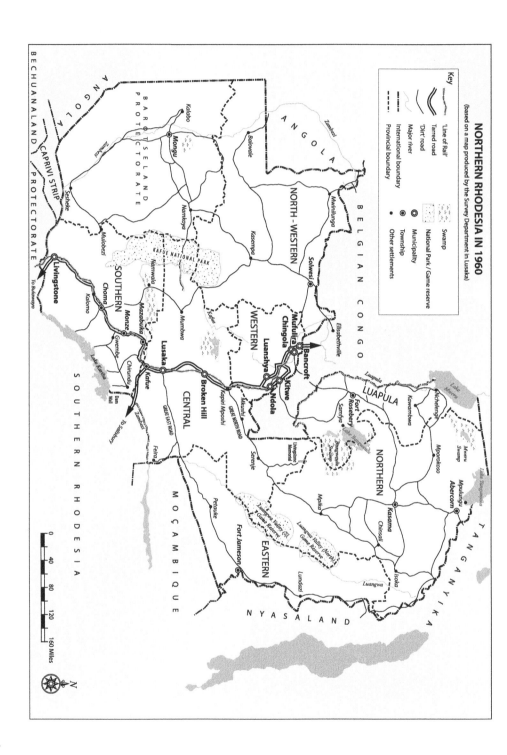

NORTHERN RHODESIA IN 1960

(based on a map produced by the Survey Department in Lusaka)

Key

'Line of Rail'
Tarred road
'Dirt' road
Major river
International boundary
Provincial boundary

Swamp
National Park / Game reserve
Municipality
Township
Other settlements

CONTENTS

1. INTRODUCTION

Remember the time when there were only three *other* countries in the known World after *Northern Rhodesia: Southern Rhodesia, Down South and Overseas?* Ron de Kock

This book is my tribute to Zambia's fifty years of Independence, but in common with most anniversaries, no matter how joyful, there is a little sadness in the background, if only that of the passing of years.

To achieve genuine Independence that was not just political but also economic and cultural, Zambia had to slough off many of the accretions of colonialism; the people figuring in this book are some of those accretions. Whatever our political sympathies had been before Independence, we had to face the fact that there would be limited opportunity for those who had enjoyed the benefits of the colonial order in Northern Rhodesia to remain long in Zambia. Apart from a few prohibited immigrants, we were not evicted, but our space for manoeuvre became increasingly constrained and gradually, for one reason or another, most of us trickled out of the country. There are, of course, notable exceptions – Guy Scott and Simon Zukas took Zambian citizenship and plunged into Zambian politics, Andrew Sardanis carved out an important business career, others continued to farm or play their part in industry, conservation or tourism and raised their children in the country but, by and large, the white colonial population eventually sought residence and careers elsewhere. Richard Hall (1966 p. 299) wrote soon after Independence, "There will still be non-African people in Zambia in considerable numbers, though it is difficult to envisage a settled population of Europeans; rather one could expect a decisive increase in the proportion of expatriates."

Memory and Memories

This book works with the vertiginous quality of memory, the way that one can be jerked back into it involuntarily or dive into it enthusiastically. It considers the comfort of memory, memory like a blanket one can snuggle into and feel safe, but it does not neglect memory as stark realisation – memory with a shudder of embarrassment or horror. What we remember and how we feel about our memories is influenced by who we are now, but that "now" implies both the present era and the present moment (everyone who lived in Central Africa recognises the gradations of the present – "just now", "now", "now-now"). Who we have become and how we feel at a particular moment are both important to what we remember and how we remember it; context matters and, since we cannot remember everything all the time, what we forget and when we forget it can be as interesting as what is recalled. Current theorists agree that we create our memories and our memories create us.

Memories can be actively sought out, but they can rise up unbidden, prompted by unexpected triggers – Draaisma (2006) quotes Nooteboom as saying that, "Memory is like a dog that lies down where it pleases". It is malleable (or plain unreliable), the product of rummaging, discarding, classifying and interpreting the stuff of the past to construct a narrative that makes sense of the present but, whilst reminiscing can be a solitary pursuit, it is often dialogical – people talk over their experiences, fine-tuning one another's accounts. Remembering is a way of drawing close to others and this book tries to catch some of the conversational spirit of reminiscence. Halbwachs (1992) introduced the idea of collective memory, the strengthening of community by means of shared remembrance, but this simultaneously identifies "outsiders", the people excluded from the common past.

People whose youth was spent in colonial Northern Rhodesia often comment that their memories marginalise them in the places where they have settled. The Women's Institute in an English village may be delighted to have a speaker on the peculiarities of housekeeping in Central Africa, but just the once – keep going on about "the good old days" and one ceases to be interesting, becoming a tedious "When we". Most people learn to self-censor, aiming to live resolutely in the present, but that means sacrificing personal depth – other than the exotic, what does one talk about when others reminisce about their youth? The difficulty of fitting in in a new country, where few have the same past or play the same remembering game, is a recurrent theme in this book. Northern Rhodesian associations, reunions, long-distance friendships and social media mitigate a sense of having the "wrong" set of memories, allowing dispersed people to communicate in situations where shared milestones mark out their history, where words and practices are recognised.

Old Age

Given that there is agreement amongst those who study memory, from whatever discipline, that it is as much to do with the present as the past, it becomes important to consider whose remembering informs this book. The majority are people who have graduated into the grandparental (or great-grandparental) generation – most are retired and less influential than they once were, many have downsized their residences and curtailed their activities. From their current standpoint, the remembered colonial past is enticing – bright, spacious and dynamic, an altogether better place than the present. In *Diary of a Man of Fifty*, Henry James, writing of a return to Italy ponders the way a place can take one back:

I seem to be living my youth over again; all the forgotten impressions of that enchanting time come back to me. At the moment they were powerful enough; but they afterwards faded away. What in the world became of them? Whatever becomes of such things, in the long intervals of consciousness? Where do they hide themselves away? In what unvisited cupboards and crannies of our being do they preserve themselves? They are like the lines of a letter written in sympathetic ink; hold the letter to the fire for a while and the grateful warmth brings out the invisible words.

Several people remarked that unless we record our memories of Northern Rhodesia they will die with us; certainly memory dies with the person, but modern psychology regards memory as a competence rather than a thing – we *do* it rather than possess it. From this viewpoint, the death of memory means that no one will ever do our remembering the way we do; recorded events, no matter how minutely described, will acquire new meanings, or no meaning at all. Whilst many of us instinctively think of our memories as being a bit like photographs or films, there is no cabinet in the brain where memories are stored – they are lost if we do not do the work of remembering, just as surely as muscles weaken for lack of exercise. The best we can hope for in terms of posterity is that the next generation affectionately remembers how we recounted our past, but they will interpret it in their own way, just as they will spend their inheritance in their own way.

Drawing on Deleuzian notions of the embodiment of memory, I argue that as our bodies age the memories we produce acquire new meanings and value, becoming more richly coloured and more interesting than the mundane events they grew out of. Bendien (2012) regards the phenomenon of reminiscence in old people as a tactic for evaluating change and a device for repositioning in a new world, rather than evidence of pathological preoccupation with what is gone that is prompted by the realisation that life is over. If we agree with her, we can think of remembering as learning to be old in a creative way that refuses marginalisation.

A member of the *Northern Rhodesia/Zambia (NR/Z)* Facebook group put up the meme, "Inside every old person there is a young person wondering what the Hell happened" – it wasn't original, but it catches the focus of this book – the dialogue between what we think we were and what we think we are. I may occasionally pull in philosophers or psychologists who have illuminated my thinking, but because I'm an anthropologist I'm happier working with encounters with real people when I try to answer the profound existential question: *What the Hell happened?*

The reminiscence bump

Psychologists maintain that around the age of sixty people experience the "reminiscence bump", starting to think frequently about the events of adolescence and young adulthood. I retired a week after my sixtieth birthday and, dead on cue, found my mind straying to my youth in Africa. I had long considered nostalgia to be a maudlin emotion of self-indulgent regret and was reluctant to spend my remaining years wallowing in a warm bath of reminiscence, so I decided to put my new-found relationship with the past to work by redefining it as ethnography. I'd taught postcolonial theory in my final years at the University of Portsmouth and embarked upon an ambitious research project to discover the afterlives of other "white" people who had lived in Zambia when it was a British colony. As the people I approached were all over the age of ten at Independence, this book is the view from old age, written from the top of the reminiscence bump.

Autobiography and Memoir

Northern Rhodesia was always an under-represented country that never inspired much literature. Though there is travel writing going all the way back to Livingstone, biographies of pioneers like Chirupula Stevenson, and ethnographic monographs from the Rhodes-Livingstone Institute, there is little to get one's teeth into regarding the ordinary lives of the ordinary European population. Occasional visitors wrote sweeping generalisations about the vulgarity of white Copperbelt society from a shuddering remove, but did not engage with it. Colonial officers and other professionals have published their memoirs, but the memoirist always writes assuming that his or her life is interesting to others, not because it is routine. Autobiography exalts exceptionalism, but ethnography does not. This book seeks to give voice to a wide slice of the former colonial population, so I like to think of it as a venture in collective memoir writing – not just the representation of varied experiences but also a cacophony of contradictory ideologies.

It would be a strange society where everyone was the same, but often it seems that those who write about imperialism assume there was a typical colonial personality (protected by a pith helmet). Charles Allen's *Tales from the Dark Continent* unashamedly reinforces this stereotype by favouring the "top division" of British African colonies (so Northern Rhodesia hardly gets a mention) and the experiences of District Officers over other colonial personnel; but anyone who lived in Northern Rhodesia knows that the European population was very varied indeed, not just in terms of the usual social indicators of occupation and education, age and sex, but also in nationality and relationship to the world outside the territory. I have captured as many different viewpoints as possible, aiming to avoid what Chimamanda Adichie (2009) calls "The danger of the single story", the what-everyone-knows story about a place and time that casts its shadow over people and events. In the case of colonialism the single story told today is often one of exploitation and brutality; I want to disturb its unity.

Many people who appear in this book have continuing relations with Zambia and affection for the country, others remember Northern Rhodesia as a lost Utopia, going so far as to frame Zambia as a usurper and despoiler. Some visit when they can, but many refuse to contemplate return, claiming that the country they loved has gone for good. In telling the story of the white diaspora, it is unavoidable that I confront beliefs and attitudes that were laid down in the colonial past, but as it is the site of my own youth, I believe that I do understand the contradictions of postcolonial melancholia. Just as colonial residents differed from one another, there are wide variations in their postcolonial selves, but there is also commonality. At its most fundamental, there is shared memory of a good climate, open landscape, brilliant light, the scents and the sounds. They lived through the same rapid political transformations and heard the same news bulletins. Beyond this, there is recognition (not necessarily admiring) of each other.

Terminology

Northern Rhodesia was named for Cecil John Rhodes of the British South Africa Company, so the appellation is inherently colonial. African people rejected Rhodesia long before Independence, but when I asked Zambian friends what they called the country before the term Zambia became part of the independence struggle, I knew it was tactless, provoking one of them to say bitterly, "I was a British Protected Person". Europeans often sidestep the problem by writing "Northern Rhodesia/Zambia" (or just NR/Z), but few people talk like this – mostly they juggle the two names, so I use Northern Rhodesia for pre-Independence stories, Zambia for post-Independence and NR/Z for a slippery continuity.

The problem of nomenclature also applies to towns – several had colonial names that were replaced after Independence, Livingstone being the one remaining exception. I intend to employ whatever place names the people in this study use, shifting between the two realities. In this I am leaning on the example of the veteran politician, Alexander Grey Zulu (2007), whose memoirs refer to Broken Hill as the site of his early political activity but switch to Kabwe for post-Independence events. Fort Rosebery, Bancroft, Abercorn and Fort Jameson will appear in this book more often than Mansa, Chililabombwe, Mbala and Chipata.

What should one call the people at the heart of this book? Back in Northern Rhodesia they were "Europeans" (as they are in Zambia today, when they aren't called *muzungus*). It was an official term for people of European descent, regardless of how many generations back. Many of these "Europeans" were South Africans who had never set foot in Europe and had no desire to do so, others were born in Northern or Southern Rhodesia. "European" meant "white", but "white" was not used officially because it evoked South African *apartheid* with its *blankes* and *nie-blankes* divisions. Though the classification ought to be meaningless by now, it was at the heart of the colonial social order. Wainaina (2006) remarks that in clichéd writing about Africa, "people" are white, whereas "the people" are black; sometimes it may seem as if I am straying close to this trap, but as this book is *about* white people, I will often drop the adjective.

The research

I received unstinting help from people who expressed enthusiasm for seeing a lost society represented and have gone to considerable lengths to provide information. Alison Poole, who transcribed notes from conversations with her father, John Orr-Ewing, wrote:

I am not surprised that you have had a good response – most old Africa colonials that I know love to reminisce about their time there! We had fun working out where he had been when and I was very surprised that with a little digging he was pretty sure even of the month he moved from one place to the next! I don't think I could do that for my own life.

What has initially been correspondence with strangers has frequently developed into acquaintanceship or friendship and I have been given generous hospitality. In such a small society it was almost inevitable that I should encounter people from my past, or people who knew people I had known long ago; usually this has been a joyful experience, occasionally it has not. Certainly, this has been an unusual research experience and one of near total immersion. Without initially intending to, I have found myself practising the fashionable "autoethnography", whereby one looks reflexively at oneself as part of the research instead of trying to hold aloof from it. When I play back audio-recordings of interviews, I realise that an outsider might find it difficult to tell who is interviewing whom as interviewees quiz me and I hear myself recounting events or remembering people I had forgotten until that moment. Occasionally I hear my voice sliding into long-lost Central African tones. Doris Lessing (1982) wrote in an essay on Laurens van der Post that there is, "A white man's malaise, an unappeasable hunger for what is out of reach. All white-African literature is the literature of exile; not from Europe but from Africa."

This book examines the experiences and emotions of former Northern Rhodesians who were caught up in the transition to postcoloniality and it looks at the post-colonial lives they constructed. It is not an apology for colonialism, but it is not an exercise in postcolonial guilt either. I believe that colonialism was an inevitable stage in world history that left its imprint upon everyone involved, in whatever capacity and with whatever ideology. I don't believe that the people who lived and worked in British protectorates were more implicated in the colonial enterprise than those who remained in Britain. I believe that history unfolds according to unavoidable economic, technological and political processes – terrible things happen in every era but there are always people struggling against the tide. I hope that this account of the Europeans of Northern Rhodesia will demonstrate that this colonial population had the same mix of good and evil as is found elsewhere and that it was made up of people constructed by their situation, trying to stay afloat.

2. WHO WERE THE NORTHERN RHODESIANS?

I don't care where they will come from, Great Britain, Holland, Germany, South Africa, Australia, America – it doesn't matter a damn ... *Roy Welensky*

The Early Days

Though we retain an image of David Livingstone catching sight of the Victoria Falls in 1855, there was no effective integration of Northern Rhodesia into the British Empire until the twentieth century:

> *Previous to 1899 the whole territory had been vaguely included in the Charter granted to the British South Africa Company, but in that year the Barotseland North Western Rhodesia Order in Council placed the administration of the western portion of the country by the Company on a firm basis; this was closely followed by the North-Eastern Rhodesia Order in Council of 1900 with similar effect. The two territories were amalgamated in 1911 under the designation of Northern Rhodesia* (Colonial Report Northern Rhodesia 1924 p. 4).

Sampson's (1956) survey of "people" (i.e. white people) who had been to Northern Rhodesia before 1902 shows there were 874 visitors (42 of whom were Portuguese who had explored part of the territory, mostly around Lake Mweru, before Livingstone's arrival), of these, only 74 were women and 48 children. Few were settlers and Sampson generously includes everyone known to have ventured as far as the banks of the Zambezi, on the grounds that they might have put their toes in it and touched Northern Rhodesia. He notes that there was something of a boom in European activity in the 1870s when 57 Europeans arrived, mostly men associated with the ivory trader, George Westbeech, who is credited with facilitating the settlement of the first missionaries in Barotseland, paving the way for the incursion of the British South Africa Company.

Sampson's choice of 1902 for his list was significant. It marked the arrival of the railway at the southern bank of the Zambezi and saw the end of the second Boer War, causing a surge in migration northwards. The BSA Company's agent had already established that there was copper in the North and in this fateful year of 1902 their consulting engineer Davey discovered lead at the site that became Broken Hill (now Kabwe). The BSA Company's *Rhodesia Civil List* for 1902 mentions North Western Rhodesia, but gives no information about its officers, other than that, "It has an Administrator, Mr R T Coryndon, who resides at Lealui." North Eastern Rhodesia seemed more important at the time, connected as it was to Nyasaland; it had 53 administrative posts and the list reveals that, "The white population is about 120."

After the opening of the Falls Railway Bridge in 1905, European settlement became easier, a railway having already been built north of the Zambezi between Livingstone and Kalomo in readiness. The line pushed up to the mining settlement at Broken Hill by 1906 and the town developed as the northern headquarters of Rhodesia Railways. The major mineral resources of the country could not begin to be exploited until the track reached the Copperbelt in 1909, two years before the amalgamation of North Eastern and North Western Rhodesia to create a single Northern Rhodesia, still under BSA Company Rule.

Rhodes had had his eye on the copper deposits of Katanga for a while and in 1889 the BSA Company obtained an African Order in Council to administer territories north of the Zambezi, land then referred to as Northern Zambezia. As early as 1890, in return for British protection, Lewanika, paramount of the Barotse people, had been persuaded to grant the Company rights to mine, trade and build railways under the Lochner Concession. Shortly afterwards, in 1895 the Northern Territories (BSA) Exploration Company's expedition discovered, as a consequence of encountering people wearing locally produced copper ornaments, that there were deposits to be exploited in North Western Rhodesia. In 1899, its agent, George Grey, found the ancient Kansanshi copper mine (Coleman, 1971); local people had certainly not lost the mine – they had strict orders from Chilwa, a retired slave trader, not to tell European prospectors about copper deposits. Then in 1902 Collier made his famous discovery of the Copperbelt sites that were to become Roan Antelope and Bwana Mukubwa mines.

There was now every reason for speeding up railway construction to facilitate both the export of minerals and the colonisation of the territory. Large-scale commercial mining did not take place immediately, old African workings were opened up and exploited before the effective development of the Copperbelt began in 1921 (Bradley, 1952). Company rule continued until 1924, when Northern Rhodesia became a British Protectorate. Meanwhile, a more or less settled European population of traders, miners, prospectors, farmers and railway workers was growing steadily.

The Colonial Era

In that foundational year of Northern Rhodesian government from the British Colonial Office, Revenue of £309,795 was raised, predominantly in licences, excise and customs duties, court fees and land sales – there was no income tax. Even allowing for inflation, this is pretty modest for opening up a new territory. The biggest single government expenditure in 1924 was £87,585 on the Provincial Administration, followed by the Northern Rhodesia Police at £47,712. By comparison, the Public Works Department, responsible for building and maintaining roads and bridges, water supply etc. spent a mere £24,053. Only the lead/zinc mine at Broken Hill was fully in operation, though the development of the Copperbelt was under way.

The first Colonial Office report for the country gives an outline, but one wishes there were more detail on the ages and occupations of those early European residents and also their geographical distribution. The language is typically colonial:

There has never been a complete census of all persons in the Protectorate, but the figures relating to the European population are known and a fairly accurate estimate of the native population may be obtained from the Native Tax Returns. By this means it is computed that the native population numbers rather more than 1,100,000.... The European population on 1ˢᵗ April 1924 numbered 4,182 of whom 1,919 were adult males and 1,016 adult females. During the year 107 births and 40 deaths occurred. The Asiatic population is estimated to be approximately 60 and the number of 'coloured' persons about 150. The total of immigrants, exclusive of natives, was 438 of whom 407 were British subjects, 15 American and 16 belonged to other nationalities. No emigration figures are available. (Colonial Report Northern Rhodesia 1924, p 5)

When the age of majority was 21 it is likely that some of the non-adults (undifferentiated by gender) were young men who entered the country alone as adventurers. "British subjects" were not necessarily people who had come from the United Kingdom or ever lived there at all; at that time the category would have included South Africans. These were still pioneering days, but they are sufficiently recent for there to be survivors who can remember listening to grandparents' tales about blackwater fever, building mud houses and fighting off lions. Essays in the *Northern Rhodesia Journal* provide much of the flavour of these days of early exploration and settlement.

As the century progressed, the European population grew and, though immigration was the most important source of increase, it became more common for white children to be born in the territory. By 1931 there were 13,846 Europeans, the population having multiplied by three in just seven years. The main source of European migrants was South Africa, followed by the UK, but the 'thirties saw an influx into Northern Rhodesia of Jewish people escaping the rise of fascism in Europe when South Africa and Southern Rhodesia closed their doors to Jewish immigration and many who had embarked for South Africa were obliged to continue travelling north. As Shapiro (2002) recounts, though considerable numbers did settle in Northern Rhodesia, there could have been thousands more had the 1938 British Mwinilunga Plan to provide a homeland for Jewish peasant farmers in the north west of the country gone through. There was already a significant Jewish population north of the Zambezi, the pioneering Susman brothers having crossed the river in 1901 as cattle dealers, going on to become the most important traders in Northern Rhodesia (Macmillan, 2005); then in 1929 small numbers of Jews expelled from Gaza made their way to the territory. Macmillan and Shapiro (1999) give a thorough account of the arrival and settlement of Jewish families, most of whom went into trade and the professions. The peasant farming scheme foundered largely as a consequence of opposition from European mineworkers who feared that the sons of these farmers would not be satisfied on the land for long but would seek work on the mines, depressing European wages. The Acting Governor appealed to the Colonial Office thus:

The result of such an experiment would be the production of a class of poor whites whose effect on native life and custom amongst other things would be pernicious ... if they were on a subsistence basis they would tend to drift to industrial centres and become competitors in labour and trade.... Elected Members consider Jewish refugees wholly undesirable ... but any of them who possess the capital which is considered essential (£1,500) could be accommodated on vacant crown lands.... At the root of this opposition is undoubtedly deep racial bias [Quoted in Shapiro, 2002 p.19]

Polish refugees, many of them children who were orphaned or separated from their families, also were brought into Northern Rhodesia during and after the Second World War. They were housed in camps, notably at Bwana Mukubwa and Abercorn and were largely segregated from the rest of the European community, though several English families employed young Polish women to look after their children. Many moved on as soon as they could, particularly to Canada, but others remained and, like the Jewish people, became integrated into the wider population. Sir Stewart Gore-Browne, in charge of the welfare of Poles, was scathing about their ingratitude, (Rotberg, 1977 p.236) but, SG-B wasn't the easiest of men himself. There is a British Pathe News item showing the arrival of Poles by train from the South and the spartan accommodation provided for them in Lusaka (http://www.britishpathe.com/video/new-homes-for-poles-in-lusaka)

We have no population figures for the war years, but 1946 recorded a European population of 21,907; a mere five years later it had shot up to 37,221. The major influx was in the 1950s – 65,277 by 1956, then the Federal Government Census of 1961 enumerated 74,640 Europeans in the last count before Independence. By then there were 2,490,000 Africans, 7,790 Asians and 2,043 "Coloureds".

As the incomer population grew, it changed in character; initially composed predominantly of administrators, farmers, hunters and traders, it became increasingly associated with mineral extraction and thus more urbanised. With the development of the towns there was a movement towards institutional completeness and it gradually became possible for many, particularly women and children, to live in almost exclusively European enclaves. It is this world of the 1950s and early '60s that is remembered by the people who are the focus of this book.

Who were these newcomers?

To this day, it is not unusual to hear the complaint that the "wrong sort" started to arrive in the 'fifties and that the character of the colony changed for the worse. The daughter of a senior administrator told me that people started coming in large numbers from, "Places like the East End of London, people who weren't used to having servants …" Actually, as always, the majority of new immigrants came not from Britain but from South Africa; the copper mines were paying high wages to entice men with experience from South Africa's gold mines and it was a matter of catching a train or driving north, knowing that a return journey was simple if things didn't work out. South Africans knew that they were not severing ties with family at home, unless they wanted it that way – Northern Rhodesia was the far end of their backyard.

For immigrants from Britain, things were different. Post-war Britain was depressing and people cited this as a factor prompting them to look abroad. Deprivations that had been tolerated as a necessary part of the war effort continued far longer than many expected – the cities had suffered extensive bomb damage, so there were housing shortages, with overcrowding and substandard accommodation; the rationing of food, fuel, clothing and other necessities was difficult to endure in peacetime. Men who had fought abroad returned to a dreary life in cramped conditions, so it is no wonder they looked for something better, especially as many had a glimpse of this during the war. Emigration to the British dominions of Australia, New Zealand and Canada became commonplace, but a minority was drawn to the challenge of Central Africa, where there seemed to be opportunity, good wages, guaranteed sunshine and wide open spaces. Not a few had been with the RAF in Southern Rhodesia and liked the lifestyle they had seen; others knew people in East or South Africa, prompting them to put Africa generally on their list of possible homes. For some, the long distance from "home" could itself be attractive, offering the escape from cloying family and a rigidly hierarchical social structure. Although it has been argued, particularly by Stonehouse (1960) that the Europeans of Northern Rhodesia did not constitute a settler population but were temporary sojourners, target workers with the intention of earning money to invest in countries they would return to, I am less convinced.

As early as 1948 Roy Welensky, then the railway union leader serving on the Northern Rhodesia Legislative Council, was demanding a closer union with Southern Rhodesia by means of a Federation, reasoning that the combination of the mineral wealth of the North and the substantial European population in the South would facilitate a bid for Dominion status, with autonomous government and an end to Colonial Office rule. Such an ambition would hardly be typical of a transitory population. Asked by the journalist Maclear Bate what he would do if Federation were not granted, Welensky replied:

"I am going to do everything in my power to bring more Europeans into Northern Rhodesia. I don't care where they will come from, Great Britain, Holland, Germany, South Africa, Australia, America – it doesn't matter a damn – just let them have a white skin and be willing to work. The very day we have 100,000 in the country we will demand Dominion status!" (Bate, 1953 p. 26)

We forget now that politicians could be so open about their desires.

Post-war it became important to bolster agricultural production in order to feed the growing urban populations; the Northern Rhodesia Government established the Land and Agricultural Bank for the extension of loans to European farmers for the purchase of Crown Land (usually leasehold) and agricultural capital development (Makings 1966). Plots were cheaply available for rent along the line of rail, with the aim of filling gaps in European settlement. Though some took advantage of low prices and available credit to try their hand at farming, it never became a major part of the economy. The bulk of the 'forties and 'fifties immigrants were recruited into skilled or semi-skilled occupations, predominantly in mining and the railways but also in building and engineering. There was a parallel expansion of clerical and supervisory workers, teachers, nurses and a smattering of other professions. Northern Rhodesia's was a predominantly working class population and its Europeans displayed few of the airs and graces that the media likes to portray as characterising the colonial way of life. Because this European working class was a mixture of British and South African, with a leavening of continental European, a hybridized lifestyle emerged that was more South African than British, even though the Colonial Office tried to discourage British Central Africa from looking south.

Federation

The pros and cons of the constitutional change that ushered in Welensky's beloved Federation of Rhodesia and Nyasaland in 1953 do not need examining in detail as they have been covered extensively (Franklin, 1963; Welensky, 1964), but the intention of Federation was to shift the balance of power in favour of the South, deferring promised progress to African self-determination and Independence. Though Southern Rhodesia was not technically a Dominion, it was one in effect, as its dealings with the British Government were through the Dominion Office not (as in the case of Northern Rhodesia) the Colonial Office. The most evident outcome of this arrangement was that the Legislative Assembly in Southern Rhodesia had greater autonomy than the Northern Rhodesian Legislative Council. Additionally Southern Rhodesia did not have a Provincial Administration composed of Colonial Office-appointed District Officers, it practiced Roman Dutch civil law and its structures underwrote European control of the country.

Unsurprisingly, closer alliance with Southern Rhodesia was vigorously opposed by African people in Northern Rhodesia (and not a few Europeans and Asians). It was seen as a device to perpetuate European rule and the local version of *apartheid* (generally referred to as the "colour bar") and was resented for the transfer of significant revenues to the south where a superior infrastructure was developed. An unintended consequence of Federation was the consolidation of African nationalism and thus the movement towards Independence. Relations between racial groups in Northern Rhodesia were already distant, but Federation intensified the division. Virtually all African affairs, including the administration of the rural areas, education and health, policing, and public works were under the remit of the Northern Rhodesian Government; but defence, European education and health, and the revenue office fell under Federal control. Income tax was levied by the Federal Government, as were import duties.

Partly because of its geographical proximity and partly because of its stronger association with the British South Africa Company, Southern Rhodesia had a close relationship with South Africa. It is still difficult to understand the relative ease with which the Federation was established, given that immediately after the war the Colonial Office was already briefing its personnel to prepare countries for self government, then Independence, and was warning new recruits that theirs would be a short career. Many of the people who figure in this book grew up taking Federation for granted and for all practical purposes regarded Northern and Southern Rhodesia as one (Nyasaland was always something of an add-on). The countries were as close as those of the United Kingdom, many European families in the North sent their children to schools in Southern Rhodesia, travelled to the better shops in Salisbury and Bulawayo, took holidays in the Vumba Mountains and saw the country as part of the same Labour market. As Joseph Mulholland said, "Our families moved back and forth from South Africa, Zimbabwe, Zambia, Malawi, Swaziland since the 1900s".

Some statistics
I am taking the 1961 Federal Census as the basis of my outline of the European population of Northern Rhodesia because this was the last count (and only formal census) before Independence, capturing information appropriate to the "end of empire". A separate Northern Rhodesian Government Census counted

the African people and we may regard this bizarre mode of enumeration as an example of the racial and political ideology from the south that would lead to the downfall of the Federation.

Geographical Distribution

The European population of Northern Rhodesia was largely urban. Eighty five percent of Europeans were concentrated in the ten towns of the country of which seven constituted the Copperbelt, where just over fifty seven percent of the total white population of the country lived:

Kitwe	12,461
Lusaka	11,806
Ndola	9,251
Mufulira	6,737
Chingola	5,575
Luanshya	5,276
Broken Hill	4,911
Livingstone	3,881
Bancroft	2,328
Kalulushi	1,113

Three thousand one hundred and forty two European people lived in townships with a white population of more than one hundred:

Choma	585
Mazabuka	428
Fort Jameson	418
Kafue	378
Kasama	285
Fort Rosebery	224
Chilanga	202
Mongu/Lealui	178
Solwezi	177
Abercorn	148
Monze	119

Finally, 8,076 Europeans were scattered throughout the country on the farms and missions and in clusters around *Bomas* (District Administrative Headquarters). The geographical distribution of population is not broken down by gender and age, but one's impression was always of fewer women and children in the rural areas.

Age/Sex

Throughout the history of Northern Rhodesia, the European population was skewed towards youth. In 1961 25,589 out of the total population of 74,640 were under the age of fifteen – so more than a third of the population was of school age or younger. A further 15,424 were less than thirty. At the other end of the scale, there were just 2,466 Europeans over the age of sixty in the whole country, only 398 of whom were more than seventy. Overall there were more males than females, but not as many as popular wisdom would have it and the ratio of males to females is fairly balanced across all age tranches. People were arriving as couples and young families – perhaps an indication that they intended to settle. The census does not separate Europeans from other non-Africans when it publishes figures for marital status by age, so there is no way of knowing whether the reputation for young marriage, high rates of divorce and separation is born out.

Age/Sex Europeans 1961

Data Source: 1961 Census of non-Africans Republic of Zambia (Lusaka 1965)

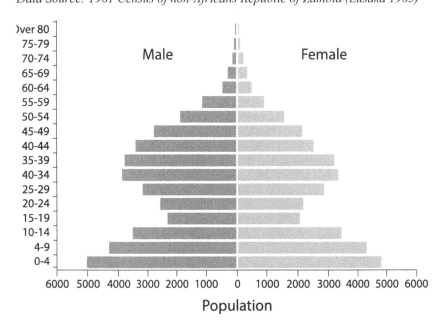

Place of birth and nationality

In 1961 48,397 out of Northern Rhodesia's European population were born somewhere in Africa; against this, only 18,900 were born in the British Isles. Though the census does not break these figures down by age, one may reasonably assume that younger people are likely to predominate in the "Born in Northern Rhodesia" group.

Place of Birth of Europeans 1961

Data Source: 1961 Census of non-Africans Republic of Zambia (Lusaka 1965)

Place of Birth	Males	Females
Northern Rhodesia	8,174	7,953
Southern Rhodesia	3,045	2,821
South Africa	12,980	12,135
Other Africa	686	603
United Kingdom	10,367	8,533
Other Europe	2,949	2,302
N & S America	421	420
Asia & Oceania	506	487
Born at sea & not stated	86	81

In terms of nationality, 28,367 people were registered as "Citizens of the United Kingdom and Colonies: Federation of Rhodesia and Nyasaland"; 21,422 were outright British Citizens and 19,417 were Citizens of the Republic of South Africa – these categories were to prove vital later on.

The Economy

Although copper was the backbone of the Northern Rhodesian economy, as Roberts (2011) points out, it did not begin to prosper until 1949, when it took off due to increased demand associated with the Korean war. There may only have been 7,480 European workers in mineral extraction in 1961, but there were 37,582 Africans and copper mining alone directly contributed 44.1% of the Gross Domestic Product – more if one counts allied industries. The downside of this was that the country was always at the mercy of changeable global demand, with corresponding peaks and troughs in pricing, resulting locally in unstable demand for labour and fluctuating wages. The copper bonuses, sometimes more than doubling an annual salary, were famous, but less attention is paid to the fact that virtually all miners of all races were on daily contracts, making for a highly flexible workforce, to the advantage of the mining companies. It also meant fluctuating government revenues. The Zambian government would inherit the consequences of this instability when the international price of copper crashed in the mid-1970s with the end of the Vietnam War.

Other economic activity in Northern Rhodesia tended to be ancillary to mineral extraction – the major function of the railway was the transportation of minerals; commercial farming fed the urban population; most industry in Northern Rhodesia was associated with mining, the railways or farming; the service sector followed the European population. A large part of the Northern Rhodesian economy fell within the subsistence sector, rural populations directly provisioning themselves.

Employment

According to the census, 24,327 European men and 8,940 women were in employment in 1961. Frankly, I do not believe the low figure for women and would hazard that many women working part-time were simply not counted as employed. The census atypically classified employment by industry rather than by occupation, so we cannot make the generalisations based on class so beloved of sociologists. Presented this way we cannot separate professionals from artisans and auxiliaries, so the municipal water-meter reader and the Provincial Commissioner would both fall into the category "Government Service". The women recorded as employed in mining were in offices and ancillary work rather than underground, but the census does not tell us this. The major fields of employment were:

Mining - 7,480 (6982 males/ 498 females)
Commerce & Retail - 6,017 (3,157 males/ 2,860 females)
Community Service - 5,095 (2,362 males/ 2,733 females) (includes teachers, health workers, clergy and lawyers)
Government Service - 3,841 (2,843 males/ 998 females)

Transport & Communications -

> 3,041 (2,462 males/579 females) (dominated by
> 1,756 employed by railway)

Manufacturing (mostly metals and transport related) -

> 2,372 (1,958 males/ 414 females)

Agriculture & Forestry -   1,508 (1,381 males/ 127 females)

The size of the Commerce and Retail group, taken together with Community Service, indicates that there had been progression well beyond the "frontier" stage and that Europeans were settling in, but, depressingly, the data reveal that this was a society without professional actors, artists and musicians.

The census provides meagre data and there are topics one would like to have information on that are missing. There is nothing about length of residence in the country, family size, households owning their homes, levels of educational attainment. We do, however, have a minute breakdown of religious affiliation. (There were: 25,253 Anglicans; 11,414 Roman Catholics; 9,042 Presbyterians; 8,458 Dutch Reformed; 7,119 Methodists; 707 Jews … through many more down to the 8 members of the Church of Sweden, not forgetting the 3,631 who profess "None").

But who were they really?

Bald statistics cannot tell us who the Northern Rhodesians really were; we may have their places of birth, ages, genders, occupations etc. but these do not explain why these particular people were living in the country or what they were like personally. Normally one would turn to the arts to get some feel for a society at a particular point in time and space, but Northern Rhodesia was notably short of artistic endeavour. However, we do know that all the Europeans who fetched up in Northern Rhodesia were looking for something better, whether they were escaping tyranny, poverty, dull routine, narrow horizons, or just meddlesome relatives; otherwise, they were the children of these adventurers. Every family had its own foundational myth and the next chapter shows that arriving was never just a journey, it was a bid for a transformation.

Probably the most famous of the men intending to achieve something better than they had been dealt were Stuart Gore-Browne, who reinvented himself in a glorious *folie de grandeur* from minor gentry into local "aristocracy" with a self-built stately home and grand estate, (Lamb, 2000) and John Edward Stevenson who mutated from telephone clerk into the polygamous chieftain, Chirupula (Rukavina, 1951). Perhaps not quite as spectacularly as these, everyone was striving to become something.

The two most visible categories of Europeans in Northern Rhodesia were the miners and the Provincial Administration – accounts almost universally depict the former as boorish, the latter as effortlessly gentlemanly; however, miners were not famous for writing their memoirs and district officers were. Representations of white miners as overpaid, uniformly philistine racists arise from a combination of class condescension and resentment – Robin Short, serving as DC Bancroft felt undervalued when posted to the Copperbelt and remarked that:

The European mineworkers ... were enjoying a copper bonus of over 100%, that is over double their mine salary and which often, for mere routine jobs, totalled two, three or four hundred pounds every month. Unfortunately this privilege did not extend to servants of Government. (Short, 1973 p. 115)

It was easy to ignore the fact that these "mere routine jobs" carried out in sweltering heat underground yielded the only real source of wealth in the territory – but admittedly the men doing them hadn't been to Cambridge.

Barbara Carr is similarly aggrieved that:

We of the government huddled in our derelict houses overlooking our neglected gardens and tried to pretend that we were shabbily genteel and very much more important in the scheme of things than our flashy, rich neighbours in the nearby mining towns ... (Carr, 1963 p. 217)

There seems to be a near universal indignation from visiting commentators that working class men could earn so much and were provided with such generous fringe benefits:

Besides being the home of a gushing and open-handed capitalism, the Copperbelt was also a miniature Welfare State conceived on lines which made the similar arrangement in the United Kingdom seem parsimonious. Houses were provided for all the workers at nominal and markedly sub-economic rents; I visited homes that would not have disgraced the Surrey hills ... the mining companies tried to soften the impact of this hot desolation for the workers and their families by furnishing them with gorgeous social and sports clubs where the subscription rates were trifling. (Dunn, 1959 p. 137)

Ronald Prain (Chairman of RST) explained that the companies did not pay their workers more than they needed to and that the year after the famous 102% bonus in 1956 when the price was £437 per ton:

As so often happens in the copper industry, this boom was followed by a recession of comparable magnitude; in 1957 the price fell to £180 ... It became a matter of urgency for the company to prune production costs. (Prain, 1981 p.115)

That pruning meant workers and all were conveniently on daily contracts. Of the famous perks Prain explains:

The development of the Copperbelt townships on 'garden city' lines had been part of a planned policy on the part of the big mining groups and carried out in close collaboration with government authorities ... They were determined to do something brand new in the mining world and get away from the traditional squalor of the North American mining camps. At first, American mining men who visited the Copperbelt were scornful of this approach; they thought that the money spent on amenities on such a grand scale was wasteful. It was not long before they were following our example. They learned the lesson that it is not sufficient for a mining company merely to have employees, but to be successful it must have employees who are happy and contented, and the more attractive their conditions, the longer they are likely to stay. (ibid. p.79)

Why so much resentment of miners? Without the benefits it would have been difficult to recruit European miners to the wilds of Central Africa, whereas the graduates of the ancient universities were queuing up to join the colonial service. The housing, schools, hospitals and clubs attracted solid family men in the 'fifties, in contrast to the earlier days of single quarters, hard drinking and brawling of the kind depicted in Courtenay's novel, *The Power of One*. Not that the new recruits were all angels.

Even anthropologists, usually so meticulous in their examination of African social life in both towns and villages, do not balk at lumping all white mineworkers together in a homogenous mass, the result of casual observation rather than engagement. Though Hortense Powdermaker had the good grace to say that she was considering Europeans only as they impacted on Africans, this did not prevent her selecting a single British mine employee to describe in detail

– someone who was aggressive and foul-mouthed, discontented with his lowly status in African-housing maintenance:

An Englishman of working class background ... his bitterness, his sense of frustration, his unconcealed feelings of violence were extreme. He talked compulsively and unceasingly about the 'kaffirs'; a deep and desperate hatred of them seemed to pervade his whole being ... he curses and kicks them if he thinks he can get away with it ... hatred poured out of Mr T and his wife like the violent torrential downpours of the rainy season. (Powdermaker, 1962 pp 77-81).

I don't doubt that Mr and Mrs T existed and we probably all met people like them but, though she recognises he is an extreme case, Powdermaker does not lavish similar detail on other mineworkers. Why did she select him as her example? Why mention that he was "working class" if he was a manual worker? She carries on, "The kick, given as a matter of course, was not an unusual form of communication between Europeans and Africans." I never lived on the Copperbelt, but I never saw anyone kick anyone else either.

Whereas memoirs present the lives of District Officers from an insider viewpoint, we typically get an external view of the miners. Administrators' accounts usually provide background on their families, their education and activities prior to joining the service, giving a fairly good impression of who they were (including their unconsciously expressed vanities), but when others mention officers of Her Majesty's Overseas Civil Service it is rare that they can resist a sideswipe about privilege, prestige and preoccupation with status.

Whilst they were a relatively small group, colonial administrators were an important part of the European community and, recruited from the public schools and ancient universities, they constituted an unambiguous elite that was significant beyond their numbers. If the miners were unjustly represented as overpaid and uniformly philistine, the PA were equally unjustly depicted as conceited and remote. Most of the PA were recruited in the United Kingdom and measures were put in place to maintain their personal and emotional ties to Britain, perhaps the most important being the requirement that they take regular long "home" leave. Frequent transfers within the country, together with the education of their children in boarding schools, worked to separate administrators from the bulk of the European population, but they were anyway socially and culturally distinctive. They were not permitted to buy land or indulge in commercial activities and from the very beginning of their service, administrators expected to retire back in Britain in late middle-age. The expensively maintained ties with the UK (along with medical care and government accommodation) served exactly the same purpose as the miners' social provision – they kept the workforce content, but they also kept them removed from the mass. It was rare for the PA or their children to pick up Southern African accents or lifestyles; they did, however, generally acquire a greater knowledge of the country, its people and its languages than the majority of Europeans. Not a few government servants had colonial backgrounds as children of the empire, with fathers serving in administration, police, army or forestry and there are several children of tea planters – such people were more intimately connected to the British Empire than to Britain itself.

By no means everyone in government service was in the Provincial Administration – there was a large number of ancillary posts of varying degrees of professionalism. Frank Bennett's *Under an African Sun* may be subtitled *Memoirs of a Colonial Officer*, but it is a telling portrait of the life of a man, "Assigned a junior clerk's job as cashier and receptionist at the Ministry of Finance's front desk" (Bennett, 2006 p.26). His main concern was to keep his head above water in hierarchical Lusaka society. Similarly Pitchford (2013), employed in the youth service, writes of working in Lusaka:

I was regularly seen jogging to work, sticking out like a sore white thumb, down the Ridgeway in Lusaka, amongst thousands of black workers. I was hauled up before someone in Establishments and given a dressing down 'for behaviour unbecoming to an officer of the Colonial Service'. (Kindle edition.)

If neither statistics nor generalisations can do justice to the nature of the European colonial population of Northern Rhodesia, perhaps we will fare better with a discordant clamour of voices articulating multiple memories in the remaining chapters.

3. ARRIVAL

A journey that will stay with me for the rest of my life *Norman Baker*

Northern Rhodesia's European population grew largely through immigration and behind the bald statistics are real people making momentous decisions to leave one home to set up another. It is no wonder that stories about the journey to the country and first impressions of it have acquired the status of foundational myths, where arriving is not just a matter of moving, it is a kind of personal re-invention. Though I initially asked about decisions to leave Zambia, people wrote much more fully about journeys of arrival, first impressions and early experiences, than they did regarding their arrangements for departure. These arrival stories are far from identical; they vary by decade, by point of departure, by the age of the teller, by mode of transport and by the reason for the move, but what they have in common is a sense of the importance of the event. This is particularly the case for those coming from Europe, crossing the equator to come to live in Africa, the continent that carries so much freight in the European psyche. The journey out is not just a passage, it is a *rite de passage* – before it the storyteller was one sort of person, afterwards another, the journey constituting the liminal stage that wrought the magic of transformation.

It seems that no one who was not a babe in arms at the time ever forgot the journey. Its minute detail is stored and recounted as the most precious sort of memory, the kind that helps one understand oneself. In common with others, my own recollections are indelible. My father had gone ahead by plane to work for the Broken Hill Municipal Council, my mother and I followed a few weeks later by Union Castle Liner. I remember her apprehension at Southampton Docks in contrast to my own excitement – she cried when the band on the quayside played *Will ye no come back again?* in drizzling rain, whereas the twelve-year old me was carelessly thrilled at the adventure before us and the anticipated romance of the African interior, but before that it would be the wonders of a cabin with a porthole, the dining room and what seemed lavish choice, the apparent sophistication of our fellow passengers, the novelty of a steward running our salt-water baths, flying fish, dancers at Las Palmas (where my mother was too timid to venture ashore), the crossing-the-line ceremony … then Table Mountain! Next, the glory of the train journey, pressing northward, my mother becoming increasingly depressed by the dust and the poverty as we chuffed across the Karoo and Bechuanaland (as it was then) whilst I fell wildly in love with the bigness and the dryness. When we arrived in the middle of the night my mother was terrified and furious because my father was not there – the station was dark and deserted. No one had told her that it was customary to sleep until morning in one's carriage shunted into a siding. For the first time I was a bit spooked too. Next morning there was my father beaming with joy! Fifty-seven years later, a sleeper car on a train unfailingly evokes that epic journey and the scent of a gardenia draws me back to that first day in Broken Hill, when the Town Clerk took us to have breakfast at his house, plucked a flower for me from a bush in his garden and showed me oranges growing. I thought I had landed up in paradise.

Judy Rawlinson was unusual in being offered the choice, aged only thirteen in 1955, whether to accompany her mother to Africa or to stay with her grandmother in "grimy post-war London", but I recognised many parallels with my own voyage, though hers carried onward and upward to the Luapula province:

Being an avid reader and picture-goer and ever the romantic, my image of Africa was of sun-parched, tawny savannahs over which a suntanned Anthony Steel strode, immaculate in bush jacket and khaki shorts, while herds of giraffe, zebra and wildebeest cantered under thorn trees in the background. I had seen the film "Where No Vultures Fly".

Judy gives a detailed account of the voyage out and the railway journey north and I regret that there is not enough space for it here but:

Finally... our train arrived at Ndola Station, the railhead. I spotted Dad in a sea of bobbing faces, black and white. He wore long khaki shorts and a white shirt, looked thinner than I remembered but his honey-coloured hair was bleached by the sun. His eyes looked bluer than ever in a tanned face. That was an amazing day.

We stayed at the Government Rest House, reigned over by the formidable Mrs Perry. I was later to learn that mud and dust were anathema within these walls, its rooms redolent of Cobra floor polish ... From Ndola we faced a 150-mile trek up to the Luapula Province on dirt roads, the worst section being through the 40 miles of Congo Pedicle ... The red laterite road stretched endlessly ahead, with hardly a curve, through low forest. MMBA – Miles and Miles of Bloody Africa .... After 40 miles we reached the exit border post and the Luapula River.... Another

65 miles, through a tsetse fly barrier and we were practically home.

But how different were these journeys, with their through bookings London/ Southampton/Cape Town/Bulawayo/onwards, were from the stories cherished by third or fourth generation Northern Rhodesians. David Gray, an electrical engineer, began his story with an account of his grandparents coming from England:

My paternal grandfather, David John Gray, arrived in South Africa in November 1899 as a member of the 2nd Battalion East Sussex contingent sent to fight in the Anglo Boer War. After the war he found that Africa had 'got into his blood' and so he was demobilised in South Africa and sent for his wife, Mary Jane Gray and their two children, Ellen and Wyndham. They arrived on one of the troop ships sent from England to repatriate the army.

The family settled in Teakworth in the Transvaal where Grandfather had managed to secure work as a ganger on the railway. Eight years and four additional children later my Grandparents decided to travel north to the newly opened territory of Northern Rhodesia. Working in the predominantly Afrikaans Transvaal where anti-British sentiment ran high had finally made them take this decision.

A 12 day train journey brought them to Mazabuka, where the station master's wife allowed them to sleep in a tent after providing them with a cooked dinner. Next day an 8 hour ox-wagon journey completed the journey. Grandfather had been accepted for the post of assistant manager on the Nanga Estate, which was run by Ben Woest on behalf of the owner, the Duke of Westminster. He saw this as a stepping-stone to his own farm and within a few years had acquired a suitable property at nearby Nega Nega through the 'Soldier-Settler Scheme'. They named the farm Honiton because of connections with lace-making and settled down to raise their family and make their fortunes.

David Gray's old school friend, Ron de Kock could match this story:

My big Afrikaner great grandfather, Piet Geldenhuys, arrived in Bulawayo early in 1896 in time to take part in the Matabele rebellion. There he met and married Francina Prinsloo, my Great-grandmother. When George Pauling built the railway line to the Victoria Falls Oupagrootjie received the contract to supply the railway workers with meat by shooting game …. When the railway line reached the Vic. Falls there was a three year wait to build the Falls bridge.

During this time my Grandmother, Petronella, came into the World on 19th December 1902.

The railway line eventually reached the site of Lusakaas (original spelling) in 1906. My Oumagrootjie said she was tired of living in an ox wagon, so her ever-dutiful husband bought a farm in the district. I understand he was one of the first white farmers there. A further six children arrived. Meanwhile my Grandfather, Piet de Lange, arrived in NR from Fort Beaufort – he met and married Ouma Petronella early in 1918. Yep! She was just fifteen, child-bearing women were in short supply in those early years. My beloved Mother, Francina de Lange was born in 1919 and four siblings followed.

My de Lange grandparents bought a small fifteen hundred acre farm six miles outside Broken Hill called 'Makululu'. Meanwhile my father, Willie de Kock, arrived originally from Komgha, then Southern Rhodesia. He worked for Rhodesia Railways in BH, met Mom there and they got married in 1936 on Mom's seventeenth birthday. In 1937 Dad went to work on the Roan Antelope Mine in Luanshya.

Some people had multiple arrivals, with a new experience each time. Like David Gray and Ron de Kock, Dr Michael James Cairns' family went back a long way, but in his case we are looking at a family with a colonial history, professional qualifications and greater geographical range:

My father, James Williams Cairns came to NR in 1926. He had spent most of his childhood in South Africa and India.... He trained as a Mining Engineer/ Geologist at the Royal School of Mines, Imperial College, London and was recruited by Anglo American for NR. The company required all their young men from overseas to be single for their first year, when he surveyed country near Broken Hill for minerals and made the first accurate maps. At the time, the only maps were made by untrained 'old timers'....

My mother, Kathleen Mary Lyons, a doctor, had been engaged to my father for three years when he left for NR. She came out alone to Cape Town in April 1927. They married in St George's Cathedral; no other member of either family was present. They set off by train arriving five days later in Broken Hill and were met by Dr Wallace, the only doctor there, who persuaded my mother to start work 3 days' later, mainly, it was said, so that his daily 9 holes of golf starting at 4pm were not disturbed by calls. She was, I believe, the first lady doctor to work in NR. Every two weeks she travelled to Lusaka by rail, being taken on a hand propelled platform, to hold a clinic there as there was no doctor. My older brother Peter was born at Broken Hill in December 1928 and I at Nkana in October 1931 before Kitwe was built.

One can only wonder at the romance of a young doctor sailing out alone to marry, then serving a new mining community in the interior – an arrival story to match *Out of Africa* but there was promotion back in England in 1935, then:

We moved to Kosovo in 1937 when my father was employed as a Mine Captain at a Lead, Zinc and Vanadium mine near Mitroviça, owned by Rio Tinto. My mother could not work there (British Medical qualifications were not recognised), so she taught me. My brother Peter travelled alone to an English school at Chateau-d'Oex in Switzerland, changing trains at Milan with a large luggage label showing his name, parents' address and destination.

In 1938 my parents decided war with Germany was inevitable and, since there were few openings for metalliferous mining engineers in Britain, my father travelled alone back to NR hoping to find employment, while my mother and now 3 sons stayed at Chateau- d'Oex, where I started formal school.

In 1939 they returned to Africa, the eldest boys to school in Johannesburg, their parents working in Nkana. In 1944 they moved to the Gold Coast then back to the Copperbelt in 1950, where his father became Personal Assistant to Sir Ronald Prain of the RST at Mufulira.

In December 1945 Peter and I sailed on the Aquitania, a troop ship, from Cape Town to Southampton. My mother and David followed in January 1946. My mother set up home in Poole and worked as a doctor in Public Health. I attended Bryanston School and trained in Medicine at Cambridge and the Middlesex Hospital, London 1950-1956 ... But Africa calls back the young medical student, who spent the long vacation 1952 working and travelling in Northern Rhodesia:

At the Middlesex Hospital I was very fortunate to meet Faith, the daughter of a Scottish Presbyterian Minister and a doctor. Faith, a Secretary who had worked in the City of London, decided her calling was to train as a nurse. We married in London in February 1957 and left for Durban in November to work at an Anglican hospital at Nqutu, Zululand under two experienced doctors.... The six months there was invaluable in preparing us for Katete, where I was to be the only doctor for the first 3 years, from June 1958. We remained at St Faiths until retirement in 1996.

Post-war

As the population statistics showed, the great era of migration to Northern Rhodesia was post-war; many of the migrants had served abroad in the forces and were finding a humdrum life in Britain was not what they had fought for. Ray Crichell, who became a fireman, expressed a *Boys' Own* ambition:

I had always wanted to 'explore' Africa as a child. This ambition was partially fulfilled when I went out there in 1946, initially as a sailor with the Royal Navy, based in Simonstown in the Cape, subsequently as a learner gold miner when I was demobbed, then up to the Rhodesias to work on the Zambesi with the old Empire flying boat service, across the river into Northern Rhodesia when that service closed down, when I then served in the Civil Aviation Rescue /Fire Service for the next twenty four years.

Brenda Butterworth was born in Northern Rhodesia where her father was Ground Level foreman at the Broken Hill mine, but she begins her story with her parent's journey:

My parents left UK the year WW2 ended. (Both were in the RAF). They bought an old army truck with another couple and kitted it out so they could travel overland to Africa – something my dad always wanted to do, especially after he spent 3 years in Iraq during the war. It took nearly 8 months to get to Lusaka, travelling through some of the most dangerous but beautiful parts of Africa.

Peter Kellett explains that the overland route was no picnic:

At the age of 13, I came to Zambia with my parents on one of the post-war overland trips from Britain. Many set off on this hazardous route with the intention of reaching South Africa, but ran out of funds by the time they reached Zambia. Nearly all the emigrant parties who set off on this enterprise did so with lots of confidence but with no experience of Africa and particularly of desert conditions. Traumatic incidents were frequent, and quarrelling verging on violence a feature of some parties. As they were all travelling to a new life, the ex-army vehicles available for little cost after the end of the war were invariably overloaded.

Because my father contracted a severe dose of malaria in Goma, the rest of the party had to leave us there. The Doctor who treated him took him on as manager of his pyrethrum plantation where we lived for a few months, but being unable to secure a resident's permit, we were obliged to travel by a combination of taxi, bus and lake steamers southwards. We met some people from Luanshya who suggested my parents try their luck on the Roan Antelope mine, where my father secured a job. By the time we reached Luanshya I had turned 14, and went to school there for the remainder of 1947.

But even a Union Castle voyage was an ordeal straight after the war, as Betty Trevor wrote in her memoir, which her son Buz sent to me (I wish there were space for more of it):

The "Carnarvon Castle" had been a troopship in the war and had not yet been re-converted. Conditions were atrocious and it was rightly known as "the Belsen ship". The passenger service to South Africa had only just been re-established and there was an enormous backlog of waiting passengers, so we were crammed in and the ship was horribly overcrowded. The two boys and I were in a cabin with 11 other women and children – no curtains, no privacy, and I felt sorry for the two very young wives each with a three-month old baby who were obviously embarrassed at having to breast-feed in these circumstances. Bim was in a large dormitory of 80 men – as far as I remember in 3-tier bunks. The sexes were rigorously segregated as much as possible – Bim had to eat in one cafeteria and we ate in another.

The search for a better life for one's family was the main motive for a move, but David Small is clear that, although prospects were better, newcomers didn't fall straight into an easy life in the early 'fifties:

I was born in Motherwell, before moving to Northern Rhodesia we lived in a tenement flat that had one bedroom, a lounge, a small kitchen and a toilet shared with 5 other flats on two floors of the building. Baths were once a week in a galvanised tub. My Dad was a fireman on the railways. My parents emigrated very simply to give us a better life. I know they considered the Sudan and also Canada. At the time they thought that Australia was too far away.

My father left first on 1st April 1952 to join Rhodesia Railways as a fireman in Broken Hill and we followed in November 1952 when he was able to get a leave house for 2 months. When I arrived in Broken Hill in late November I was

8 and my brother was 4. After another leave house, my parents were allocated their first house, as housing was owned by the railways. The house was what was called a "wood and iron". It was built above the ground, supported on iron railway sleepers to keep away the white ants; it had corrugated iron external walls and roof, with wooden floors and internal walls. It had a veranda most of the way round the house, 3 bedrooms, lounge, dining room, kitchen and bathroom. The toilet was at the bottom of the garden and was a dry bucket, which was emptied every night from the sanitary lane. There was limited electricity for light, the stove and the fridge ran on paraffin and water was heated by an external wood-burning stove. I'm not sure whether my parents thought it was an improvement on their accommodation in Scotland but to me and my brother it was a new world complete with servants – unheard of in the UK.

So too for Kate Smith whose family was to move from an urban life to take up farming:

We left England when I was 7 years old. My father had gone ahead some months earlier and mum, sister, Trish and I followed in September 1955. We had lived in a terraced house in Oldham – nothing special and, like most kids then, played in the street as we had only a very small yard at the back of the house (and an outside loo – the norm then).

We sailed to Cape Town and then took the train for a 4-day trip to NR. Even at that tender age the vastness of the place made an impression on me, and Africans would approach the train selling woodcarvings. Upon arriving at Kitwe we travelled to Itimpi to live on a farm our parents had rented and there began the most fantastic childhood I could have ever wished for.

Over and over again the story is of stepping into the light, escaping poverty and restriction, whether as a single person or a family, and that escape is depicted in terms of a journey and arrival. Michael Page's policeman father joined the mines:

My mother, younger brother and I arrived in Luanshya, in 1956, my father having gone there a year earlier. My father, from a large working class family was a policeman on the beat in Bournemouth, England after serving in the Air Force and my mother, the only child of a working class family that had left Wales for Bournemouth during the Depression. My father was earning nine pounds a week, low even in those times, riding a bicycle for transportation, and struggling to survive with two small children. They were, of course, seeking a new and better life. Emigrating, and to "darkest Africa" as well, was a brave thing to do in those days.

But family journeys could be motivated by desperation as well as hope; Norman Baker wrote of travelling for nearly six months with his mother towards the end of the war:

My father was killed in a bombing raid over Bournemouth .... I have no recollection of ever knowing him .... My mother had been born and brought up in South Africa before the war. She decided that it would be better for all concerned if we rejoined her family in Africa who had by this time moved to Broken Hill in Northern Rhodesia ... it was eventually agreed that we would have to travel in a military convoy but at our own risk ... eventually we set sail in September 1944 ....

[At the time Norman was aged just 6. Because of mines on the Cape route, the ship was diverted to Alexandria; they lived in a transit camp at Suez for 6 weeks, then in another camp at Ismailia. They set sail again, landing eventually at Mombasa to begin an overland journey to Nairobi, thence into Tanganyika, across Lake Tanganyika into the Belgian Congo]

We then took the train from Elizabethville and crossed the border into Northern Rhodesia at the end of February 1945 and the end of a journey that will stay with me for the rest of my life. On arrival in Ndola we were signed over to my grandparents and family by the military escort.

Bob Huntley is the sort of man one imagines making it in the colonies – he says himself that he always had an entrepreneurial spirit and, orphaned during the war, knew he had to be able to look after himself. After school in England he had joined his mother's relatives in Southern Rhodesia, started a business dealing in agricultural futures in South Africa, becoming briefly a paper millionaire in his twenties before going seriously bust. "Zambia saved my bacon ... " he says – he went to the Copperbelt as a miner to pay off his debts and recoup some of his losses but was swiftly recruited onto the staff of Anglo-American.

A simple statement like Eddy Stern's, "I was just under 3 when I arrived in N.R. with my parents in 1939," conceals the grief and suffering that must have accompanied his family's journey from Germany. Joe Behrens, another German Jewish refugee, recounts his start in Northern Rhodesia, travelling, aged eighteen, with two slightly older cousins; they were literally penniless and were never to see their parents again. When I met him for tea at the Museum of London after reading his deposition in the archives there, he told me how the family had managed to obtain tickets for Cape Town for the three boys, assuring them they'd follow on when they could. Neither South Africa nor Southern Rhodesia would admit them and, with train tickets and packs of food supplied by Jewish groups along the way, the boys travelled northwards to the only country that would admit them. For a while they lived on a farm outside Lusaka, established by the Jewish community to provide basic shelter for the refugees whilst keeping them out of town. Behrens maintains that the NR Jews, whom he referred to as the "off-comers", helped out of a sense of duty but did not welcome the "new-comers". *"There wasn't much ... how can I say...? We lived side-by-side rather than together."* The wider European community wasn't interested in employing the incomers who worked, on sufferance, for local Jewish businesses – stories of local wariness of the "new-comers" are reiterated in Shapiro (2002). From this unpromising start, Joe Behrens went on to set up a successful electrical business, the best cinema in Lusaka and the much loved drive-in. He also maintains that his treatment in Germany and being shunned on arrival in Africa determined his views on Northern Rhodesian race relations.

This arrival story does not stop with the three young men. Joe had relatives in South Africa whom he visited once he was established, even flying his own small plane down to attend a wedding, where he met and fell in love at first sight with Eva. When he offered to bring her up to Lusaka to see how rough things were there, she declared that she didn't care, she was marrying the man, not the place. When the war ended, Joe was able to trace the one member of his family who had survived the camps – his sister was weak and her feet had been amputated as a result of frostbite. He brought her to Northern Rhodesia and she married one of his friends; they subsequently moved to Australia.

George Lazarevic's father came from Yugoslavia and, having been a sailor for eleven years, arrived in Northern Rhodesia in 1938 to work in the copper mines. His mother came from Poland after grueling experiences. They met in Bwana Mukubwa and married in Nkana/Kitwe in 1945:

When the British brought out the Polish refugees it could have been an evacuation out of Siberia rather than Poland itself – I am pretty certain the former. She, her younger sister and her mother spent four years in Siberia – having been captured by the Russians – cutting timber and living on basically bread and water. I know a lot of the journey was on cattle trucks via India and what was then Persia.

Arrivals of people from continental Europe always reflected different post-war conditions from Britain's. Dominic Fuciarelli wrote:

I was born in July, 1948 in a small farming village called Gagliano Aterno, in Abruzzo , Italy . When I was a couple of months old my father left for NR where he was employed by a builder in Chingola. He left behind myself, my mother, and two older sisters. We did not see him again until December of 1954 when he had made enough money to bring his family over. I was six years old before I met my father. In those days many families were separated for long periods of time as the men searched for work. Many people from my village settled in Hamilton, Ontario, but my father chose Africa because one of his relatives had gone to NR a couple of years earlier and wrote saying that there was demand for people experienced in construction.

We finally arrived at the port of Beira in Mozambique and transferred to land by small boats where I finally got to meet my father. He had travelled by train from NR to meet us and we were soon on that same train for a three-day journey to Ndola. It was extremely awkward for me at first. A total stranger was now giving me orders and everyone around me was speaking gibberish. I did not speak a word of English, or any of the African languages. My older sisters, who were in their teens, were in total shock at having left all their friends behind and cried for weeks. We arrived in Ndola, where my father's boss, Mr. Gusovic, was waiting with his car. He drove us to Chingola and we took up residence in the house my father had built in the six years he spent away from his family.

Wartime disruption of career resulted in many men looking further afield. Michael Wagner was three years into articles as a charted accountant when the war broke out and he was called up. Taken prisoner in North Africa in 1942 he spent nearly two years in camps in Italy before escaping to join Italian partisans. Following the war, two more years of articles then a career in accountancy had lost its allure:

I was nearly 30 and, wanting to get married, I accepted an offer from the Colonial Office to join the Colonial Administrative Service. In December 1946

*sailed to Cape Town en route to Northern Rhodesia to become a cadet in
the Service where I had nearly 23 enjoyable years.*

Alan Chattaway tells of a father who was typical of many returning
servicemen:

*I went to NR in 1952, November, aged almost 7. My Dad went 6 months
earlier by Union Castle liner to Cape Town, then train to Luanshya. He had
applied for the job to get away from Britain's poverty after WW2. During the
war he'd been in North Africa, Middle East and India, and had learned that his
health was better in warm climates, so he applied for a job as an operator at the
Roan Antelope Copper Mines power station. During his 6 month trial period he
regularly mailed mom and me Koo peaches and Nestlé's canned thick cream (it
came from the UK, but was unobtainable there due to rationing and the export
drive to pay off war debt). RACM offered Dad a permanent position and paid for
flying mom and me to join him. It took us 3 days, with two overnights and several
other refueling stops.*

The injustices confronting older demobilised servicemen motivated Graham
Snow's parents to look further afield:

*We emigrated to NR in 1952, with the intention of staying there, I was only 4.
My dad was a bank clerk, and was called up for the army. He served in Europe
and got bombed on the troop ship* Lancastria. *Over 4000 men lost their lives.
Fortunately my dad could swim and was rescued by a French fishing boat. He
then served in the Falklands. He spent 5 years serving his country. After he was
demobbed, he went back to his old job, and applied for promotion. He was told
he was TOO OLD!!! He had been at war for goodness sake! Through friends of
friends he heard that the colonies were a good place to be, and that there were
opportunities in NR. So he packed up his family and we sailed to Cape Town,
then got the train to Lusaka. My mum recalls arriving in dusty Cairo Road, and
seeing a horse rail outside the Grand Hotel thought it looked like a Wild West
town. She said she wanted to get the next ship home!*

Quite often the attraction of the Empire is associated not with the war but
the difficulty in contemplating returning to routine life after the rupture caused
by National Service, still in operation until 1957 in Britain. Anthony Noel is an
example:

I was just 21 when I sailed from London to Cape Town to join the Northern

Rhodesian Government as a junior trainee, having completed my National Service with a year in Nigeria. This experience increased my desire to work in Africa, initially stimulated by my readings of the David Livingstone Diaries; in retrospect perhaps a rather naïve starting point! From Cape Town the train took four days to reach Lusaka, and then I was driven by Land Rover a further 600 miles along the great east road, to a place called Katete, close to the borders with Nyasaland and Mozambique.

Derek Dutton also felt the need to get away:

I had never settled down after my RAF service in Singapore, so I wrote away. Had an interview and accepted, set off from Southend Airport in a Dakota for a three and half day charter flight to Darkest Africa. People laugh when I tell about the three and half day trip but although I have flown the big jets, which was the best flight of my life… The charter flight people had not told them we were coming…. My friend and I saw Immigration three days later. They nearly had a fit when they found out I only had £1 by then, but I had a job and accommodation so they let me stay.

An "anything-but-this" attitude could provide the motivation for the young men joining the NRP. Chris Lyon a bank clerk before National Service decided that there was more to life:

I left grammar school with three 'O' levels and started work at the Head Office in London of the then Standard Bank of South Africa. I was called up for National Service in 1953 and, after training, was posted to a radar station outside Newquay in Cornwall as an RAF policeman … National Service upset a lot of young men's views of their futures and I was no exception. I went back to the bank and realised very quickly that I could not carry on in banking for life. The bank would have sent me to work in Kenya, Uganda, Tanzania, both Rhodesias or South Africa but I would not survive in any of these countries as a bank clerk. The Evening Standard *had in its 'Situations Vacant' pages adverts for at least half-a-dozen colonial police forces which grabbed my attention every evening until I took the plunge and applied. I narrowed down my choice to either Bermuda or Northern Rhodesia, but I did not like the look of the Bermuda uniform, so I went for Northern Rhodesia! I joined the Northern Rhodesia Police in October, 1956 as an Assistant Inspector.*

Paul Wheeler had worked for Harrods Estate Agency before military service, but a return there did not appeal to him; he worked as a barman in his uncle's pub in Reading, where he also played for Reading FC in the days before footballers earned a fortune, enrolled on a hotel management course but was restless. A friend had joined the Kenya Police and this inspired him to apply; he was accepted into the NRP in 1950. Later, two of his sisters came to visit him and both married in Northern Rhodesia.

A colonial background

The British public schools educated the children of the empire and reproduced the next generation of colonial officers. Colin Heape's account has echoes of William Boyd's *Any Human Heart*:

I was brought up as a "child of Empire", living with my father and mother in the West Indies during the war. My father was Colonial Secretary to the Duke of Windsor in the Bahamas. We came home to the UK in 1945 and I was sent to school. I did not see much of my father again until he came home for good in 1949.

A career in the Colonial Police was one of the suggestions given to me by the careers advisory service when I left school in 1955. I had volunteered for the Royal Marines and served with them for my National Service from 1957-1959. I was coxswain of a landing craft on Christmas Island during the final H-Bomb tests in 1958.

As a boy, I had listened to my father's stories about Africa. The Colonial Office had posted him to British Somaliland in 1919. So I had a Colonial background and was proud to serve the Empire. My father took me to the Colonial Office and I talked to his friends there. They told me that there was a worthwhile career in Rhodesia for young men like me. But by 1959 many politicians had already decided that the Empire was a millstone round the neck of the British Government. The Crown Agents officially recruited me for the Northern Rhodesia Police and I signed a contract that I would serve the Federation of Rhodesia and Nyasaland. I was flown out to Lusaka in August 1959 via Cairo and Entebbe.

David Anderson was another man with a colonial background:

I was born in Singapore in June 1939. When the Japs took Singapore my father was captured and later died in a P.O.W. camp in North Borneo. My mother and I managed to get away on the second last boat to leave and we managed to reach England many months later.

*From 1948 – 1951 my mother and I lived in South Africa but we returned
to the UK so that I could attend my father's old school. I did a year's teaching
(unqualified) in Scotland immediately after leaving school and then joined the
B.S.A.P. in 1958, stationed in Bulawayo. I went 'home' in November '61 – from
a Rhodesian October (suicide month) to an English winter. I took the train to
London, the tube to Trafalgar Square and then walked into Northern Rhodesia
House and joined the N.R.P., flying out in January '62. Decisive action!*

Tim O'Hara had an Indian background and a colonial career seemed natural:

*I believe I was the only Learner District Assistant recruited from an Irish
(Republic) school! I was keen to get an early chance to see the World, maybe
because I was born in India, the son of a tea-planter, and only returned to our
family farm here in Sligo when I was 9. My parents could not afford to send me
to university, so this was perfect for me.*

Mark Shelldrake, another tea planter's son had come to Northern Rhodesia
with VSO when he left school. He'd originally hoped that they'd send him to
India for a year before going to university but he took to Africa, discovered the
life of the Provincial Administration and, with a strong recommendation from
the DC he'd worked alongside, applied from London to become an LDA.

Making a break

The Empire was always a refuge for people who did not feel at home at home
and wanted to make good on their own terms. Robert Olive's story is one of
finding contentment by moving a long way away from his family:

*I was born in 1938 and my father abandoned my mother when I was two. I
had two older siblings and what with the war, post-war austerity and my poor
mother's health, life was very basic and we underwent considerable hardship
during my first fifteen years – along I suspect with many others at that time.
The upside of this was that I was sent away to boarding school courtesy of the
Catholic Sisters of Mercy and made it to grammar school when I was eleven…
When my mother died I was fourteen, and I had to go and live with my father
and his new wife. This was not easy, I felt trapped mainly by reason of my age.
My father was disgusted at my O-level results and insisted that I leave school
and start work… In due course I served for three years with the Royal Corps
of Signals and, whilst deciding whether to renew my army contract, spotted an*

advertisement in the Daily Telegraph *for Police Officers to serve in NR. I had had no more idea of becoming a police officer than flying in the air, but my brother was a detective in the Worcester City Police, and this seemed like a real escape opportunity – become a Police Officer AND see Northern Rhodesia (wherever that was...) So I arrived in Lusaka in April 1960 after an all-night flight, an absolute greenhorn with not much idea of life inside an ordinary family or outside an institution. Boarding school experience, plus the bonus of three years army service, rendered a five month training course at the NR Police College a relatively easy time.*

Newspaper advertisements really did seem to be effective in setting young men dreaming about a better life in Africa. Brian Robinson, too, had the *Daily Telegraph* to thank for his release (and banking does seem to have prompted them to seek greater excitement):

Before I joined the NRP I had served in the Metropolitan Police as a cadet, I spent 3 years in the Royal Military Police and just before I left for NR in 1958 I worked for 8 months in a London bank, for which I was totally unsuited. I was short of self-esteem and self confidence. I was engaged to Pat, with no prospect of marriage on £32 per month net. On the way home on the bus I read an ad in the Daily Telegraph *for Assistant Inspectors in the NRP at £900 per annum! I spent 3 eventful years there, where I had great responsibilities. Pat and I married at St George's Church Luanshya and 14 months later our daughter was born in 1960.*

Unlike the policemen, Robert McChesney was unusual in coming without a job or contacts, but he too was drawn by an advertisement:

In 1956, aged 28, I left my home in Liverpool and travelled to Africa 'on spec', having read in publicity produced by the Federal Government of Rhodesia and Nyasaland that there were opportunities for work in the Rhodesias. After an apprenticeship in U.K I had had jobs in electrical engineering, including three years at sea. I took the train to Bulawayo, where I worked for a short while ... I got a lift with a caravan salesman who was going to the Copperbelt and, once there, I started to look for work, which I discovered was not easy. Eventually I found my way to Ndola and the NRG Public Works Department, where I was offered the post of Electrical Works Supervisor in Kitwe.

Sarah Greening was a rare American immigrant:

I arrived in Northern Rhodesia in late 1962 as the young American bride of a District Agricultural Officer I had met while a student intern at the Foreign Training Division of the US Department of Agriculture in Washington, DC. I was 22; he was ten years older. He had been working in NR already for eight years, whereas I was merely a recent graduate of a degree course at a New England women's college with little experience of the world outside formal education. We were married near my home in Wilmington Delaware, and immediately flew from there to England, where we flew out again to Kenya. After our honeymoon on the Kenyan coast, my adjustment to married life began in earnest. I did not find it particularly difficult as I had already seen Peter's house in Mazabuka from my visit earlier in the year. Being young I treated all that was to come as an adventure.

Women generally came to Northern Rhodesia as wives and there were those, like Faith Cairns and Pat Robinson who came to marry. Given the norms of the time, the concern for "reputations" and the strength of gossip networks, these brides, like Ruth Spindler, often came with their wedding gowns in their luggage and married promptly upon arrival:

I was born in York, England and met my husband-to-be there in 1958. He was a sergeant in the Army and had applied for a position overseas through the Crown Agents as an Assistant Inspector of Police in N.R. In Sept 1958 he flew out to Lusaka, NR to take up training there (no sweethearts or wives allowed). We had become engaged in August 1958. I flew out to Lusaka in March 1959. We married at Trinity Methodist Church officiated by the Rev. Nightingale. On going to NR, I was terrified of seeing snakes – luckily I never did. I was fascinated by the country; Lusaka's main street Cairo road looked a lot like the movie sets for old Westerns.

Relatively few women came on their own as young professionals, Philippa White being unusual in that she grew up in Mozambique and intended her time in Northern Rhodesia to be short:

By the time I finished university in Cape Town my parents had moved to Salisbury, Southern Rhodesia. I graduated in December and my course in London was only starting in September the following year. My parents encouraged me to apply for a temporary teaching post. This was the time of the Federation of Rhodesia and Nyasaland. Having hoped to get a posting in Salisbury, I was horrified to be offered a teaching job at Chingola High School. This was 1962.

My first reaction was to turn the job down. My father talked me into it saying I might "meet my fate". He said I could dine out for years describing how I taught Latin near the Congo border at the time of the trouble there, with Baluba tribesmen probably waving their spears outside the classroom window. So off I went on the bus feeling pretty apprehensive and never imagining that I would live there for nearly 40 years!

Her "fate" was Patrick White: Patrick was born and brought up in South Africa. When he left school at age eighteen he hitchhiked northward hoping to get a job. This was in 1955 and he had ten pounds in his pocket and a lot of hope in his heart. When he got to Chingola he managed to get a job with Chingola General Engineering as a boilermaker apprentice.

Children often laid down memories of what may seem like trivial details of arriving, but they are things that bring home the reality of the small person wondering at the big country. Barbara Jacobs came from Glasgow when she was nine and is insistent that her memory of that momentous event is intact:

I remember a long layover in Madeira. It was 1961 and in those days, planes had to stop over to refuel. We stopped in Madeira – for 5 hours. I remember that they opened the gift shop for us, and my parents bought me a Spanish doll. Then I remember sleeping on the hard benches, head cradled in my mother's lap, my precious Senorita cuddled in my lap.... I remember arriving in Africa. I remember stepping off the plane into that – hot Africa.... We were bound for a mission station, 7 miles outside Chisikesi, which is 20 miles outside Monze, which is the arse end of nowhere, beyond Mazabuka.

And there, I spent the happiest years of my life. And I do – I do remember that car journey, when I was 9, after a 24 hour flight and a gawd knows how long drive. I can clearly, DISTINCTLY, remember the clear African night sky through the back window of the car. I can remember my big brother softly, but insistently kicking my ankle ...'Wake UP, Kid!'

Not everyone took to the country straight away. John Anton-Smith a tropical agriculturalist was initially disappointed after the West Indies:

I have a love/hate relationship with NR. In part it was due to my earliest experiences. I hadn't appreciated the effects of the dry season. As I journeyed from Cape Town in September I looked out for signs of agriculture and could scarcely see a blade of green anywhere and I got more and more depressed the further I went North. I had just come from student accommodation in Trinidad, set in a lush botanic garden. The soil was incredibly poor (which is why I was sent there) – it wasn't until the rains came and the bush flowered, that I cheered up a bit and grew to love the country.

Perhaps in answer to the question why European people went to Northern Rhodesia we can say, for nearly as many reasons as there were Europeans there – everyone was pushed, pulled or just drifting according to their own circumstances. So long as there was a British Empire, Northern Rhodesia might be a long way off, but it wasn't really very remote – it was one colonial option among many for those in the UK, whereas it was just the far end of an ongoing Great Trek for South Africans. Certainly it was an adventure and a new start, but the language and the legal system were English; British qualifications were recognised, the schools sat examinations that were set and marked in the UK, the currency was sterling. With a bit of effort, settling in wasn't hard.

4. WHAT WAS IT LIKE?

I forgot to tell you what was probably the best thing that living there did for me. I felt like a PERSON, an individual. It was so nice to be able to walk down the street and be known as me! *Derek Dutton*

Although people don't usually want to listen to "Whenwes" reminiscing at any great length, they do often ask, "So what was it like living in Africa?" I think the answer they want is a *Leopard in my Lap* story about one's home petting zoo, but living there was normal at the time, whatever one makes of it now. I want to think about the ways that, so very many years later, people have talked and written about their recollection of living in Northern Rhodesia and through into Zambia. It is not particularly erudite to observe that one's experience depends very much on who one was and when one was there, as well as where one lived – but it needs remembering.

Major variations in European lifestyles in Northern Rhodesia depended on the country's geography, its transport geography in particular. By Independence there was still just the one railway line (Livingstone/ Lusaka/ Broken Hill/ Ndola) followed by a tarred road, with another branching off to connect Lusaka to the Federal capital. There were no other tarred trunk roads. Virtually all commercial and industrial development was oriented towards the line of rail, settlements off it were just administrative headquarters and agricultural centres with limited retailing, medical and social provision, approached on unmetalled roads, dusty in the dry season and treacherous in the rains. Journeys were routinely lengthy and fraught with punctures and breakdowns. For many Europeans, the smaller settlements became like islands, surrounded by a sea of unknown Africa.

When asking for memories, it's the "interesting" things that people recount – one hears little about plentiful clean water coming out of taps, or lavatories that flushed into sewers, but by the late 'fifties that was the experience of most Europeans. Far more often the stories come from people who recall boreholes and sanitary lanes with nightsoil removers. Everyone has a few "frontier" stories, these becoming more plentiful the further away the storyteller is from the line of rail and the further back in time. The stories of the pioneering days that were handed down to grandchildren make one wonder at the speed with which conditions changed. David Gray writes of the 1920s and '30s:

Northern Rhodesia was a dangerous place with snakes, spiders, crocodiles, leopards and lions all posing a threat to the unwary. My Uncle Jack was attacked by a wounded leopard and barely escaped with his life. Six months after that incident, he was helping my father swim a newly acquired herd of cattle across the Kafue River when the dugout canoe in which they were paddling began to fill with water. They abandoned the sinking canoe and struck out for the bank some 20m away. My dad reached the bank and turned to see where Jack was but only saw his hat floating down the river. Jack had been taken by a crocodile. His body was recovered 3 days later and an 8 foot croc was shot close by.

In the late 'fifties Diana Greyvenstein still emphasises the out-of-town:

I married a Luanshya lad and I loved Luanshya right from the beginning. My husband's family lived on a farm off the Ndola-Kitwe road, quite a bit inland on a rough corrugated road, and when the rains came it was a quagmire. The farm itself had no electricity, or running water. They cooked on a wood stove, used a coal iron to do the laundry, tilly lamps. Being young and having no fear, we would venture out into the bush over the weekends with friends. We would collect grass and leaves and place blankets on top for our beds and a great fire in the centre. Yes, we did hear lions roaring and the cry of the hyena.

Is this "ordinary" or "extraordinary"? It is familiar to many people. By contrast, Ron James says of nearby Chingola in the 'fifties:

Those years could just have easily been spent in a South African mining town, so similar was Chingola to them at the time. Chingola was very up to date and had all the mod cons of the time (for white people, that is). NR could have been another Province of South Africa ... I am not sure why I am so nostalgic about Chingola and the general copper mining area. It is probably more the era of the '50s in that whole combined part of Africa, including the Transvaal where I was born: the wonderful weather, the freedom of roaming around in the bush/ bundu after school, and so on. Added to that, is my realisation that my father was just there for the money. He was waiting for the opportunity to go back to South Africa and start a motor business. So, although that took 7 years, I get the feeling we were just part of a contingent of contract workers – much like those in Dubai these days. We weren't committed to NR, we were not citizens.

Colonial Style

We probably know more about the working and private lives of district officers and the police than other categories of Europeans in Northern Rhodesia. The Provincial Administration (PA) constituted Northern Rhodesia's elite so many others, in and beyond government service, emulated their lifestyle Anthony Noel described his initiation:

Katete was a relatively small but prosperous district where the emphasis was on agricultural development and craft training. I say prosperous because large quantities of groundnuts and maize were exported by lorry, so there was a significant amount of cash in circulation, sadly this is no longer true; in their annual report the local mission hospital talks of 'one of the poorest districts in Zambia'. For me, after a few weeks finding my feet, learning the local language, Chinyanja, was the first priority, so my boss, the District Commissioner, sent me out on tour on my own. The concept was for a district officer to visit every village each year, to check the census and tax records, to be seen and to listen. However, like most governmental targets before and since, it was never achieved.

The plan was for me and one or two messengers to be taken in our 3 ton lorry to the start point in a minor chief's area, and then left to engage our carriers and to proceed on foot or cycle to all of his villages. There were no maps so the route planning fell to the senior messenger. "Surprisingly" the messengers, our local policemen who accompanied me, could not remember a word of English once we left the Boma, so my learning curve was steep. The District Messengers were a vital part of the administration. A splendid body of men, many with experience in the Burma campaign, they had constabulary powers of arrest and often went out alone great distances to investigate and get their man! They also had the same unofficial role as the NCOs in the army, to indoctrinate the junior officer in to the ways of getting things done.

Adrian Forrest gives a description of one of the old style DCs (the sort that stories of empire are full of, but who were a dying breed) and of the people one might find on a small station:

My first tour in NR was entirely in the Southern Province. My first station was Namwala. It was a beautiful and most interesting district, but socially it was an odd mixture and not a particularly happy place, the principal reason being that the DC was a dreadful snob. He was a very wealthy man who had no need to earn a living and was happy to let you know quietly that his private income was much greater than his salary. He never ceased to run down NR. Among the white population (there were ten houses and I was the only bachelor) there was a wide range of social types who might have been turned into a more homogeneous group if the DC had made a slight effort to break down the social barriers.

Before I went to Africa I was told, "You have to be a special sort to like Africa!" I soon realised that that was not accurate. Among those ten households there was an extraordinary variety. One man (slightly hunchbacked) worked in the Water Development Dept and had previously been a professional old-time dancing instructor in the Tower Ballroom in Blackpool. Another had worked as a postman in Liverpool. Yet another had previously been a medical orderly on a Welsh coal mine and was known to the DC as 'The Poxter'. His only job was to deal with venereal disease because it was so prevalent throughout the district. The DC despised him and was openly rude to him. When the DC wrote his annual report in, I guess, 1953 he reported as follows – 'Perhaps, if I were Julius Caesar entering the Namwala District, I would proclaim "VENi and VD but heaven knows when I will say Vici!"'. Two others were much older and had shot and drunk their way round Africa for thirty years or more. My memories of a further resident are that he never ceased to say how he hated "the munts". Another, who was a Building Foreman had served in the Royal Navy all through the war and then, having emigrated to South Africa in 1946, worked his way up through Africa and was busy building many houses at Namwala. Of all the Europeans on the Boma he was probably the one who got on best with his African staff. After one year at Namwala I was transferred to Mazabuka and my place was filled by a new cadet, who could not stand Namwala, and moved out after one week. I am not sure how he managed it but he was so unhappy that he persuaded the bosses to let him go home. The DC put an entry in the District Notebook – 'A new cadet arrived on the station and left again five days later, having gone mad!'

Forrest then moved on to something altogether more normal:

My second posting was Mazabuka… I did not feel really settled and was not upset when, after six months at Mazabuka, I was quite suddenly transferred to Gwembe, a district entirely in the Zambezi Valley. I found Gwembe much more agreeable. In eighteen months in the district I worked with two DCs who were much more friendly and helpful than at Namwala and Mazabuka. Everyone worked to make it a happy station; we played tennis in the evenings and bridge after dark when all were present. The European population of Gwembe, at the time of my arrival, consisted only of the DC and his wife, another bachelor and myself.

Don Smith's notes about his career are evocative – he catches the life of a young LDA (Learner District Assistant), a post the Colonial Office invented when it knew that it could no longer offer recruits a career, just an experience:

Provincial HQ Kasama for six months. Rosemary taught in the "European" school. Deputy PC Derek Goodfellow gave us wedding present of baby German shepherd dog. Dominated by PC, DC, Paramount Chief Chitimukulu relations. Bemba tribe universal. Much more office than touring. Suddenly posted to Mporokoso. Best place for us by far. DC Ian Mackichan very welcoming. Natural swimming pool with tropical birds flying over – incredible. Much touring particularly up to Sumbu on Lake Tanganyika. Different tribes – Lunda and Lovale and all very friendly. After a year, a succession of DCs and a huge deterioration in relations. Kaunda and UNIP making selves felt. One night Game Dept with records going back burned to the ground. DC's thatch in flames also. Usual touring by bicycle continued. Each village in an area visited in company of local chief, headman, our district messengers and chief's kapasus. Census called. Men only, women sat far off. Native authority books checked – taxes on bicycles etc. General chat about anything from animals wrecking crops to minor legal situations. Always friendly in the villages, so it seemed.

Robert Olive found his induction into the Northern Rhodesia Police socially transformative:

The five month training course at the NR Police College was a relatively easy time and I passed out well-versed in Law and with a decent standard of Chinyanja. The main benefits of this brief sojourn, however, were my starting to learn the social skills needed (and which I sorely lacked) to maintain one's position, and indeed one's standards, let's be brutally honest here, as a WHITE BRITISH COLONIAL OFFICIAL! Separated from the sheltered environment of a Police Officers' Mess and placed into the small farming community of Choma, I became aware of my almost complete lack of social awareness and general etiquette when dealing with the day-to-day workings of a small country Police station in Africa. Most of the (white) public were either true colonial settlers going back in some cases to the 19th century, South African and Rhodesian farmers and British civil servants (District Commissioners and Boma staff in general) plus, of course, the Police community. Many of us young policemen were bachelors and were in the same boat – NR Police was not an 'old school tie' organisation – most being ex-Army and not used to the class differences which we experienced. This is not to say that we were in any way set apart or ostracised by other whites, indeed we were made most welcome and enjoyed wonderful hospitality, since the ultimate class defining factor was of course, colour.

It was a great advantage for me to see at close hand 'how the other half lived' since we (the whites) moved constantly in the same very close circles. This was largely due to the very small numbers of whites in Choma (perhaps 30/40 farms) plus the 'township' essentially the Administration etc. Early 1960s Choma featured no English-speaking radio, of course no TV, merely bar life, and lots of sport, huntin', shootin' and fishin', and much dining out. This usually took the form of formal dinners at the Police Mess or the Boma, and especially in the homes of local South African and Rhodesian farmers who were extremely hospitable, and by their very difference to us Brits were quite exotic with their bush and hunting skills. I doubt I would have enjoyed the same rapid learning curve on all fronts on the Copperbelt, due to the much denser and more diverse white population, but without doubt my first three years in NR served as my 'University of Life'.

The small settlements were more often written about in memoirs than the towns, even though a minority of the population lived in them. There would usually be a club and a few shops, run by Asian or Greek traders, stocking just basic supplies. Normal life placed an emphasis on self-reliance, good networking and strategic planning – European people who lived in small settlements either loved or loathed them, depending on temperament and their attitude to improvisation.

Colin Carlin was aware of the social differences between Abercorn and the rest of the country, it was more "English" and had a rather different notion of prestige from the rest of the territory:

I think Abercorn was different from the line of rail and more like East Africa. We went to Mbeya in TT (Tanganyika Territory) *and also had connections to Iringa. The TT settlers in Sumbawanga to the north of Abercorn between lakes Rukwa and Tanganyika used Abercorn as their supply base. The other big differences was that we were then the HQ for the International Red Locust Control Organisation that operated largely in East Africa – the Rukwa valley and further north toward the Malagarasi swamps north of the Kigoma to Dar-es-Salaam line of rail. They also operated on the Mweru Wantipa Swamps in Luapula province of NR. This brought eminent scientists to the village.*

Some of the older Abercorn "characters" had drifted down from the Lupa Gold Fields on the Ruaha River in central TT and the 1945 Labour government's failed ground nut scheme also in TT. There was an interesting clash of interest and personalities between the English Settlers, the the "PA" (whom the settlers thought of as "suburban") and the Red Locust "types". (Some of these, in the language of the settlers were very brash and red brick and very left wing!) An interesting time was had by all at the Africa famous Abercorn Arms Hotel. It was rumoured that the NR Admin kept South Africans, especially Afrikaners, out of the Northern Province so as not to "spoil" the locals with their racism. Some of the Settlers had interesting contacts in London so Members of the House of Lords or MPs would occasionally come and stay for private visits. The PA was terrified of the Gamwell sisters who could, and did, get questions asked in the House if they did not like what the Governor or the PC, or even the poor DC, was doing!

Robert McChesney being an electrical engineer employed by the PWD, naturally expected only to be posted to the towns where there was an electricity supply, however when he and Connie, his teacher wife, returned from long leave in 1960:

I was astonished when the Establishments Officer told me I had been allocated Mongu. I thought there had been a mistake but he said I was wanted there for the Royal visit. Connie decided it was a joke. But no. A small power station had recently been installed in this tiny settlement in the middle of the Barotse flood plain ... Barotseland was a great place if you were interested in hunting, shooting and fishing. It was also the place in which you could study the old Africa, its ways and its people. I loved game fishing and Connie became interested in the sport purely for dietary reasons, as freshly caught bream was a great supplement to the tinned and dried foodstuffs we had to have delivered

53

from Lusaka every six weeks or so – a rather erratic supply system as it depended on the state of the roads, which could be under water for long periods of time. Connie was lucky enough to have a teaching post at the 41 pupil European school which spared her the endless tea and coffee parties which were the lot of many colonial wives.

We lived in an old BSA Company house that was basically a living room, dining room and bedroom (with dressing room!) surrounded by gauzed-in sleeping porches. The bathroom had the only shower in Mongu. The lean-to kitchen with the inevitable Black Monster cooking range was as hot as a blast furnace. Connie did all the cooking, including the bread making, and some of our finest meals were produced in that kitchen.

Mongu was a unique place with its Paramount Chief, Sir Mwanawina Lewanika and its ku'omboka ceremony. The whole way of life is dictated by the inundation and receding of the Zambezi. The 80 or so Europeans who lived and worked there all seemed to have been handpicked for their eccentricities. Many of them loved the bush and would live nowhere else.

Like Barotseland, the remote Luapula Province retains a special allure, especially because of the Luapula River and Lake Mweru. As a young police officer, Robert Olive laid down fond memories. On the map the river forms the boundary between the Province and the Congo, in reality it joins them:

I have many memories of crossing to the Katanga side aboard either the pontoon or, for long weekends aboard the H.M Customs launch.... We had one Tubby Tolson based in our enclave. He was officially Border Customs Officer, sported a full set of whiskers and wore full 'naval whites' and peaked cap, complete with scrambled egg. Talk about British eccentricity – all this in the heart of Africa, landlocked and all!.... I visited the other side to liaise with Wilfrid Vermeersch (Belgian equivalent of DO) and take them tinned milk and other stuff for their children as there was absolutely nothing 'European' for the little ones during the Katanga uprising. There was of course plenty of fish, rice and local vegetable products. I have a picture in my mind's eye of redundant dugouts submerged at the water's edge, full of manioc, leaching out the dangerous acid which is present in its skin if left untreated.

There were many expat Greeks living there, mainly involved with store-keeping and fishing. They built huge boats, chiyombos, all by hand, and plied up and down to Mweru, to various drying stations along the river. On one occasion we went over in the Customs launch and went ashore in just our weekend gear of shorts and shirts for a few beers, to show the flag and keep our communication channels open, when we were invited to a Greek wedding, sweaty shirts and all. Well, it really was just like the films, a really over-the-top Orthodox wedding, followed by the biggest party I have ever been to, just about the whole town were there. The other side (Congo) was far more racially integrated, rather like Portuguese East and West, so the whole thing really was WILD and went on until the small hours, Greek bands (awful) Congolese bands (wonderful) all colours singing and dancing together peacefully without any signs of racism or class distinction, and all spilling out onto the street!

The country had relatively few farms, most fairly near to settlements, but farming was seen as culturally important, representing the dreams of freedom that drew people to the country. We have already met Peter Kellett's family on their overland journey from Britain immediately after the war – Peter recounts the huge responsibility he was given when still very young:

On leaving school I worked in the copper mining industry for three years, on Nkana and the Roan Antelope mines. In 1952 I preceded my parents to the farm we had bought in Abercorn. As there was no house on this property, I lived in a grass hut while carrying out my father's casual instruction, innocent of specifications, to build a house for the family ready for their (not all that much) later arrival. At the age of 19, I managed to build one which was much admired, which I count as one of the few successes of my young life, particularly as I was simultaneously in a steep learning curve related to cattle management, butchering (which involved the hazards of customer relations), a milk delivery and trying to protect my cattle against predatory carnivores. The prevailing belief of cattle farmers of 50-odd years ago, that lions, leopards and hyenas were dangerous vermin which it was one's duty to shoot, would be incompatible with today's emphasis on wild-life conservation, to the extent that I now feel uncomfortable in mentioning this to people, especially in that it would entail having to admit that it was an exciting activity for a young man barely out of adolescence.

Farming ate up many of those dreams – there were just so many things to go wrong and more people went bust than made their fortune. John Steers' father was looking for a less confined life than a clerical post offered:

In my first year of school my father resigned from the NRG and tried to grow tobacco on a farm he leased outside Fort Jameson. The farm belonging to Alan Carr, Norman's bother. This was a disastrous venture and my father then joined the Township Management Board as its secretary, the equivalent of Town Clerk...

My father tried market gardening on a 10 acre plot in Makeni but was not very successful and returned to accounting. He had done accounting by correspondence while with the NRG. The plot had been owned by an Afrikaans family and had a small banana plantation and lovely avocados trees. Next door was an elderly Afrikaans couple with citrus trees. The toilet was a drop pit and not very appealing. My kids do not believe me when I discuss what we went through in the old NR. My mother was still with the Federal Department of Heath having been the hospital secretary in FJ ... In 1960 we lived in Bancroft for 2 years where my father was employed as the manager/accountant of the Chibuka native beer brewery and the mill. My mother worked for the Town Management Board.

In 61/62 we returned to Lusaka where my father bought another 10 acre plot in Teagles Makeni and started producing dressed chickens.... Unfortunately an owl got into the pens and the chickens, from day old to 10/12 weeks old when they were ready to eat, caught Newcastle disease and all died within days. This happened within a year after he started. So he was back to accounting. My mother returned to the Department of Health.

The Towns

The towns had a distinctive colonial geography, the most obvious spatial division being along racial lines with separate housing zones for Africans, Europeans, Asians and "Coloureds." Whilst African housing areas did not merge into the European sectors, virtually all accommodation in European and Asian sections of town had servants' quarters on site, so there were African people living in European areas; there was, however, no question of their being socially integrated and they needed to be able to produce a *situpa* (pass) proving their right to be there.

Since mineral extraction was the country's *raison d'etre*, mine workers were at the heart of the society and the Copperbelt the powerhouse of the economy. The mines were famously good employers providing a range of benefits for their employees (both black and white, though segregated). These included almost free health care, including their own hospitals, highly subsidised clubs, canteens and sporting facilities. Where there were mines there were swimming pools and cinemas that other European townspeople could use, and miner affluence led to better shopping provision than elsewhere.

Mine workers were the aristocracy of labour, but railway workers came much lower down the heap. Robert Plain was dismissive of his father's role:

Dad "worked" as a plumber in the works yard for the Railways… He travelled up and down the line assisting the maintenance of the provision of water supply facilities for steam locomotives at various small points within 150 miles of Broken Hill. The water supply points usually were just a railway crossing, with maybe a small station run by a station foreman assisted by a platelayer and a pump attendant, plus enough labourers to do the heavy work. The hamlets were there so that the locos could top up their water supply every 20 miles or so. Normally there was a siding which had a metal water tower with a square steel water tank on top which gravity fed the water to a water column. When on the line Dad usually had the use of a "Caboose", a sort of home on wheels containing sleeping, eating and cooking facilities. The "Caboose" came with a cook boy, which was just as well as I never saw Dad cook anything. Dad supervised the same gang of boys who did all the work – Dad just kept an eye on them when he was sober, when he wasn't they carried on anyway and got the job done.

David Small's father was able to move from railway to mine employment, then up the hierarchy:

In 1955 there was an open pit mine opening up in Chingola that required qualified drivers, as the ore was hauled out of the pit by locomotive. Money would obviously have been a big factor as part of the wage package was a copper bonus that was determined by the price of copper which at the time was very high. When my father was 40 he managed to get onto a training course for work-study officers, a system being introduced into the mines to improve efficiency… he started studying seriously by correspondence course for a career change and by the time he was about 45 he was a Fellow of the Institute of Work

Study Engineers. I will always admire him for this, to take up studying at 40, having left school at 14, must have been a major challenge.

Whereas the mines of the Copperbelt had initially been worked by men arriving alone from the south, by the early 'fifties families were coming in greater numbers, with resulting shortage of accommodation. Many people talk of waiting to be allocated a suitable place to live, sharing with other families, squeezing into one room in a hotel, moving between leave-houses, or occupying mine single quarters. Geraldine Mackey describes the impact this had on her family:

My parents spent my first years in Mufulira struggling to become established. My brothers, aged only 8 and 9, became boarders in Luanshya convent, as my parents had to wait for a house to be allocated to them. For the first few months of my life, my mother and I lived illegally with Dad in his single quarters accommodation. Eventually we received a mining camp house and we all lived together again, but our first real "home" was a new house, 8 Quorn Avenue, which we moved into in about 1959.

The single quarters were regimented rows of huts without kitchens; the men who occupied them were expected to eat in the mine Mess. One can only assume that the authorities turned a blind eye to women and children out of necessity, but it was not just miners who faced housing shortages: Eve Anderson talks of how her family had to move from one unsuitable residence to another before finding the ideal place:

My father, Bruce Keith Anderson was a big fish in a small pond – he was Manager of Ingersoll-Rand and spent most of his time shuffling between the Copperbelt and the Congo. The early years after the war were not easy – I remember my parents being shunted from one house to another when people were on long-leave as there were no houses to buy or to rent – in twelve years they had 27 moves! We occasionally lived at the Rutland Hotel, also Haddon Hall and Glenstray. At 'Glenstray" we had an outside 'thunderbox' – an awful thing at the bottom of the garden. In those days the loos were in a straight line and bordered on a sanitary lane – once a week a sanitary lorry used to call and empty all the buckets. I loathed going and was terrified especially at night because there were spiders around – also lizards and snakes. It was all very primitive and disgusting!

One day in 1952 my father told us that he'd bought a house in Nkana Road that had just been built – and what excitement. We moved in with hurricane lamps and no water but it was home! We were all very happy there – my mother made a wonderful garden full of plants and shrubs and colour and at the back we had mango, pawpaw, avocado, lemon and guava trees. And right at the back of the garden there was an enormous, I mean ENORMOUS, ant-hill.

Independent artisans came up to the Copperbelt to make their fortune. Norman Seton's family went initially from Britain to Southern Rhodesia, but his father realised that there were better prospects on the Copperbelt:

We started off living in a house on the block where Dad had set up the new concrete works. I remember the windows being glassless with only wooden shutters that opened outwards. They had crosses cut out in them as the house was originally built by a missionary. We used to eat a fair bit at the Nkana mine mess, as Dad was not a great cook and also he did not have a great deal of time for cooking after a day at the factory. Homework was by Tilly lamp. We did have hot water though, from the Rhodesian boiler, that was an old 44 gallon drum with a wood fire under it. Prior to Mum and my brother joining us, Dad moved to a real factory in Freetown Road and we had a two room flat at the back of the factory, it had electric lights and an electric geyser for hot water. Alpha, the dog, used to sleep under my bed on an old mealie sack.

Meanwhile, Dad purchased a 5 acre block of land out of town in a township called Itimpi. I think it was crown land and sold for 5 pounds an acre. Dad was building a house on the block and running the business and supervising me all at once. I guess he was fairly well worn out with all this. Mum and my brother Richard arrived sometime late in 1957. I recall the house was only just liveable when they arrived. The bedrooms had doors on, but there were still full cement bags stacked in the lounge.

Thanks to an extensive building programme by both employers and the municipal councils, pressure on European housing eased by the late 'fifties, but because highly subsidised (or free) accommodation constituted part of most major earners' salaries, owner occupation was generally restricted to self-employed professionals and business people. The big employers built their own districts within the towns, mine and railway townships being the most distinctive. In most towns one would describe the districts by employer, rather than by class – men lived among their workmates and women and children would also identify themselves as being mine/ railway/ government/ municipal; within the European community the usual relationship between housing and social status did not occur. Land being plentiful, most Europeans lived in fairly spacious (but not huge or luxurious) bungalows surrounded by large gardens. Well appointed kitchens and multiple bathrooms were unusual and virtually every house had metal roofs and polished cement floors, the better to resist white ants.

Because Government employees were subject to frequent transfers, their housing came equipped with "hard furniture" from the Public Works Department store. On small stations, where everyone knew all of the housing stock and contents, people would swap less desirable for more desirable when someone moved on, so there were frequent complaints about the standard of the accommodation allocated on transfer. PWD furniture was simple and without upholstery, but it was well designed and made in local hardwoods – people brought their own rugs, cushions and curtains, so home was not so much a house as the contents of some packing-cases. Gardening would be done with no great expectation of seeing long-term results and, indeed, plants in pots and tins constituted a significant part of many families' *katundu*.

Few others relocated as often as government officers, so their accommodation usually came unfurnished. Some furnished their homes extravagantly, particularly on the Copperbelt, which was often accused of encouraging ostentatious lifestyles, but most lived fairly modestly – for absolutely sure, I never saw the now popular, supposedly colonial, safari-style furnishing in the homes of Northern Rhodesians. Unlike Southern Rhodesia, private swimming pools were uncommon, but some senior mine staff and a few privately owned homes had them.

Social Life
Something people coming to the country found different about the Northern Rhodesian lifestyle is the way that one's home generally *wasn't* one's castle. People spent a large amount of their time out – socialising at clubs, participating in sporting activities, camping, picnicking, hunting; on the other hand, homes were open to friends dropping in or invited to dinner parties, sundowners, coffee mornings, pre-prandial drinks, *braaivleis*.... This relaxed social life, never to be replicated later, is what most Northern Rhodesians say they miss most. Part of

this sociability was due to very few Europeans having extended families in the country – friends were much more important than relatives and friends were made easily. We need to remember that there was no television anywhere in the country until a station was opened on the Copperbelt in the early 'sixties (just a single channel mainly showing old American programmes), extending to Lusaka a few years later. Even radio reception was poor. Geraldine Luscombe, whose parents had initially left her in England for her schooling, sums up the life of a young woman in Broken Hill:

On their leave in 1962 they took me back to BH with them. Then followed the best two and a half years of my life! Such a different lifestyle to the UK. Dances at the Elephants Head in full evening dress; sundowners at the Mine Club after a rugby match; cinema three times a week; and who can forget the wonderful days spent at Mulungushi Dam? They were simple but such special times.

Stewart Burns paints a picture of the life of a bachelor on the Copperbelt:

Once my schooling was over I joined the Standard Bank for no other reason than their starting salary was Forty two pounds eight shillings and fourpence, as opposed to an Apprentice's salary on the Mine of £15. Those of us who joined the Bank were classed as "the elite" amongst our fellow school-leavers who had gone to the Mine and been apprenticed, as we had cash a-plenty and rarely ran out of money before we ran out of month. The meeting place after work in the afternoons was Michael's Café in the centre of town where we would quench our thirsts, buy our cigarettes, and exchange the news of the day. A year after joining the Bank I was transferred to their Bancroft Branch. Bancroft was in the throes of resurrecting itself from the dead as the Mine had been closed for a couple of years due to mudslides and generally bad economic conditions ... As with most mining towns social life in Bancroft revolved around the Sunday Night Sundowner Dance at the local Mine Club.

Robert Butterworth contrasts the relaxed social life in Livingstone with the greater formality and hierarchy of Lusaka:

In 1957 I joined the Federal Government of Rhodesia and Nyasaland as a Tax Officer. My first posting was to the Federal capital, where I received some training, before proceeding to Livingstone, in Northern Rhodesia, where I arrived just before my 23rd birthday. To me Livingstone was Paradise: the Victoria Falls, the Zambezi river, plenty of fishing and a bit of shooting – wonderful! Add to that the transition from miserable, austerity-blighted, Britain, to the luxurious, reasonably priced beef steaks, and crayfish tails that arrived in refrigerated rail wagons from Cape Town... [There he met his wife, Eilonwy, a nursing sister] *.... What a place to do your courting! Wonderful weather all year round, lunar rainbows over the Falls, snorting hippos in the Zambezi, delicious, affordable, food and drink at the Falls Tea Room, or Livingstone's four comfortable hotels .... Livingstone was rapidly developing as a tourist centre for the Falls, with excellent restaurants, clubs, and pubs. Then came a transfer to the capital:*

Lusaka, in 1960/62, was different. There were clubs and pubs, but much entertaining took place in people's houses. Capital city NRG officers and their families were very socially restricted and pretentious, with a concentration on rank, salary, place of birth in Britain, accent, and education that did not appeal to us. Also, during our 2 years there "Politics" (a word rarely heard in Livingstone) became THE absorbing topic of conversation at work, and at dinner parties in the evening. I grew to hate the place, but Eilonwy, with a satisfying professional life at the European Hospital, where she was 2i/c of the maternity ward, was much more tolerant and relaxed.

Clubs

Clubs (and being "clubbable") were important. The major employers – the mines and railways had their clubs, often with excellent sporting facilities; there were also town clubs and sports clubs, all with their clubhouses, organising regular fêtes and dances and all subtly calibrated by status. Major charities like the Red Cross were well supported, as were the churches. All these acted to reinforce the structures and predominant values of European society but few operated across the racial divide and when legislation was introduced to ban discrimination on racial grounds from public places, clubs were quite specifically exempted.

John Plimmer reminisces about the hard drinking at the highly subsidised Rhokana Mine Club:

Oh how I remember the "long bar" – many a lengthy session was spent there. The miners came up at about 3.30 p.m. and many headed for the bar. A lot used to stay until thrown out on the veranda at nine thirty (early closing so they would make the early shift next morning). I remember spending the whole night there and going on early shift for the cage-man to tell us next morning,

"You chaps stink of alcohol – you're bloody drunk still". Then there were the characters – I remember Martin Thorgalson, a huge Norwegian ex-whaler ... Us youngsters were always trying to get Martin in a fight with a big Afrikaner, but they were too smart for us and we never managed it. Some of the boerjies *came in at three thirty and slammed ten shillings on the bar counter and the barmen would place a bottle of brandy and a jug of water for them. They didn't go home till it was finished. One chap spent so much time in the bar, when he went home blind drunk his wife locked him out. Those were the days. Looking back at our Rhokana mine club, I wonder, did we have hard drinkers or was it just socialising?*

There were a few well-meaning inter-racial clubs, floundering soon after they were formed. Colin Morris remarks on their being inherently doomed:

I went along for duty's sake to a number of multi-racial groups of one sort or another. They seemed a complete waste of time. We draped ourselves around a room, perching cups of tea on our knees and laughing over-heartily at one another's weak jokes, grimly determined to be all pals together. We trod delicately around any of the issues which were a real cause of difference and went home exhausted from the effort of trying to pretend that there was the slightest common ground between us... It was all terribly nice and utterly futile. (Morris, 1961 p. 18)

"Culture"

By the 'sixties the major towns had cinemas; these were well patronised because of the lack of TV and the *bioscope* loomed large in the lives of urban children and adolescents. The films took a while to arrive after their release and there wasn't a hope of anything that wasn't main-stream. People remember the formality of a visit to the cinema in the early days; I recall a woman in a long velvet dress, wearing a tiara and I don't think it was ironic.

Beyond this there were the little theatres; amateur dramatics were taken seriously throughout the British Empire and Northern Rhodesia was no exception – the standard was often high and the auditoria usually packed, but it was noticeable that both actors and audiences were predominantly British and middle class and that interest in the theatre did not extend across all social groups. The productions tended towards the colonial classics of Rattigan and Gilbert & Sullivan, though occasionally directors were permitted to be a bit more adventurous, but when the Broken Hill *Venus* staged *Murder in the Cathedral*, there were complaints in the interval from those who'd assumed it might be more like *The Mousetrap*. Noel Wright was an adventurous director:

If I'm asked to name the things I most regret having to leave behind for the rest of my life, the Venus Theatre in Kabwe would be on the list. It was one of the social hubs of the town for us expatriates, and without a doubt the main cultural hub. Over many years its members teamed up to make it an amazingly well equipped venue, and to produce shows of varying, but sometimes outstanding, quality. It was matched by a similar theatre, some of them even better endowed, in every town of comparable size on the line of rail.

The *Lusaka Playhouse* was the cultural heart of the capital and its central role is described in *Goodbye Africa* by Desmond Bishop (2009), a stage-struck schoolboy who went on to a career in Australian and Zimbawean TV. All of Lusaka's European population in 1962 remembers the lavish production of *The Merry Widow,* directed by Gill Wheeler. Otherwise, however, provision was poor – no art galleries, only occasional touring classical or jazz musicians in the biggest towns, thinly stocked bookshops and record selections limited to recent(ish) hits in electrical goods stores. Public libraries were late to be established by the municipal councils and many were heavily reliant on donations of unwanted books, though some of the clubs had small libraries. Sarah Greening says of the club in Fort Rosebery:

I administered the library system for a while, which meant I could order new books. I quickly learned from the grumbles that ensued not to order the books I wanted to read, but to stick to the romances and thrillers that most people preferred.

Domestic Staff

Most European households employed domestic staff and, for women in particular, this was often the only relationship across the racial divide. The combination of intimacy and inequality implied always makes for difficult interactions and obviously most new arrivals in the country from overseas had no experience of servants, often resulting in arrogant and uncaring behaviour on the part of employers. Obviously, people who treated their staff badly did not write to tell me about it – but most of us have memories of some atrocious employers. David

Gray describes a very new world for his pioneer grandparents:

Now the Grays had property, a chance to live off the land, and servants! Granny had 12 house servants, all known as "boys" whatever their ages. One house boy, one cook boy, a kitchen boy for washing up, a laundry / ironing boy, a wood gatherer, a mail runner / general factotum, a dairy hand, a boy to tend the donkeys and chickens, two water-boys to draw water and transport it from the windmill in the garden to the house on a hill half a mile away and two gardeners.

This sort of household was far from the norm in the towns of the 1950s and '60s, and in many families the relationship could be affectionate, if inegalitarian, as Rose Heesom recounts:

When we lived in Broken Hill, a wonderful Malawian man, Simon Zulu, came to work for us, he brought with him his wife Lucy who gave birth to three children during their time with us. We absolutely loved Simon and Lucy and their family and they appeared to love us just as much, they were part of our family. Simon taught Barbara to eat 'sadza' and I still remember her as a tiny toddler sitting on the kitchen table eating it with her hands, just the way Africans did. Lucy taught John to fry and eat flying ants, I never did get a taste for either! But I did like the fried hibiscus leaves we used to pick from the shrub and cook over the little wood fire.

I remember taking the servants for granted – Simon cleaned the house, made our beds, washed and ironed our clothes, cooked our meals and tinkled a little brass bell to summon us to the table when dinner was ready ... and cleaned up afterwards. In those days did Simon and Lucy have the luxury of electricity in their kia, did they have an electric hotplate or stove on which to cook, did they have somewhere to shower or bath? I don't know, I didn't question it then, but do remember Lucy cooking over a wood fire and bathing her babies in an enamel basin at the front of their kia.

The relationship with staff was not always based on trust and, though servants were asked to look after children when parents went out in the evenings, people talk of locking up their sugar and marking the gin bottle. Some have said that employing staff was predominantly a matter of adapting to local convention. Sarah Greening, arriving as the young American bride of an Agricultural officer in Mazabuka (which she describes as "set in a landscape somewhat similar to the American southwest) saw her husband's long serving cook as being on her side:

But my role as housewife and dona to Peter's cook of some years was one with which I was totally unfamiliar. Perhaps that was an advantage. With no preconceptions I was able to acquire the allegiance of Jackie, a Muslim from Malawi, who had been trained well by a previous dona and knew much more of cooking and looking after house and home than I did ... I was privy to his opinions on Peter's bad temper (infrequent and deliberate after standards had slipped too far), his work colleagues, and our negligence in not locking our doors, which Jackie did for us when we went away as there were certain 'bad Africans' around. He also told me the African names for various bwanas. Peter had two – the man with the maps, and 'do not argue with him because you will lose' This was the beginning of an easy relationship that lasted throughout my years in Zambia.

Dudley Brown, a former member of the PA, thought that people in Britain overrated the importance of domestic help.

When we first came to England people accused me of missing Zambia only because of the servants. They completely missed the point.

And Noel Wright observed of settling down in Australia:

I thought having to do without servants might be a problem, We'd been spoiled... bearing in mind the long hours they put in, how could we do all those domestic chores on top of our new jobs? It turned out to be not so hard. Mechanisation and division of labour were the key.

Hard Lives

As everywhere, trying to set up in business wasn't always easy, as Faith Brentnall shows:

I was born in Chingola on the Copperbelt in 1953 and am the youngest of 4 siblings. I have 3 older brothers who were all born in South Africa. Times were hard in SA and in 1948 my dad decided that relocating to Northern Rhodesia would be a good and necessary move for his family. He started work at Nchanga Copper Mine as an electrician and worked there for 11 years. He broke service in about 1959 when we moved to Kitwe where he went into business with his brother Conrad. They had a funeral business called "Oelofsen Funeral Directors". I remember my uncle Connie used to make the most beautiful coffins, I also remember being a naughty child and I would lie in the uncompleted coffins and test them out for size! ... My mom couldn't stand it and things didn't work out for the two brothers and in about 1960 we moved back to Chingola and my dad went back to the mines where he stayed until he retired, in 1972 I think.

Many people discovered a more affluent lifestyle in Northern Rhodesia than they had previously experienced in South Africa or Britain, but it could exact a heavy toll. Michael Page's experiences are far from unique:

Our family experienced, as so many other families did, a new and in many ways much better life. My father was initially employed as a pit boss, leading a team of labourers in the copper mines. He had no experience in this type of work but he was white, which qualified him as a boss in those days. Later, my father joined the police force and eventually became the local Chief of Police. Going from a pretty grim working class life in the UK to a middle class life in the sun, with large house and garden, servants, golf, barbeques and all, was wonderful for us. Materially, we had a very good life indeed. There was a camaraderie among the expats, understandable as most had come from a similar background and had been brave enough to make a major change in their lives. There was, however, a darker side. The combination of easy lifestyle, ready money and much leisure time allowed many to indulge in a social life that included heavy drinking, both men and women. Both of my parents became alcoholics, my mother seriously enough that she ended up hospitalised for many months (no rehab in those days) to try to dry her out and she was never the same again – eventually dying of the results of this illness. Now, with the benefit of a little more life experience, I can recognise that this was a serious problem.

There was little in the way of a welfare system in Northern Rhodesia and disaster could strike hard; mutual assistance was important within the European community. Brian Townsend's family was helped by a complete stranger, a man who was well known for this:

In July 1959 my father decided to take our family on a road trip to Kapiri Mposhi. Just north of Broken Hill we had a horrific car accident where the whole right side of the car was ripped off. My mother and sister, on the left-hand side were unharmed. I had a severely lacerated face and my father had 10 broken ribs and a punctured lung.

We were taken to Broken Hill hospital. My father and I were both admitted. My mother was in a panic – it was the first time she had been out of Lusaka and knew nobody in Broken Hill. She also could not drive! Then up came a man on crutches asking what the problem was and she tearfully explained to him the predicament. No problem. My mother and sister were taken back to his farm outside of town and were taken care of. They were driven to the hospital every day. Once I was released after a week, I also went back to the farm before we were driven home to Lusaka. That man was Johnny Milliken. He had had a motorcycle accident which had partially paralysed him and, because he had been in hospital for so long, he would wander around the hospital every week to see if anyone needed any help. My father was in hospital for six months. Every weekend, one of Johnny's nephews would drive to Lusaka, pick us up and take us to Broken Hill to see my father. We would stay at the farm and be returned home on the Sunday. Johnny was a saint as far as we were concerned.

But, as Joseph Solomon demonstrates, life for struggling Europeans was not as tough as for people classified as "coloured", straddling the two main communities, sometimes accepted, generally not:

We travelled from South Africa to Livingstone, and we lived with some relatives of my step-father in a black location called Linda, in a semi-detached house that consisted only of two rooms and a small attachment that passed as a kitchen, there was a toilet about ten metres away, with cold water showering facility only. Not long after that we got our own two roomed semi-detached house and conditions improved slightly.

Back in Northern Rhodesia my step-father never ever worked again. Times and life were tough, but I, as a child never felt the hardships, but in retrospect it must have been difficult for my mother, as we had had a comfortable life whilst we lived in South Africa. I remember days where we had to wet dry bread and my mother putting sugar on the bread to make it tasty, and evenings where we would sit and watch the neighbours having supper in the hope they would invite us to join them, which they did...

My step-father was not making any effort to find work and I assume out of desperation, my mother turned to the African Welfare Department, because in 1960 we were sent to boarding school in Southern Rhodesia, run by German Catholic nuns in Makwiro, about fifty miles from Salisbury. Again we had to travel by mail train to a siding with our mother where the nuns had to pick us up. I remember it being a rainy day, my mother, two older sisters and my half sister

sitting in the back of a hooded pick-up, saying our final goodbyes and waiting
for the train that would take my mother back to Northern Rhodesia. I later learnt
that my mother hadn't eaten for the whole journey, a total of four days.

After Independence

As the next chapter will show, around the time of Independence most Europeans
were taking stock of the situation, wondering what things would be like and
whether they could stay for any length of time. Although those with the most
deeply entrenched racial prejudices left, many found daily life virtually unchanged
at first. For others there was new-found liberation as the colour bar came tumbling
down and many of the new "expats" arriving as advisors and professionals had no
experience of the old social structure. Those who stayed moved from permanent
and pensionable employment to short contracts – this brought home the temporary
nature of their relationship with the country, so most started to think strategically
and to save more enthusiastically for an uncertain future.

John Cribb of the NRP provides an example that is both typical and
exceptional. He approached Independence as *Aide de Camp* to the Governor, Sir
Evelyn Hone, a man for whom he had enormous respect. In this role he witnessed
the transfer of power. Deciding to stay on for a tour in the Zambia Police after
Independence, he was asked to remain at State House to form the new Special
Duties Division, responsible for the protection of the President. Though this
was a police division, it was a paramilitary force amply funded by commercial
(particularly mining) interests that were concerned there should be no threat to
political stability. He remained in post until 1968 when he decided that this was
not a job for a newly married man, but this sensitive position was taken over by
another non-Zambian, Frank McGovern, an Irishman with long Special Branch
experience. McGovern had been closer to Kaunda and other leading politicians
before Independence and was to remain at State House until 1976.

After Independence terms of employment on the Copperbelt became even
better than before as mining companies enticed staff to stay on contract. Robert
Butterworth moved from government service to a senior position with Anglo-
American. He describes the conditions put in place for expatriate workers in the
new era, by 1975, as Mine Stores Controller:

We had a 4 bed-roomed villa complete with swimming pool for which I paid the kwacha equivalent of £5.7.6d a month (and that included water and electricity). My salary was £1000.0.0d (a month) before the great inflation! Chingola, where we spent 13 years, became our home. Neither of us had the slightest desire to live anywhere else. Both of us had interesting, satisfying, jobs AAC were fantastic employers – they did everything to keep their workers happy and productive, including very high pay, generous leave provision, wonderful housing, and health facilities of a much higher standard than that which pertains in the dear old NHS, here.

John Steer's family's fortunes picked up in the post-Independence boom:

My father in the early '60s started doing the accountancy work for the Zemacks who owned the Victoria Hotel in Church Road Lusaka and two second class hotels in Stanley Street Lusaka. My father rented one of these, the less salubrious, for a time and then the better one till 1970 but with generally non-white clientele. In early independence the government was holding seminars for everything going and most of those attending stayed at the Annex and were paid for by the GRZ. My parents made a small fortune.

Not leaving until 2000 Philippa White looks back:

When I think of life in Zambia when we first lived there and how it was when we left it is truly incredible! The schools I taught in had white pupils and the Africans were in separate schools. The only Africans one met were doing menial jobs. At the time of independence there were exactly 100 black university graduates in the whole country! One's friends at the golf club and in the organisations one belonged to were all white. By the time we left there had been a complete turnaround. Most of our fellow Rotarians were black or Asian, schools were entirely multi-racial and most of my golfing friends were black girls.

How to sum it up? Living in Northern Rhodesia varied for colonial Europeans, some had an easier time of it than others, some accepted the colonial structure, many exploited it but others worked against it. There were, however, things in common – the wide open spaces, the climate, the possibility of reinventing oneself, the sense of a challenge – nearly everyone still yearns for these.

5. I FEEL SORRY FOR THE CHILDREN OF TODAY

A wonderful place to grow up in, I always felt safe and happy there and spent many contented hours in the bush on my own *Julie Swenson*

It is a cliché that in childhood the sun always shone, but for people who grew up in Central Africa, *it really did.* A common refrain from former Northern Rhodesians is that their childhood was very special and that, by contrast, today's children have an impoverished existence. Facebook groups echo this sentiment and comments from members concentrate on the "Do you remember whens?" of childhood, interspersed with remarks insisting that computer games and malls are no substitute – the next generation must wonder how such happy young people managed to turn quite so grumpy. One answer is that many people do think that they were snatched from Paradise, banished from the Garden by a new regime and obliged to make their way, wandering in a harsh world. The other answer is, of course, hindsight – perhaps it wasn't entirely perfect?

Children, though born equal, are soon sorted into their different niches, so one shouldn't be surprised that among the European children of Northern Rhodesia there was considerable variety in experience and opportunity, just as there was for their parents. We can, however, say of all of them that their childhood in this particular colony was unlike the one they would have experienced elsewhere. Few European people who grew up in Northern Rhodesia share the childhood experiences of the people they now live amongst; many regard that as a privilege, others feel deprived.

For Europeans, it was a young country; the 1961 census of Europeans shows that there were 25,589 children under the age of 15 (34.3% of the white population – by comparison, in Britain currently just 17.3% are under 15). We can add another 2,903 who were under 18. Few people had extended family close by, so though children grew up knowing about grandparents these had little substance, other than as senders of birthday presents.

Young savages
When asked about growing up in Africa, most people tell stories of adventurous childhoods, running barefoot, climbing trees, shooting with catapults and

air guns, making dens and tree houses, riding bicycles and breaking rules laid down by their parents and teachers. This is the image of untrammelled freedom that we treasure and the memoirs that are emerging about growing up in Northern Rhodesia often recount hair-raising stories (I'd particularly recommend Ian Hassell's *Hamba Gashle*, Conrad K's *The Shadow of the Tokolosh* and Anthony Bruce's *The Consequence of Memory*). It was not, however, necessarily more than ordinary child's play. Leslie van den Brink summarises the routine:

Life was fun for a youngster of 12 years old. I remember we had a big ant hill in the back garden and plenty of mango trees, I always ended up getting mango sores around my mouth until I realised about having to wash up after every fruit. When I used to go to the matinee either on Wednesdays or Saturdays we used to take all our comics so that we could swap with each other and coming back home just waiting to play the hero we had seen in the latest picture at the Bioscope. We spent most of the afternoons at the Mine Club swimming pool where we were chaperoned by old Wattie Watson. The first year at Luanshya I went to Rivercross primary then on to Luanshya High. I am afraid that I was never very clever at school and never got out of the lowest grade but I finished school with a first class pass so that I could start an apprenticeship.

What people emphasise about being a child in Northern Rhodesia is extraordinary freedom. Rose Newman's sentiments are echoed by many – those bare feet being almost a universal symbol:

We took so much for granted - the freedom to run, mostly barefoot, wherever we pleased, being out of the house and playing outdoors until it got dark.

Many children became familiar with the bush, roaming whenever they had the opportunity. The towns were all small enough for the bush to be close by and Julie Swenson stresses how easy it was for a child to be happy in this context:

No matter where I go and how many places I have lived in, Northern Rhodesia will always be home to me. A wonderful place to grow up in, I always felt safe and happy there and spent many contented hours in the bush on my own (exploring and adventuring!). I was an only child so enjoyed my own company and had a wonderfully imaginative childhood – I was and still am a voracious reader... We got TV in the early '60's but no one ever stayed home because of it – just too much to do. Lots of sports, good exercise and plenty of fun.

It was often a pretty ramshackle existence, beautifully described by Mik

Wright who was never to give up his independent and free-spirited lifestyle and is now a craft shoemaker in West Virginia:

We lived out at the airport at Ndola. Dad was a master welder and could fix anything mechanical. A panel beater by trade. That's how they used to take the dings out of cars. There were only about another 5 houses out there. We had two men, a "houseboy", his name was Jim and a "garden boy" whose name was Isaac. Jim was a Zulu and used to do everything in the house, including cook. I loved him, he taught me to speak fanagalo *a language he had learned when he went to work in 'igoli', the gold mines in Johannesburg. Isaac taught us how to make a kati, which is called a slingshot here, out of old car tubes and bits of leather from old shoes to hold the stone. We had great times shooting at the huge lizards that were all over the place. We also killed and ate a lot of birds. We were always on the rampage fighting wars and killing things, being big hunters. The place was called Kansengi – I think that's how you spell it. There were only two seasons that I remember there. Hot and raining or hot and no rain.*

When I was 13 my dad sent me out into the bush, up near Nyasaland, with an old Boer who was working on the roads up there for a month. One weekend the old man took me out with the big gun and showed me how to stalk and shoot a huge buck, a hartebeest that stood twice as high as I did. It was an amazing feeling, sorrow and awe for this huge animal that I had killed. The old man said that it was "for the pot" there were about 20 men and some women to feed.

Trevor Snyman, another boy who spent as much time as he could in the bush, writes of his conversion from would-be hunter to conservationist when he was just 12:

My trusty pellet gun accompanied me on all jaunts into the bush. My dad used to hunt with his friends on trips into the bush. I guess that my pellet gun was my attempt to emulate him as a hunter. On a sadly memorable day I was in my beloved bush, looking for something to shoot. I carefully tracked a black bird that I saw high in the trees, slowly following it until it settled in the branches above. I aimed carefully, suddenly the big hunter, and squeezed the trigger, loosing off the pellet. The bird, I now know it must have been a Forktailed Drongo, fell to the ground, not dead, where it lay fluttering. I panicked, suddenly feeling like hell, sad at having hit it, and not sure what to do. Aware that it was suffering at my hand, I used the butt of the gun to kill it. I sat down and cried, unbelievably sad at the loss of the little creature, and ashamed at having been the instrument of its death. I picked up the little limp body, still crying, and resolved to never again shoot at any creature. I buried the little bird, made a cross of twigs, and went home. The pellet gun still accompanied me on my future trips into the bush, but henceforth my targets were tins and stones, inert targets that I could not kill. Later in life I can still feel the sadness at having killed this bird.

Children were generally left to their own devices in the assumption that they were safe in the small European towns, so there are frequent references to freedom to roam, riding bicycles everywhere, but girls in particular were expected to know their limits. Eve Anderson gives an example of a transgression that probably terrified her parents:

I must have been about 10 years old when I hitchhiked to Luanshya – the Ndola swimming pool was closed for repairs and I wanted to train, so I just stood on the side of the Ndola/Luanshya road and hitched a lift. When I arrived at the Luanshya pool the superintendent there recognised me, asked me how I got there and then phoned my father. Needless to say my father arrived about an hour later furious with me!

Otto Gilbert is one was of many who played in the residue from the copper refining process. He is a mining engineer now:

There were a number of dormant slimes (tailings is the proper word) dams around Nkana and these were good spots in which to run amok and have fun. The grown ups never visited these areas – as technically they were dangerous – so we were able to excavate small cubbies and generally be able to have a free hand doing nothing in particular – they were just fun places. We were out of sight and were actually quite harmless.

Kate Zonkie recounts the antics of a tomboy:

I did my schooling in NR, Kitwe. Oh those were the days! We had to walk to school every day with our shoes tied around our necks, to save the leather! As children were wont, we got up to mischief, picking mangoes off the trees on the way, or mulberries, then denying it was us, not remembering that we had the tell tale signs around our mouths. There was a stream at the bottom of the hill where we lived and we would go and play there every afternoon, catching tadpoles, putting them in jars and watching them transform into frogs. We rode our bikes with such daring in the street, weaving in and out of the driveways, chasing the neighbours' cats, just being hooligans.

My father worked on the copper mine in Nkana and so we had the slimes dams around us. We were not aware in those days of the dangers that were there, for us it was a magical place, where we could find caves and make dens, or play at finding treasures in the caves. There was always running water at the bottom of the dams, almost a jade green water, but that did not deter us, we would jump in and try and swim against the flow, which at times could be very strong.

My high school days were revealing to me and I had a hard time of it. It was not a mixed school ... WE had to do deportment, and learn to be 'ladies'. WE had to learn to cook and sew and housekeeping! ... I did get through most of my years at Kitwe Girls High, but the last term of high school I bunked – I had had enough of it.

John Tyne was more conscious of the danger of the slimes dams:

Because there was no physical compacting of the 'tailings', the dams were similar to sand dunes, quite solid to the touch but unstable if burrowed into. So, of course we used to do just that, making little caves in the side of the dams where we spent many happy hours fantasising about robbers etc. with scant consideration for the possibility of a cave-in, or getting sick from coming in contact with the chemicals in the sand.

A number of youngsters lost their lives when their caves collapsed, hence the strict warnings from both the corporation and parents. Another incident I experienced with my brothers, was where my eldest brother was almost lost in 'quick sand' on one of the dams. It was only by good fortune that there happened to be some other older boys nearby, who came to his rescue that he wasn't actually sucked down. A really close call, which we did acknowledge by avoiding that particular spot, but that didn't stop us playing in other areas.

Another dangerous pastime was going to the mine scrapyard, handing over a packet of cigarettes to the old watchman and getting a whole bunch of detonators which were about the size and shape of a cigarette. On one occasion, we got a whole box full in their original packing. These were easily set off by touching the wires to either end of a torch battery ... Unfortunately, there were some accidents and one guy lost a bunch of fingers and an eye, when he stuffed some detonators into his bicycle's handlebars and set them off.

A little less wild

The "wild child" story is the official version of growing up in Africa, and we all know how to tell the tale. Like all standard narratives, it is true in parts, but only in parts. In a *Science Studio Interview* the philosopher A.C. Grayling said of his childhood in Luanshya:

> *... the two main entertainments that people had, adults anyway, were adultery and golf. And for somebody like me without television and not much else to do, reading... when I was about twelve, I went into our little local library, which was a very eccentric little library. It consisted of all the books that were left behind by British expats who had died of tropical diseases ... So there was a complete set of Plato's dialogues ... The first one I read was* The Charmides, *which is about temperance, and I was bowled over by it, thought, this is absolutely wonderful.*

Grayling was, of course, exoticising his childhood by referring to the library being stocked through the early death from tropical diseases by the previous owners of its books – it was probably stuff people didn't want to pack when moving and he was certainly glamorising the Copperbelt by making it sound like Kenya's "Happy Valley", but he was far from being the sole intellectual.

In reality, most of the children were not little Mowglies – they went to schools where they were prepared for Cambridge School Certificate, as well as being instructed in the importance of wearing their ties straight. Though some girls in Northern Rhodesia shared in the boys' adventures, parental fears often kept most close to home and by their early teens they were learning the elaborate forms of fluffy femininity that seem always to be highly developed in "a man's country" (and 30-yard petticoats just didn't go with tree climbing). Although he spent a lot of time in the bush, Mik Wright was also an urban teenager:

> *I went to Llewellyn High School. I was always more mature than the kids my age and met and became friends with a guy called Chris. His father was a boxer and his big brother was a musician in the local orchestra and played classical clarinet. His friends had a band called 'The Young Ones." Peter played the sax in their band and used to go back quite often to the U.K. He brought back LPs by the Beatles and the Rolling Stones. Our lives would never be the same. Soon Chris and I had to have our own band called The Echoes; the older guys tolerated us hanging around and we learned from them.*

Living in the sticks

Penny Giorgio highlights how different it was for a girl living on a farm, rather than on the Copperbelt:

My family was on the Veterinary Research Station there and then moved to the family farm in Muzoka, a small railway siding village consisting of our beef, maize and chicken farm with bakery and shop for the local folk, a group of Asian traders and the inevitable beerhall. My early memories are of a free spirited and happy family life with my older brother and with intercourse with neighbouring farming families in the area between Mazabuka and Zimba. Our farm community consisting of some 30 home, shop and farm workers was a very close one, and a protective cloak was placed on my brother and me by all these wonderful people whether we were out riding or fishing or walking through the bush. It was idyllic and I am eternally grateful for this start to life among great people and the wildlife that was prolific at that time.

I was educated at home with correspondence courses by my mother until, at five I was sent as a boarder to Beit School in Choma. My brother was sent to Lusaka to school. This was a difficult time – too young to cope without the family and, although I did somehow achieve both scholastically and in sport, I do not remember this time with joy. Difficult years of drought and floods in the early 'fifties put paid to the farm for my parents and, although we retained ownership, we moved to Lusaka where I completed my education at Jean Rennie School and made life long friends who sadly are scattered over the globe. Among the wonders of teenage life was work with the Operation Noah project of moving animals out of the flood brought about by the Kariba Dam project.

Karen Horn talks of the loneliness of farm life:

When I was one year old we moved near to Mbala (formerly Abercorn). We had a farm there, a cattle ranch. My brother, who is eighteen years older than I am and at that time a young man, looked after the day-to-day running of the farm and my father owned the butcher shop in Mbala, where we sold the meat from our cattle. This job at least kept us in food, but with not much left over for luxuries. During our last few years in Mbala we left the farm to live in town. We were happier there, my mother was not as lonely and I had friends to play with. Prior to the move I boarded during the week with a family my parents were friendly with. This worked out very well, as I had playmates, and I was able to attend the small primary school.

Until Federation, both African and European education were administered by the Northern Rhodesia Government, though some of the (slight) provision was in the hands of missionaries. The last Colonial Office *Annual Report on the social and economic progress of the people of Northern Rhodesia* before the war (1938) showed that:

For the education of European children there were in 1937 controlled schools [i.e. government approved] *at Livingstone, Choma, Mazabuka, Lusaka, Broken Hill, Ndola, Luanshya, Kitwe and Mufulira, offering primary education up to Standard VII, with the additional subjects, Latin, French, Algebra, Geometry and Science in Standards VI and VII. There were controlled schools at Fort Jameson, Mulendema and Silver Rest offering primary education up to Standard V.* (p. 25)

It was evident that the colonial government made the assumption that most European children would be limited to artisanal employment and did not need educating beyond primary level. Those seeking full secondary education had to be educated outside the territory. High school education came late to the country and many parents were never convinced of its value, having been denied it themselves. Robert Trail says of his schooldays in the 1940s:

The school only went to Standard Seven and it is hard to believe in those days that you left then and went to work – average age was 13 or 14 years, the boys to the mines and the girls to the Mine Offices. You knew every body in town, that is how small the town was. All the children went to Frederick Knapp School, from the General Manager's son to the lowest of mine workers... My childhood was wonderful, with my pellet gun and dog Duke, I roamed the bush around town. On my bike I visited friends all over. I went fishing at the Kafue river seven miles away, swam at the rapids with friends and went to the Bioscope Wednesday afternoons and Saturdays. I feel sorry for the children of to-day.

When I got to Standard Seven I became a boarder at Prince Edward School in Salisbury until Matric. It was not easy in the 1930s. As a child I had malaria a few times. Because of the tsetse fly, there was no cattle, so no fresh milk. But they were wonderful days and we became self reliant and confident. We were well educated and well trained. Friends made in those days are still our friends today. The downside is because of circumstances our children now live in America with their families and are American citizens.

The Federation had at its heart the growth of a white settler population in Central Africa and progressively introduced the infrastructure to facilitate this. Attention was paid to raising the standard of European education in order to maintain the advantage Europeans had over Africans, so new high schools were established in the major towns, extending provision up to Cambridge Higher School Certificate (university entrance) but many, particularly farm children, still started school late and left early, after two or three years of high school.

Just a bit rough?

There is, however, no denying that some parents regarded the children in Northern Rhodesia's schools rather "common" and would not contemplate educating their own children in the country; this is hardly surprising in the light of their comments deploring the post-war arrival of large numbers of people with a working class background. Furthermore, children who didn't have one already, inevitably picked up a Rhodesian accent and knowledge of South African slang in the local schools. Writing about joining primary school in Ndola in the late 'forties Stewart Burns encountered the famously terrifying figure of Frederick Knapp:

He was a tall and imposing figure – the typical Headmaster of the Billy Bunter comics. My initial memories of my schooling were of unpleasant teasing by my fellow schoolmates as I was the possessor of a very broad Scottish accent which they found either amusing or unintelligible ... I very quickly learned to get rid of the Scots accent and adopt the Rhodesian manner of speaking, to the total horror of my mother and father.

Children also encountered the hegemonic view of the racial structure of their society, held by many of the teachers as well as their fellow pupils; unsurprisingly, the schools were the society writ small. In 1956 when the UK House of Commons held a debate on *Northern Rhodesia (African Development)*, much of which centred on the role of education, James Johnson MP quoted from the Northern Rhodesia Government *Report of the Committee upon Racial Discrimination* and said:

I do beg the Minister and all Hon. Members present to listen to this, because it is an all-white Committee speaking about their own people:

"One of the biggest educational problems is what to do with children who in Europe would dig ditches, hew wood and draw water. This type of European knows that his white skin is his biggest asset." (I assume I can hear the tones of Stewart Gore-Brown.)

Fortunately not all teachers regarded their pupils with the contempt that the LegCo committee demonstrated (or perhaps they did and decided that Latin would be the best civilising agent) but discipline was strict, especially for boys.

Hans Dielissen wrote:

*At King George VI High School the naughtiness carried on, indicated by the amount of canings we got by the head master. We all kept track of how many we had with strokes on the back of our ties. Discipline was a big thing at school, tie straight, socks up, long shorts and short hair, if any of these things weren't right the prefects would pull you out of line and you would have to go to the head master at break and be caned, first sign the book, then your head under the table and then the strokes with the cane. I'm sure Mr **** enjoyed caning us.*

After independence in 1964 a lot of Africans started coming to the school and a lot of people were moving away to South Africa and Rhodesia, we stayed till 1967 when my parents sent me to boarding school in Bulawayo Rhodesia. I had just turned sixteen a few days earlier and had had a real free life, it was like being sent to jail for me. It didn't last long, within two days I had run away, hitched back home, got beaten up by my dad and taken back, that only lasted one day ... it did ruin my whole education. This time I didn't go home as I knew my dad would murder me, I moved in with my brother who lived in a lodging house in Bulawayo. Within a day the police were at the door but they left me alone as I had just turned sixteen and didn't have to go to school anymore. The next day I went to the employment office and found a job fitting auto glass.

Barbara A concurs with this impression of institutionalized violence:

I started school at age three with American nuns at Sacred Heart Convent, then went to Chingola Primary and High Schools. The schools were strictly whites-only in those days. In my junior years I was a happy enough kid, and particularly enjoyed going to ballet and tap-dancing classes and appearing on stage. By the time I reached high school, however, the only extracurricular activities that seemed to matter were sports, which I was hopeless at and loathed, and that soon branded me as a misfit. At Chingola High, discipline was haphazardly enforced, yet corporal punishment (cuts, or caning, on the buttocks, back of legs or open palms) for major and minor infringements alike was common (even for girls) and sexism and bullying were rife, even encouraged as it was seen as a way of "toughening you up".

Being an only child, my parents were not that keen for me to go away to boarding school, but the truth is that I would have done far better academically had I been sent to an establishment that either encouraged girls to excel or nurtured individuality. Whether my parents were aware of some of the less savoury aspects of Chingola High School, I can't say at this distance in time. What I do know is that while a handful of teachers were excellent, many of them were second-rate, even sadistic, being transient individuals on short contracts who had little commitment to the school or the welfare its students. About 20 years ago I met one, then retired in Australia. I hadn't known her personally as she had taught the streams doing commercial subjects, but I felt a certain vindication when she said words to the effect: "How ever did you cope? In all my teaching years that was the worst school and the toughest, most terrifying kids I ever encountered anywhere – and the other teachers weren't much better either!" It says something that a shy introvert like me managed to learn anything at all and survive! Apart from being appalled at the notion of getting physically slapped about by teachers who turned a blind eye to bullies, my own teenagers were astonished when I told them that there were no such things as school counsellors or remedial help for those slipping behind; no excursions (other than for sport) and no graduation ceremony or social events such as a "prom" dance. We sat final exams and just walked out of the gate and awaited the results in the mail from England three months later. I do not look back on my days there with any kind of nostalgia or sentimentality.

I'm delighted to say that neither of the schools I attended were quite this bad, but it is a pattern I recognize; friends in Britain are amazed to discover that there was no music, no art, no physical education and even sport was an optional after-school activity that most of us opted out of. Arriving after my time, Tony Sparks wrought a minor revolution:

I had a life that had been shaped by music, theatre and dancing. So there was this 17-year-old of "artistic" bent, which as you will see caused me problems during my last two years at King George VI High School. The day I arrived at my new school auditions were being held for a production of "A Midsummer Night's Dream" to be directed by the English teacher and I was given a part. The review in the local paper, the Broken Hill Observer, said something along the lines of "...perfectly cast as Puck".

Apart from the Shakespeare, there seemed little else happening – not even a teacher who could play the piano! At the end of the first term the headmaster was retiring and, as nothing had been arranged in the form of a farewell, I asked if I could do a variety show for his last day. It proved to be such a success (particularly with the boarders as it gave them extra curricula besides the odd sport) that the word spread to parents who wanted to see what their offspring had been up to. First day of the new term, and a new headmaster wanted to meet the head boy and girl and prefects. His first question was "Who was responsible for the concert at the end of last term?" One of the local ministers of religion had heard about it and complained that there had been a strip-tease – true, behind a sheet with back lighting and wearing a swimming costume!

Dancing, accompanying the singers, directing the show – getting my photo on to the front page of the Observer by doing a Charleston lip-synching impersonation of Pinky Pinkham – Wrong! That was a signal that Tony was a bit of a sissy and along with some verbal abuse could be picked on – including being dragged off to the loos one day by a group who proceeded to make me put on a dress to wear to my next lesson (Afrikaans). But I had a stubborn resilience and kept it to myself, never complaining to my parents or anyone in the school. Today, it's much easier to know about and recognise what it is to be gay, particularly for those who grow up in an urban environment.

This lack of education in the arts was echoed by Stuart Mclean but, like many people who survived it, he considers the strict discipline a valuable part of his education:

All of my education was in Northern Rhodesia, at Lusaka Infants School, Lusaka Boys School, Fort Jameson School, Gilbert Rennie, Hillcrest High School in Livingstone and back to Gilbert Rennie. The education offered to me was second to none but sadly I didn't really take full advantage of what was on offer. I left school with three A levels but didn't go to University as I should have done. The education was wonderful and every advantage possible in an education system was available to us, academically and in sport. Possibly the only area that was weak was music, drama and the arts. The teachers were well qualified and committed and brought a lot of ideas from successful education in the UK. I recall almost always being very much encouraged by the teachers… One of the advantages of life at school in NR was that, although there were people from all strata of society, in many ways it was a classless society. As a result it was possible to mix with families who had different standards, ideals etc. and this allowed me to adopt some of these ideas, a facility that would never have been available to me had we remained in Scotland. There I would have probably been restricted to people of a similar background to mine. Discipline was strict, we wore uniforms and were expected to behave in an acceptable way both at school and in town. For example as a boarder at Hillcrest on trips to town uniform, including a boater, had to be worn and you were expected to raise your hat to your elders, white only!

The twin Jean and Gilbert Rennie Schools in Lusaka were regarded by most as being the best of the state high schools, partly because good teachers could more easily be retained in the capital, partly because many of the pupils were the children of civil servants. The cricketer, Phil Edmonds describes Gilbert Rennie to his biographer as:

An absolutely magnificent school where the facilities, academic and sporting, were extraordinary – and all for £3 a year. I suppose, looking back, that it set itself up to create the leaders of tomorrow: the basic Oxbridge philosophy of education. Indeed most of the masters were Oxbridge and the main cricket field was called Parker's Piece after the cricket field in Cambridge. (Barnes, 1986, p.6)

Edmunds is inflating the Oxbridge count, but the school did have a more English flavour than those to the north and it succeeded in gaining university entrance for virtually all who wanted it. Boarding was not solely a matter of elite education outside the territory, a number of the state schools had hostels providing for the children of farmers, missionaries and people living in the small settlements. Neville Isdell enjoyed Gilbert Rennie:

I was in love with Africa, so much so that … I decided to stay behind in Lusaka at boarding school when my parents took another six-month leave in Belfast. I lived at the Gilbert Rennie School and under the British system was assigned a first-year student, called a 'fag' who as part of an initiation process had to fold my clothes, make my bed and run any other errands I might have.

I played rugby, cricket, tennis and soccer. At the time I wanted to become a geography or history teacher.

Jean Rennie was altogether less "English". Marion Fuller-Sessions, the daughter of a District Commissioner who would go on to be Governor of Somaliland, hated it when she was sent to board at the school for a short while, finding the daughters of Afrikaner farmers who predominated in her dormitory uncongenial. She prayed each night for an escape and was delighted when, after five weeks of misery, a place was found for her at a private school in Southern Rhodesia.

Though most schools for European children were government run, there was a small number of mission and convent schools, day and boarding, the latter taking both sexes at primary level and girls as far as Cambridge School Certificate, but not to higher level. Most of the stories about convents are of strict discipline and it was believed by many parents that they offered a superior education. I have yet to see the evidence, other than in needlework.

Going away to school

The tradition of sending children to boarding school outside the country was initially established as a consequence of the lack of local provision. Private boarding schools, particularly in South Africa and Southern Rhodesia, were affordable by senior mine staff and professionals, many of whom, with some justification, doubted the standard of the local high schools when these were eventually introduced. The English-style public schools (in the confusing English sense of private schools) in Rhodesia and South Africa were a solution to the problem of keeping children relatively near home, whilst obtaining an internationally respectable standard of education. Boarding became fairly normal as Robert Webster points out:

I think the most profound effect on my life was that the colonial lifestyle and location meant that the correct thing to do was to send the kids to boarding school. I was schooled at a Jesuit College in Salisbury, Rhodesia...a school with high academic and sporting standards. (We still have reunions around the planet...) I got a great education and that set me up for University and easier job choice for the future. The downside was that when at home, I had a live-in nanny who probably showed more affection than my parents. ...that is not to say that our parents did not love us, they just ended up not knowing how to show it. We had a comfortable life and the lifestyle was wonderful...lots of open space and skies, laid back outdoor living, fun and a simplicity that all combined to teach us about the most important things in life.

But a man who would rather not be named contributed a rather different view of the consequences:

Due to the farms being fairly isolated all the community's children had to be sent to boarding school from about the age of seven. In my brothers' and my case we went to primary school in Mazabuka, high school in Livingstone and then much further afield in Pietersburg, South Africa, a three day train journey away. This was a particularly negative aspect to our growing up in NR. For a child to be sent to boarding school at the age of seven is a traumatic and barbaric experience and led to an unnatural relationship with our parents as we never really went home again and had a normal relationship and time with them as a family. All time together was telescoped into holiday periods. And when school was completed we immediately went on to further learning and finally employment, again a long way from home. So we in effect left home at seven and now I wish I had more time as a family unit with my brothers and parents.

Jane Leach used the trope of postcards from the past to isolate incidents from her childhood:

I pick up one card after another. Each one is a vivid story of a childhood in the Colonial Service. The school in Kasama. The lion skins pegged out on the front of the small two roomed building which served for all the various ages of us kids.

Soon to be followed by the 2,000 mile journey for me and my 11 year old sister, when I was 10. Back down that long winding road because she had a hole in the heart and could not afford to get malaria. The first leg was by air. There we stand – dressed in Wykham School uniforms on a runway in the middle of the bush. A Dakota taxis in and we climb on board. Mum and Dad wave good bye. We two girls took this 2,000 mile journey on our own. Dakota to Ndola to catch the train to Pietermaritzburg.

One year later it would be at Ndola where my sister died in her father's arms after a debilitating four day train journey from Pietermaritzburg, with my mother and me. She had been dying slowly as the train chugged North. At Livingstone

*and Lusaka the train conductor desperately tried to contact a hospital for an
ambulance to meet us. The platform at Lusaka was bare and dark, so on we
went. An unmarked grave for a 12 year old, and still three days to get home. A
sorrowful night stop at Mpika, the Crested Crane Hotel.*

*Three years later, my two younger siblings and I would catch a Thatcher and
Hobson bus. Mum and Dad once more waved their children goodbye, on our
way to school on our own, in the care of the bus driver. We sat in a compartment
reserved for Europeans in a bus for African people.*

Families were liable to educate their sons rather than daughters, as Rose
Newman suggests:

*John, being the boy and therefore more deserving of a better education (!!)
was sent to Falcon College, near Bulawayo, where many of the Copperbelt boys
went for their high school education, either there or to St Stevens college. The
sarcasm is tongue in cheek, as I don't at all begrudge John his education, he was
by far the academically brightest of the three of us! I wouldn't have wanted to go
off to boarding school anyway and I received, locally, as adequate an education
as I needed for my interests and ambitions.*

Those who hoped that children attending private schools would be better
behaved than those who stayed behind would be disappointed. The school train,
dropping off children as it made its way down to the Cape was notorious. Otto
Gilbert describes the journey:

*Once or twice a year we would be packed off to boarding school, most of
us in South Africa. This was usually the highlight of the year's activities as we
could run wild for the duration of the journey, usually 3 to 4 days depending
on the destination. The trains were, of course, the old steam Class IV Garrat
locomotives operated by Rhodesia Railways and the accommodation was in
compartments or coupés. Second Class travel meant 6 bunks in one compartment
or four if your folks were well heeled and you were first class. The Dining car
was strategically located in the centre of the train so that the boys' section could
be segregated from the girls. Chaperones monitored the movements of either
sector quite rigorously. The only times the girls and boys could get together was
when the train was negotiating some very steep gradients and it was possible
to step off the moving train and run forward to overtake the dining car and re-
board the train. Making the return trip sometimes proved quite hazardous!*

On the southbound trip, we would alight at Livingstone Station, hire a taxi and hot foot it over the Victoria Falls Bridge to be dropped off at the Victoria Falls Hotel, at that time one of the grandest Hotels in the Empire. There we would lash out for some cold drinks and snacks with beers for the older and more forward youngsters. At that time the Falls Hotel was still owned by Rhodesia Railways. The railside hawkers in Bechuanaland near villages like Mahalapye and Gaberone were always the subject of a fair amount of torment by the schoolies who would bargain for their curios and wares right until the train's departure from the siding, usually still in possession of the item, with no intention of returning it to the vendor.

Robert Plain was explicit about the vandalism on the school trains and the contempt for African children:

Travel to Muir College was by train and each one way trip took four days, first by Rhodesia Railways to Bulawayo, leaving Broken Hill in the dead of the night and arriving in Bulawayo about mid-morning a day and a half later where we had to change to South African Railways. South African Railways always put on a couple of old coaches for us as some of the boys were somewhat wild and boisterous and on occasions damaged the coaches. [One boy] was particularly mad as he would climb out of the compartment window and into the compartment next door while the train was on the move. On one trip our compartment door was ripped off its hinges, it was not us, but we got the blame anyway... On the return journey the train would stop for long periods at places in Bechuanaland. This was great fun as we would heat up pennies with a candle before tossing them out to the piccanins begging at the carriage windows. We sometimes bought night apes but they always escaped, where they went is still a mystery. The train usually arrived in Bulawayo in the early evening of day two and we would have to lug all our gear through the Customs Hall where it was checked and a large white chalk cross or tick made on our luggage. The Rhodesia Railways train north left later the same evening. While crossing the Falls bridge many of the green leather bolsters were consigned to the bottom of the gorge as the train crossed the bridge. In late 1956 and early 1957 the Africans had begun sabotaging the railways lines by removing sections of railway track resulting in derailed goods trains, many of which we saw as we crawled by on the temporary track past the wrecked train. Drew & I left Muir College after two years as Mum and Stan could not afford the fees anymore and I think I was getting close to expulsion.

Going "Home" to school

The children of officers who were posted to remote areas and transferred frequently needed a stable education and the United Kingdom had the valuable function of ensuring that the next generation of the colonial elite was exposed to European society and the values ingrained by the public school system. To retain the right quality of officers, fees and travel to schools abroad formed part of the contract of members of HMOCS. Jeremy Paxman, noted the importance of the role of the public schools in the British Empire and his comments are as true of Northern Rhodesia as elsewhere:

Creating and running this enormous enterprise required a certain type of individual, which gave Britain its idiosyncratic public-school system, designed to produce not intellectuals but "sound chaps" – capable, dependable and resourceful. They were to be oblivious to discomfort and able to inspire respect, for through them was the reality of the British Empire to be made clear. (Paxman, 2011 p. 10)

Despite the undoubted advantages, the cost to the children was that they were far away from their parents; this could be traumatic. In the days before flying between Britain and Northern Rhodesia became normal, long sea and train journeys would have eaten up the whole school summer holiday of children at school in Britain, so children might be separated from one or both parents for long periods, as what Jane Gardam (2005) poignantly calls "raj orphans". Patricia Englert was sent home at the age of eight and did not return to Northern Rhodesia until she was thirteen, seeing her parents only when they came to Britain. She writes:

I went to NR in 1938 at the age of 8 months and stayed there through the war years until 1946. My father John Frederick Passmore, was in the Colonial Service... I shared the common experience of boarding school and holidays with my grandmother and periodic separation from my mother of nearly two years and my father of nearly 3 years during the years of my education. My older sister and I had the summer holiday of 1951 with my parents when my father was stationed in Namwala.

Although she and her siblings came home every year for the long holidays and also saw her parents when they were on leave, Val Kenning explained that in shorter holidays they had to go to a guardian – at first elderly relatives, later a woman was paid to look after them. At *exeat* weekends and half-term they had to rely on the hospitality of school friends and Val tells of the humiliation of her school's practice of putting up lists of the colonial children requiring invitations, going daily to check whether someone had signed against her name. Such miseries were concealed from her parents because letters home were censored, but in any case she said she didn't want to worry them.

Often the experience is described stoically, and that is precisely the quality that the education was intended to foster. Lorna McMullen, the daughter of a member of the PA wrote:

When I was just about to be nine (1950) I was sent to school in Dorset and did not see my parents for the next three years which, although it was a normal thing to do in those years, seemed to me rather traumatic. My early years in NR were a great privilege. Great friendships were formed which have lasted all my life. I think it has helped me through life to realise how fortunate I am to have had these early years.

Jane Galloway told me in an interview that when she and her sister flew back from Britain aged thirteen and fourteen they had not seen either of their parents for eighteen months; after a long journey they were both crying as the plane landed, her sister afraid their parents wouldn't recognise her, Jane afraid she would not recognise them.

Mothers, in particular, suffered from separation from their children, even though Brian Heathcote, the son of a Provincial Commissioner says he had no problems himself when he went away to school,

I was packed off to boarding school in UK in 1962 aged 9. Only saw my parents then in the Xmas and summer holidays, Easter being spent with our aunt in Tilford Surrey. I can't remember being particularly *homesick and enjoyed my prep school in East Sussex. I remember the very snowy winter in UK 1963 and being delayed flying back into UK due to a closed airport. My Mother never forgave my father for packing me off to boarding school at such a young age, but it was felt a better education would be found in UK than Africa.*

Really remote places

There were small settlements where virtually no European children were to be seen outside school holidays because of the need to send them to school. Missionaries were generally stationed in remote areas so sent their children to boarding schools; their stories are often stark. Priscilla Flower-Smith's account makes one realize what great sacrifices were required of missionary children:

My parents, May and John Stanley Lougher, married in Nigeria, in 1930 after getting engaged in Britain. Four years later they came home 'on furlough' and went back in about 1937, but to the Belgian Congo this time, leaving my elder sister and me behind in a missionary children's home, as they and others like them were not allowed to take children to disease ridden countries. (Priscilla was one year old at the time).

A missionary background was not always puritanical, as Jane Leach shows:

I changed schools I think 10 times. Formerly at Indaleni Mission in Natal, my father fled from the apartheid system to serve as an Education Officer in the British Colonial Service. We were four children in this clearing in the bush. Kasama – The Chishimba falls were a wee way out. There was club house, of course, where Mum won lots of tennis cups and acted in the amateur dramatic society... Where has the PWD man who married the nurse gone? Lynette and I were the flower girls and our long dresses brushed up the caterpillar hairs from under the huge fig tree and we spent most of the reception in tears. No one could be bothered to stop the drinking to see to us. Nor could Mum and Dad be bothered to get home from the drinking after the tennis to see that us kids had the house open and the Tilly lamps lit. So we sat at the back of the house with the servants. One of the wives of these servants went down to the river to collect water and came home minus one arm, the other having been taken by a croc. She made no fuss!

Yves Grebert was the son of French missionaries in Barotseland who mostly enjoyed his unusual bush-based boarding school experience:

I was the last of four kids to go to boarding school in the family, our younger brother was too small do so. Being 4th in the row undoubtedly made my life easier, I was only there for my primary school as after then we headed back to Europe. We all attended Silver Rest School outside Lusaka, on the great east road in the middle of the bush and the commercial farming. In the late 'fifties, early sixties, this all white school founded by an Afrikaner, Van Wyck, was attended essentially by surrounding Afrikaner kids from farms, a few coming from the Copperbelt, and us a bunch of missionary kids from Barotseland. In the typical old fashioned boarding school, we learnt the Victorian discipline and rigour of those establishments – one that marks any childhood.

Due to the distance from home (600km), we missionary kids could not return home on weekends nor "long weekends" – we travelled to school by flying to Lusaka (on the Dakota-DC3's) – stayed at school three months in a row. We learnt to correspond with our parents (correspondence always has since then been an important part of the social family life) – principally a Sunday obligation, writing in French, a language that we had never learnt to write, but were helped by some of our teachers who had had some basics! Though we could not go home frequently, the advantage was that we were invited by our local commercial farmer friends on special long weekends. What a great opportunity and an eye opener it was to go out on these huge farms....kids driving cars/jeeps, going hunting in the bush, playing with tamed monkeys, duikers, owls, etc., swimming in dams, fishing, having to butcher the pig or the goat for a "braai" We were faced, in some instances, with some rough Afrikaner farmers & lifestyle where drinking was part of life and sometimes ended up in jagged situations (things that in the missionary world we were not exposed to!!!) ... a whole bunch of adventures remain impregnated in our memories. We also realized that their relationship with the blacks and their treatment were not the same as in Barotseland and the missionary world. Things started to change at the time of independence. Most of our commercial farmer friends left the country to go south.

Although some children went to boarding school pitifully young, others had no other children of their age around them. Jenny Boutwood writes about being the daughter of the DC at Sesheke:

I was the only child of school age on the Boma, and my mother taught me by correspondence course. It was very frustrating trying to concentrate on arithmetic, with which both my mother and I had problems, while from outside came the sound of younger children playing happily in the garden. But it was exciting getting the large brown envelopes every month, with all the things for me to do; a lot of it was colouring.

Menna Uttley's father was an agricultural officer and the family lived on a remote research station in the Southern Province:

Our life at Mapangazia was truly idyllic. The house was large with a veranda three quarters of the way round. This veranda was very important to my sister and me. It was here where strange human tissue (dried baby's umbilical cords) was hung in tiny wicker baskets by the "witch doctors" when we first arrived, and it was where we studied by 'School on the Air' and were taught by our mother. At certain times of the year enormous spiders would make their webs in the corners. In the rainy season we would watch the rain come into the veranda and I thought of Noah's Ark and that the rain would never stop. As well as spiders there were always intriguing animals around. Some locals showed us a dead hyena lying in the back of a truck and it was here that our dog 'Elizabeth' was bitten by a Puff Adder and took three days to die.

Occasionally we would have visitors at Mapangazia, once the Governor came to visit. My sister and I spent a great deal of time practising curtseying. On occasions such at this my mother would get out her special tea set of eight brightly coloured cups and saucers (we still have these today). On visits that were unplanned we could see a vehicle approaching along the dusty road around a couple of miles away – time enough, my mother would say, to make a plate of fresh drop scones. Once a month a tractor and trailer would go to Mazabuka to fetch provisions for us and we waited excitedly for its return as often my father would have bought us new dress material which my mother would then make up for us.

It was at Mapangazia where, although we took Paludrine for protection against malaria and were tucked up each night under a mosquito net, one rainy season my sister and I contacted malaria. We were very ill and unable to stand.

A tough life

The Copperbelt in particular had a reputation for hard drinking, behind some of the childhood freedom there was child neglect, often concealed by servants feeding European children from their own kitchens. Homes could be violent as hard men meted out punishment to their wives and children. Corporal punishment was routine in homes as well as at school, one informant telling me about her friend's father using the *sjambok* on her for trivial offences and boys expected regular beatings (which they now seem to think were good for them).

These things, unsurprisingly, emerge more often in memoirs and novels than in letters to me, but Linda Hayes wrote:

I came from an abusive alcoholic background and was out on my own from the age of 16, fending for myself. I left Zambia with my whole life in 2 suitcases just 3 days after I turned 25 and landed in the USA not knowing a soul.

Ron Heyes hints at more than he reveals:

I was born in Bulawayo in 1929 and lived with my father in Luanshya from 1933, in the Cato Huts, [single quarters], and was brought up by a Matabele man by the name of Jeffrey whom I loved very dearly. He taught me how to cook, fish, hunt with both gun and bow and arrow and fight so that I was never in the position to be bullied. My father was a shaft sinker who worked all the hours under the sun. He sunk Beatty shaft in Luanshya and C shaft in Nchanga. I have many real and hairy stories to tell of life as a "wild" child in Northern Rhodesia, including witnessing the attempted murder of a man sleeping with the wife of Swede Pearson, the unbeaten heavy weight boxer of Northern Rhodesia for many years (he even beat the redoubtable Roy Welensky, whom my mother was sleeping with for many years when she was the housekeeper of the Luanshya Hotel).

Robert Plain, too, refers to family violence and break-up:

I couldn't help but notice Dad would argue with Mum when he got back from the golf club drunk and on one occasion he beat Mum up, after which she Drew & I went to the Police Station late that night. The Police officer asked Mum if she wanted my Dad charged but she didn't, so the situation got worse instead of better. On my ninth birthday my birthday cake was shoved into Mum's face by Dad, that was my last birthday celebration...

Independence

Just before Independence, racially segregated schooling came to an end. There was a massive expansion of high schools throughout the country. Like many, Rob Wilson, who had always previously been a day-scholar, was sent south of the Zambezi:

After Zambia's independence in 1964 I was sent away to boarding school in what was then Rhodesia because GCEs were no longer being done in Zambia. It's hard to go from a day school to boarding at the age of 14, but at least there were a few of us doing it. Falcon College did provide a lot of opportunities besides education, and I really enjoyed rugby and photography. Another bit of history happened – Ian Smith declared independence from the UK, and we all had to get used to a rather different life as sanctions bit.

The time came to leave Africa – my parents left for the UK and a few months later, when I'd finished at Falcon, I headed south on the train for Cape Town, en route to England. I lived in Zambia for nearly 18 years from birth. Looking back it was so many things: unreal in today's more sensitive world, but a real adventure at the time.

Margie Robinson voices the sentiments of European children attending schools in Zambia, where suddenly young men and women were enrolling in order to catch up on education that had previously been denied them:

I don't have many good memories of Zambia, I did my high school in Mufulira and must be honest I was so unhappy there, I remember only the men in their twenties in Form 1 and the girls getting pregnant and carrying to full term. My father was very strict and would not allow me out much, most of the kids back in the 1960's went to South Africa or Rhodesia to do their high school years but my father, being a missionary/minister, couldn't afford to send me away to school, so I mostly only remember the bad times. I think the good time was when we got into the car and left Zambia and moved to South Africa. That was in 1970. And in a second email:

Teachers felt at exam time we should know better, yet we were mostly ignored during lessons, only in Science do I recall the teacher giving the two white kids a bit more attention. I remember our classes had more than 30 kids. In primary school I was quite sporty, but when I got to high school, I did not really enjoy athletics, the black kids were quite fit, and tall and strong, so I did not partake in any sport.

African friends

It should be pretty clear by now that European children had little opportunity to know African children as equals, though pre-school children often had close relationships with the children of their parents' employees and learned local languages playing with them. Hilary Broughton, living on outstations as a PA child, told me she spoke ciBemba and ciLala before she knew English, all her youngest friends being African.

Similarly Mik Wright recounts that living out at Ndola Airport:

My brother and I got to know and play with the black kids our age, ran around the bush all day, learned how to catch rats by finding their holes and blocking all the exits but one then pushing sticks down into the other holes and as they came out the open one we would bash them with a club. When we had enough, we would take them to one of the kid's kias and their mother would cook them up for us to eat. The process was quite simple. Hold them by the tail into a big pot of boiling water over the fire and all the hair would drop off, then gut them and fry them up with some chili and onions. This all eaten with a scoop of sadsa with our hands. My mom was always mad at us when we came home too full to eat her dinner, having eaten with "the kaffirs". My good friends. I missed them when we moved into the town.

David Gray:

Being an only child I was fairly lonely and my parents used to employ a young Black boy of my age during the school holidays to be a playmate. This child called Moffat hobbled into our lives looking for gardening work at the start of one school holiday and returned each year for four years. He had a deformed right knee having been shot by police quelling the 1939 riots. Moffat was strapped to his mother's back at the time. We got on well together conversing in a mixture of English and 'Fanagolo'. I wonder what happened to my friend after he outgrew this cross-cultural association.

The idyll

The word "idyllic" appears in many descriptions of childhood in Northern Rhodesia – the memory that remains with most people is of the sunshine, the open spaces and the freedom. Barry Woodhams, writes of life on the 85,000 acre Veterinary Research Station near Mazabuka:

I guess my childhood on the ranch was idyllic – horses, swimming pool, shooting, walking etc. As it was a research station there were lots of vets I could travel out with – they were always keen to have a 'gate opener and closer' with them in the Land Rover. The laboratories on the station gave me an interest in all things living, as there were entomologists, vets, biologists all actively working on the ranch. There were not that many children on the station (many sent their children back to the UK for school). We were sometimes the only family on the station – my father ran the pathology laboratories. I learned my love of bird watching in my early teens from a vet and have never lost this love. This early experience I am sure has significantly influenced the rest of my total life.... I did a degree in biochemistry and then a PhD. I am a biochemist and have spent the whole of my working life in pathology – initially in London University then in the NHS.

Buzz Trevor's is the image most people want to cling to. Another son of a veterinary officer, his is the classic Africa story:

I think that Mongu was the only place in Northern Rhodesia that my mother did not particularly like, but for an 11 and 12 year old boy there can have been no better place in the world. We lived in a large rambling, thatched-roof house set on the hill overlooking the flood plain of the Zambezi. My dad and I rode virtually every day. The roads were so bad in Barotseland that sometimes my dad did his fieldwork on horseback. I cannot imagine a better place for riding horses – open bush and sandy underneath so if you did fall off it was relatively forgiving!

For several months of the year the Zambezi flooded and water extended as far as the eye could see. Different from the ocean or a lake, the flood plain was a mass of vegetation and abounded with birds. It was truly a magical place. From the base of the hill, channels were cut through the reeds so you could get out to the river proper by motorboat or, what I preferred, in a makoro.

Another memory is the fruit trees. Oranges and mangoes were absolutely prolific. Everyone just helped themselves – they were the best... First and foremost, I recognize that I had the sort of childhood that is not afforded to many people. The freedoms and experiences I had are even more remarkable when I see the circumscribed and ordered lives that children nowadays lead. At the same time, I realize that I was fortunate to live in a particular narrow window in time and my good fortune was actually privilege based on my skin colour.

6. A MAN'S COUNTRY?

A single woman on the permanent and pensionable establishment may be required to resign her appointment in the event of her marriage *NRG General Orders*

It was often said that Northern Rhodesia was a man's country. Taken literally, one might well respond "Not all that much so" – the population imbalance was not great, but the structures and values of European society were loaded in favour of males and to understand European women's lives in Northern Rhodesia, it is necessary to put them into the context of prevailing sexual morality, family values, career opportunities and racial fears. The achievements of second-wave feminism, which radically changed assumptions about the "natural" role and status of women in much of the world, post-date the colonial era, so it is essential to recognise that some of the apparent strangeness of the experience of European women in Northern Rhodesia is a matter of time rather than place. It was a time when, for most women anywhere in the world, status largely depended upon a husband's position and older single women were an anomalous category. We do, however, need to recognise that colonialism and geography put their gloss on the gendered experience of life in Central Africa.

As to whether it was a good place and time to be a woman, that is a loaded question – it all depends on what one wants from life. As I look back, it seems that ideas about "proper" behaviour, reputation and assumed dangers did impose rather a lot of restrictions on women's activities, particularly their ability to move about independently, but at the time it was not just normal, it seemed rather pleasant to be courted, escorted and "looked after". Certainly there was a good social life and women were usually at the centre of this, planning events and keeping things going. Much of this seems positively Victorian now, but one era should not judge another. It is interesting to think that Independence came to Zambia around the same time as the first stirrings of the gender revolution and that in Northern Rhodesia it was racial imperatives that gave European women an increased political voice. It was, however, no coincidence that across the globe, national liberation movements, black power and the women's liberation movements developed in step.

It is a cliché that colonial women were more rigid in their racial attitudes than their menfolk, that they were sticklers for etiquette and were fanatically hierarchical – like all clichés it contains elements of truth, but it is not the whole truth and I find it shocking when serious commentators fall into easy generalisations, demonstrating prejudices that they would not make in other contexts. So, for example, Edith Turner, working with Victor, her anthropologist husband, assumed that she could bracket all the white women in the territory together, writing, "Our colour gave us higher status ... I was *not* going to be like the colonial ladies." (p.58) But these "colonial ladies" were straw-women of her own construction – she could not just wish away her own racial status in a rage of voluntary anti-whiteness. Had she looked more closely, she would have found white women from a range of backgrounds, with varied occupations, holding different political opinions. Some would be single, some married, widowed or divorced and they would be performing a variety of paid and unpaid roles; she might even have liked one or two of them.

It is necessary to think how European women came to be in the country; they fall into three obvious categories, those who grew up there, those who came alone and those who came as wives (it was not used then, but the current term "trailing spouse" reflects the status). The first of these were socialised into the norms of the society, whether they abided by them or not, the others had to integrate themselves. Just as women who came to the country could gain freedoms through arriving, many brought up there dreamed of achieving their own independence by escaping abroad.

The old days

David Gray wrote about his mother's experience as daughter-in-law in the Gray's extended family farming at Nega Nega in the 1930s:

The big social event of the year was always the Kafue Agricultural Show and there my Mom and Dad met in 1928. Mom was of German/Danish descent and was visiting a Danish relative from a nearby farm who attended the Show. My Mother and Father married in Cape Town in 1933 and returned to Honiton Farm. Grandfather Gray was taken seriously ill with intense stomach pains so a letter was written to the doctor in Lusaka and he duly arrived by train several days later. It was decided that an operation was necessary so the riempie *settee was stripped of cushions and a large enamel/iron basin was positioned beneath to catch the blood. Chloroform was administered and the operation proceeded. Now my Mother had been having a torrid time of living with her in-laws, being of German descent and with WW 1 still fresh in their minds, Mom was not welcomed with open arms. They called her 'the Hun' within earshot. However, in his time of need, Grandfather elected that Mom should do the nursing and his own daughters should be spared the gory details. The investigation revealed stomach cancer and the doctor decided that he could do nothing further. Grandfather died four days later.*

Ron de Kock sent me the family memoir he had written for his children; his maternal grandmother, Ouma de Lange, is the undoubted star of his stories about the early days. She and her husband bought land in 1933 to the south of Broken Hill and developed a farm they named *Roosboom* :

The presence of cattle at that early time in this area meant that it attracted leopards, as the calves were easier to catch. Aunt Sue recalls a time one evening when everybody was sitting outside around an open fire and a leopard came rather close. He was presumably interested in the dogs who were barking like crazy. Aunt Sue says that she hid in the house away from the danger while Oupa ran to get his .303 rifle. She heard later that her mother got fed up with this leopard so she grabbed a burning length of wood from the fire and walked towards it brandishing this fire stick before her, shouting at him to "Voetsek jou verdomde luiperd!" (Go away you blasted leopard) *The leopard got the message and pushed off to safety before Oupa de Lange came outside with his rifle.*

Ouma de Lange had to provision her large household, including the farm staff, across an annual cycle, budgeting the maize meal that was the staple. She made nearly everything the family needed, the bread in a home-made wood-burning stove, the boerewors from a home-slaughtered beast, the soap from animal fat and soda. She was also no stranger to violence:

The Broken Hill Hotel had thirteen steps from the street level that took you to the veranda and hotel entrance. It seems that Ouma was standing on the top step while a black African was standing on the step below. He said something that Ouma didn't approve of so she let fly with a roundhouse right. This walloped him off his feet so that he fell backwards, landed on the bottom step and cracked his skull. I think bond was paid to keep her out of jail. She must have appeared before the Magistrate and explained her side – probably pleaded self-defence.

I wish I had more space for the deeds of this woman who'd married at fifteen then set off north in an ox-drawn wagon before the Victoria Falls Bridge was built, but perhaps I digress – things had calmed down a bit by the high point of colonialism in Northern Rhodesia.

Careers for Women

Although the Colonial Office occasionally recruited high profile women, it sent none of them to Northern Rhodesia. As a schoolgirl, I was interviewed for a Northern Rhodesia Government Scholarship and the officer responsible asked what I'd meant by "Provincial Administration" as my preferred career. Surely everyone knew what the PA was? I realised then that I couldn't actually be anything I wanted if I tried hard enough; he laughed and told me girls couldn't join the PA because, "A District Officer has to go out and talk to chiefs in the bush." There was not one woman District Officer, not even in those parts of the country denuded of men by labour migration.

More men than women responded to my request for information about living in Northern Rhodesia and life after leaving the country and their replies often conveyed the normality of the situation where men's roles were central. Many women who grew up in the country told me their parents thought it was not worth educating them and of a culture that assumed that few careers were open to women. In 1962, the year I left school, just fifteen European and two African girls in Northern Rhodesia took A-level examinations in the country (though there were more at boarding schools outside).

Betsy Prince-Stott, who finally fulfilled her ambition to become a teacher when she moved to New Zealand, was always near the top of my class in Broken Hill, but was obliged to leave school immediately after Cambridge O-level, even though government schools were free. Ruefully she told me:

I played lots of sports, including swimming and I represented NR in Softball, Basketball and especially Hockey (School and Open Women). I loved learning and did well at school, but when my parents decided I did not need to go to University, I started work in the Standard Bank.

A "suitable" job to fill in the years as a talented woman waited for a husband to come along.

Similarly, Veronica Guest wrote:

We did not get career guidance at school in the 60's. The only opportunities we knew that were open to women were secretarial work, nursing or teaching. Most young men became apprentices at trades on the mine. I had to leave school after completing my GCE as there was no higher class after 1965. This was because most of the whites had left and so M-level was no longer offered. Many parents sent their children to complete their schooling in Southern Rhodesia or South Africa. Besides the fact that he could not afford it, my father was still of the opinion that it was useless educating girls, as they only got married and became housewives. While many of my classmates did indeed marry their high school beaux soon after leaving school, my father was mistaken about me, I never married and had to support myself my whole life.

Priscilla Flower-Smith felt that the reason she was not allowed to stay on at school was not simply that her missionary parents could not afford it, but also:

I suspect that the feeling that I was a girl, and therefore would get married, came into the calculation. Odd, when you think of it, when both parents had the benefit of further education. I had to wait thirty years before I could go to university, Royal Holloway for my first degree and then, when I was sixty, a doctorate in history from Exeter University.

Priscilla went to work in a local bookshop when she left school after Cambridge, then as an accounts clerk for a wholesaler. She yearned for higher education and applied to St Anne's, Oxford but met and married Malcolm, an NRP officer. After Independence he joined the British army so they led a peripatetic life, but clearly her ambitions lay dormant; when her youngest son entered the sixth form she finally felt able to enrol for a degree.

A contributor to *The Donas Remember*, a book compiled by police wives, wrote:

Because there were few girls and many boys, most of the girls married very early at about sixteen years of age. I was determined that I wouldn't and would go to university. My father died, so this was impossible and I decided to train as a nurse. My mother pointed out that I was far too squeamish, so I applied for jobs in Barclays and Standard Banks. I was offered jobs at both and went to Barclays. This meant living in Mufulira with my sister rather than out at the farm. I cycled everywhere and one evening I was stopped by two policemen in the police Land Rover because I didn't have a reflector on my bike… this was my introduction to my husband, Dave. (Schofield ed.,1993.)

These stories demonstrate the way the scarcity of grants put a young person's career ambitions at the mercy of family circumstances or prejudices. (I know I'm lucky – not only did I land a rare scholarship, I had no brother to fulfil my father's frustrated ambition for a degree.) Young women wanting to pursue a career knew they would have to leave the country to qualify and afterwards most would seek work outside, as there were few opportunities for professional women in Northern Rhodesia.

Women's careers

There were, however, prominent women doctors in the country, several but not all, were missionaries and by no means all were spinsters either. I have already mentioned the pioneering work of Kathleen Cairns who came out to marry her mining-engineer husband. There was also Audrey Gray, the daughter of missionaries who qualified as a doctor before she married the missionary Merfyn Temple, in 1946, working alongside him until just before Independence. And few who met her ever forgot the redoubtable Hope Trant, who went on working in the Northern Province into her eighties. I know of no women lawyers or accountants before Independence.

In all departments, the Northern Rhodesia Government service was dominated by men but no one seemed to question this. A glance at the Staff List for 1963 is depressing – in most departments one reads through the ranks to "Clerical Officer" before finding a "Miss" or "Mrs" after the name (men did not get the suffix "Mr" – male being the default mode). Article 53 of *General Orders*, NRG stated:

A single woman on the permanent and pensionable establishment, or serving on agreement for a tour of service, may be required to resign her appointment in the event of her marriage, and a widow may similarly be required to resign in the event of her re-marriage.

It was assumed, however, that it was more a matter of "will" than "may". I cannot find one married non-temporary woman on the Staff List, but Article 54 does explain that a (hypothetical) permanent and pensionable married woman officer "… will be eligible for the same conditions of service in respect of leave, passage privileges and medical attention *in respect of herself only* as a male officer." (Italics in original) So, a married man could claim passages and health care for his wife and children, but a married woman could not claim for her husband and children – we are getting a clear picture that married women were ancillaries.

Most junior clerical grades in government, were filled by locally recruited European women and, in rare cases, by African men. The majority of these women were married. For example, the NRP employed 156 personnel in the general clerical grades, 147 of these were European women; all those who were married were graded "Temporary Local Appointment" and the few unmarried women were "On Probation". "Temporary Local" staff were not pensionable and had few employment rights.

In NRG, the majority of officers in the Executive Grades were men and, like those in the superior Administrative and Professional Grades, most were recruited in Britain with full HMOCS entitlements (health care, pensions, home leave with passages paid etc.) A few unmarried women were recruited in Britain on the same terms – Liz Dunn told me in an interview that she was recruited in the UK as a stenographer on permanent and pensionable terms and after a short while was promoted to Executive Officer in charge of the Secret Registry of the NRP. In this post she had 14 subordinates, enormous responsibility and was in a politically sensitive position, but she delayed her marriage until after her post was Zambianised, otherwise she would have lost her severance pay and pension – she did not say "might have lost".

Nurses and teachers constituted the majority of the single career women coming from outside Northern Rhodesia. Most were employed by the Federal Ministries of Health and European Education or the mining companies but some came as missionaries. *The Society for the Overseas Settlement of British Women* (founded in 1919 to provide for the excess of unmarried women after the First World War) encouraged the emigration of single working women to the colonies, funding passages and providing hostel accommodation. In the case of Central Africa, the society usually brought women to Southern Rhodesia (as more "civilised"), but some realised on arrival that there were good employment opportunities in the north. The Society became particularly active in the aftermath of the Second World War, appealing to single women who had experienced the relative freedom of life in the services and were reluctant to slip back into the role of dutiful daughters in their parents' households. Independent single women could enjoy a career and an excellent social life in Northern Rhodesia – but the cliché was that there weren't many independent single women, because they soon married policemen. Another contributor to *The Donas Remember* wrote:

In 1956 I was a night sister at the Aberdeen Royal Infirmary. In those days there were no married women nursing at the Royal Infirmary and I looked at my colleagues, all old maids, and thought this could be me for the rest of my life. We had a very restricted life and I suppose I wanted to do my own thing. Because there was a two year waiting list for assisted passages to Australia, she signed up for the Federal Government Nursing Service with a friend who was engaged to an officer in the NRP, then: *I met my husband on a blind date in June 1956.*

Working, if only part-time, was normal for women in the urban areas and this was facilitated by the convention of employing African men as domestic staff. Jobs were plentiful for European women because the unofficial colour-bar favoured their employment in the non-domestic service sector – they worked in shops, offices, hairdressers, restaurants and as self-employed dressmakers, cake-makers etc., but if they strayed beyond conventional "women's work", they were almost invariably in subordinate roles. It was a society that, on the whole, assumed that women should choose a portable career that would allow them to fulfil their destiny as wives. They married young and tended to worry if they were single at thirty. The story of European women in Northern Rhodesia is largely the story of wives.

Government Wives

NRG, however, thought of wives as a distraction from the business of running the country.

Article 63 of *General Orders* states:

An officer on first appointment must obtain the Governor's express permission before he is accompanied or joined by his wife. Such permission will not as a rule be granted, except to officers appointed to senior administrative or professional posts, during the first six months of an officer's first tour.

But Article 64 insists a wife should not expect official consideration when she arrives:

An officer will be posted at the station at which his services are required, irrespective of the fact that he is accompanied by his wife or that married quarters are not available there. If an officer is hampered in his movements by the presence of his wife, that will not be taken as an excuse for failure to perform his duties properly at any station at which he may be posted.

The burdensome wife should, however, rally to the flag and play an important role in terms of hospitality, welfare and educational work. Because of frequent transfers it was difficult for the wives of District Officers to follow careers of their own but when husbands were given urban postings they might find work. Government wives were expected to pack up the household possessions regularly, adapt to new houses and new people and, above all, they were expected to improvise and not be phased by whatever difficulties or shortages presented themselves.

Andrew Sardanis, who ran a transport company operating in the North Western Province, is skeptical about the value of the work done by the District Officers, but he is full of praise for their wives:

I admired the spirit of the PA wives. British middle-class girls would arrive at a remote station miles away from anywhere. They took the harshness of their new environment in their stride. They coped with the insects, the mosquitoes and the snakes, and with the lack of shops and supplies. Their groceries would arrive from Chingola, once a week after a journey of two or three days. These would include meat and butter packed in salt. In the hot season these smelled – the reason why casserole was the main dish of the stations. (Sardanis, 2003 p. 40)

Emily Bradley's (1950) book *Dearest Priscilla: Letters to the wife of a colonial civil servant* is written from experience in Northern Rhodesia and West Africa and was regarded as *The Bible* for British young women taking on the role of wife to a District Officer. It is far-fetched and must have terrified prospective brides. Bradley is adamant that women aren't really necessary to the colonial life, where men have servants to take care of their housekeeping and, since they are there on sufferance, they'd jolly well better fit in on men's terms:

Nothing is so cruelly disheartening to a man, when he is prepared to enjoy his life and his work in what is still largely 'a man's country' than a miserable wife. It spoils everything for him, his home, his leisure and inevitably his work. Nor is there much that he can do for you when it is the very fact that he has an absorbing job to do for the greater part of the day that seems to be the cause of your unhappiness. Most government office hours are from 8.00 to 12.00 and from 2.00 to 4.00. These are the hours that you must fill for yourself, when you are alone and there is 'nothing to do'. (p. 85)

I'll refrain from making sarcastic comment about those grueling six hour days at the *Boma*, but Bradley is full of "good advice" about things like underwear:

Crepe-de-chine and satin can be far too hot for the hottest weather. Fine lawn and tricolene that you can cast to the wash-boy are much more satisfactory.... you are going into a man's world and your feminine fripperies will be the first to suffer. You will be forever making new underclothes, and learning the routine of turning nighties that have gone at the top into petticoats and the latter into panties. (p. 35)

Change often, don't become a slut...! Long skirts against mosquitoes in the evening .... Sitting about in loose garments is not good for your figure and it is all too easy to fail to take enough exercise because it is too hot. (p. 38)

As if a nicely brought up English gel would need telling not to slouch by her DC's wife! (And surely the said nicely brought up gel would wash her own underwear?) Joking apart, *Dearest Priscilla* does put its finger on the core problem, she was an "incorporated wife" (Ardener, 1984), always on duty as an unpaid servant of the Empire, expected to maintain standards and subject to constant surveillance. It was best if she had a colonial background herself and knew what was in store. There were, however, considerable compensations; they might be away from electricity, reliant on dried milk, tinned vegetables, bush meat and home-baked bread, but there was an undeniable cachet attached to an outstation posting and often a packed social life revolving around a small club and entertaining. Wives would have to adjust to a rigid social hierarchy that depended on their husbands' ranking, being careful not to usurp the preferred role of a more senior wife when it came to official functions and charitable activities.

Sometimes it takes an outsider to comment on the peculiarities of a social situation; Eileen Sadler, the wife of an education officer wrote in a letter to her son:

Michael was now a member of Her Majesty's Overseas Civil Service. There is a large book called Standing Orders ... I think we adjusted to the English people with whom we worked and lived, but I often wondered what they thought of us South Africans. Our immediate colleagues were friendly and helpful, but there was a certain snobbery in the service and class distinction – public school and all that. I once overheard two young wives introduce themselves through their husbands' public schools. I could not believe what I was hearing. (Sadler, 2013. Letter 27)

Buz Trevor sent me some beautiful accounts about life in the 'forties and 'fifties, written his mother Betty Trevor, the wife of a veterinary officer. She describes a dinner party that mortified a young hostess at the small station of Abercorn:

The big social event was the visit of the Governor of Northern Rhodesia. The D.C. had to move out of his house into his little guesthouse, and there were very strict rules of procedure and protocol. We were usually invited to the Dinner Party, which was not a really enjoyable affair as everyone was afraid of making a faux pas. *The first we went to, it was a new D.C. and his wife had carefully instructed and rehearsed the staff; for example His Excellency had to be served first before even his wife. Well, the soup was hot and delicious, then, oh horrors, instead of the fish, H.E. was handed a bowl of strawberries because for some unknown reason the houseboy thought it would be a good idea for them to come next!*

The post of game ranger surely must trump both District Officer and colonial policeman in the imagination of the boys in dreary Britain – the Northern Rhodesia Government had a whole service called the Wildlife Department in which being an elephant hunter was a fairly normal sort of job. Many game rangers had wives, two of whom have published their memoirs, both fascinating on the practicalities of rearing a family in challenging environments.

Barbara Carr's (1965) *Not for me the Wilds* (disparagingly referred to by her husband as "Bugger the Bush") describes, in minute and petulant detail, life married to Northern Rhodesia's most famous game ranger, Norman Carr – she starts by complaining that she prefers fashionable London society and stylish hats to life in the bush and never stops moaning about scarcities and hygiene, being required to entertain people she considers boorish, or the loneliness when Norman was away. She could have accompanied him but hated roughing it in camp and one can only conclude that the silly woman married the wrong man.

Kate Morris has a very different personality and joined in wholeheartedly with setting up a new station in the Luangwa Valley, rearing abandoned young animals and learning to cook in difficult conditions on tour. She buckles only under the most extreme pressures, writing of the terrors of a caesarean section when the anaesthetist had to be brought in from Nyasaland to the small hospital in Fort Jameson (the nearest town to their game camp in the Luangwa Valley) then the anxiety surrounding caring for her baby when her husband was away on tour. When the sleeping baby narrowly escaped an accident she reached crisis point:

Now I was right in line with that Game Warden's wife whose book "Not for me the Wilds" was yet to be published. The stiff upper lip of the flag waving Brit didn't come within a hair's breadth. I was lonely, exhausted and terribly unsure and I broke down and wept... The anomalies attributed to the lot of a Game Department wife were the cause of many a marital split. Often based in out of the way places, and abandoned for long periods to one's own devices, one became resilient, resolute, tough. Wholly responsible as mother, father, mentor, disciplinarian and nurse, problems had to be faced and crises solved. Yet upon the appearance of the macho man it was assumed that all these traits be quashed and the wife dissolve into the helpless little woman. Neither full time wife nor working woman, it was an impossible role. (Morris, 2000 p. 55-6)

The wives of officers liable to be posted to remote districts, could not expect to have their children with them for long – as the previous chapter showed, sending children to school outside the country was normal. One woman told me that, as they bravely waved goodbye to their children at Lusaka Airport, mothers would be careful to wear dark glasses. Betty Trevor, again, considers the problems of educating her sons:

There was no school in Abercorn. We knew that there were several excellent schools in Southern Rhodesia but they all had long waiting lists and we stood no chance of getting a vacancy. Similarly the well-known Prince Edward School in Nairobi was restricting its intake to those living in East Africa. We had been told that the Correspondence Course operating from Salisbury was satisfactory, so we enrolled the two boys there. I took it very seriously, working with them both every morning. But perhaps I was intolerant; perhaps the boys were above average – anyhow, for us it did not work out... I was unable to get the boys transferred to a higher grade so I abandoned the course.

Meanwhile we had heard of a school at Mbeya in Tanganyika, 200 miles away and we wrote off there. We were fortunate as our two were the last to be accepted from Northern Rhodesia... there was a Vet in Mbeya and Bim [her husband] *was able to make a clever arrangement to visit him for 'consultations' three or four times a year. This meant we could drive the children to and from school in Government time and in Government transport. Oh how we enjoyed those trips... If Bim could not manage to wangle a trip, the boys had to go on the weekly bus. The driver and passengers were always very kind to them, but we used to worry a lot as the bus invariably broke down and they would all have to spend a night by the side of the road, and it was known to be bad country for lions.*

Town Women

The outstations may be the stuff of colonial legend, but the majority of European women lived in urban areas where, by the late 'fifties, living conditions were comparable to (or higher than) those in Britain or South Africa. The acute accommodation shortages of the immediate post-war years were easing in a rush of house-building and the housing, though hardly palatial, was usually spacious and modern. Gone were the days of "thunder boxes" and "sanitary lanes"; clean running water was normal, as was electricity; using Rhodesian boilers to heat water and cooking on wood stoves was becoming rarer in town. Gardens were generously sized and most grew fruit and vegetables at the back, flowers in front. Gardeners and house servants were employed across most income groups, meaning that many traditional female household tasks translated into supervising. It varied considerably how much of the cooking was done by a housewife, but there was a lot of cake baking and specialist cookery whilst the preparation and routine stuff was often delegated. Even in the larger towns, entertaining was predominantly within the home, so the role of hostess could be an important one.

Because of the poor provision of household furnishings and fashionable clothing stores, many women made their cushions and curtains and did their own dressmaking, so a woman who did not go out to work would not necessarily be entirely at leisure. In many ways the European women of Northern Rhodesia's towns embodied old-fashioned norms of femininity, paying attention to the more decorative aspects of homemaking and finding ample time for caring for themselves. They were expected to be coiffured, made-up and stylishly dressed

– women in Northern Rhodesia's towns most definitely did not aim to look like Michaela Dennis in her khaki drill.

Many middle-aged women belonged to associations like the Women's Institute or played an active role in church fund-raising and social activities; some did practical charitable work. The Girl Guides had an enthusiastic leadership focusing on Betty Clay, the wife of a senior member of the Provincial Administration (also the daughter of Robert and Olave Baden-Powell). Ranger (1980) cites the importance of the Scouts and Guides in the construction of an imperial ethos in Northern Rhodesia, but by the 'sixties the movement retained few teenage girls.

Accommodation

Women's wages were almost universally lower than men's, on the assumption that they were not major breadwinners. The 1960 edition of the Information Department's publication, *A brief guide to Northern Rhodesia* states that a shift worker on the mines (always male) could expect upwards of £90 a month plus bonuses, and a young man in a government junior clerical grade £54 a month, whereas a woman (not necessarily young) in the same grade would receive £43. The guide goes on to say that a family of two adults and two children, "Would find it difficult to maintain a reasonable standard of life in a town on the line of rail on less than £60 to £75 a month" (p. 61) – this sum did not include housing costs as most men were provided with free or highly subsidised housing by their employers; few women, however, were in employment that entitled them to housing. Single nurses, teachers and the other professional women who came to the country in their own right would be granted accommodation, often in a hostel or sharing a house, but it was usual for young women who had parents in the country to live with them until marriage. So, married or single, most women lived in male-headed households and, working or not, most women were dependent on men. Because of the restricted range of employment on offer, the low remuneration for women's work and the lack of rights to accommodation, divorce or widowhood made it difficult for women to remain in the country unless they swiftly remarried. Jon Horley's mother could not stay, although she had a job:

There are lots of wonderful memories of an outstanding childhood up to 1964, when Mother and I had to leave, as my father had died on leave in the UK. I'm afraid that rendered us homeless – his job with the NRG meant that the house they provided wasn't available to us.

Fay X was unusual in that she came as a small child to Northern Rhodesia with her single mother shortly after the war, but her story throws into sharp focus the many structural difficulties faced by a woman trying to cope alone. Accommodation was always a major problem – when they arrived from UK it was to live with an uncle, aunt, two girl cousins and her maternal grandmother in the two-bedroomed rondavel accommodation the mining company deemed adequate for her uncle's family. Resentment of the interlopers was almost bound to build up in such cramped conditions. Only occasionally, did her mother's secretarial work confer housing and then it was designed for a single woman. Fay went away to a convent school. When her mother married, her husband became eligible for family accommodation and, for the first time, Fay had a room of her own, indeed a bed of her own. The marriage, however, like many on the Copperbelt, was an abusive one and marital breakdown lurched into more housing crisis. Fay's is a long story of humiliation and struggle, which only resolved itself many years later, far away from Africa, but in her own words:

Not everyone was 100% happy in the early days. My own story was that it was hell at home because my mother married a South African who was raised to be a racist and chauvinist. Also the law about separation and divorce under the Protectorate Govt. was controlled by the D.C. and he had the power to order a women to reunite with her husband under a rule that men could sue for 'restitution of conjugal rights'.

[That law relating to restitution of conjugal rights also applied in UK until the *Matrimonial Proceedings and Property Act* of 1970.]

Fay commented further:

"I have found some of my schooldays friends and they knew/know nothing of my real life. I was in the Choir and the Drama Group and put on a facade of normality. I often wondered how many others did."

Under escort

It is difficult now to remember the moral norms of those days before the contraceptive pill, equal opportunities legislation and changing notions of gender. It was not just in Northern Rhodesia that assumptions about female dependency underpinned the protection of women and the suppression of their autonomy, but there was a feeling that women were especially vulnerable in this racially divided society. It was never made as explicit as in Southern Rhodesia, where moral panic about potential attacks on white women by black men led to legislation in 1902 imposing the death penalty for *attempted* black on white rape (but not the reverse), but there was an underlying fear causing many European women's lives to be spatially and temporally restricted, escorted when leaving the home after dark or venturing beyond the confines of European settlement. The middle-aged American anthropologist Hortense Powdermaker was required by the mine authorities in Luanshya to take a minder with her when doing field-work in African housing areas in the early 1950s; they asserted that she ran the risk of rape (Epstein, 1992 p.18). To this day, when I tell former Northern Rhodesians about research experiences driving off the line of rail and living in villages "alone" (i.e. with no other Europeans) most are incredulous, but I regret that my teens were spent confined to town.

The combination of protection from danger and the pressures of the rigid sexual norms of the day meant that there was close surveillance of European girls and young women. Probably it was a matter of time rather than place but, in the small Northern Rhodesian towns, reputations were important and were sanctioned by dense networks of gossip. Where there are repressive sexual norms, there are often abusive relations. Several men have hinted to me about a "darker side" to their lives when they were teenagers – I am not so naïve as not to understand them.

Young women coming out from Europe to marry would usually spend a night or two in the home of married friends of their fiancés before a wedding, today one would expect the sensible thing would be to live a while in the country, trying the lifestyle out in advance of commitment – it would not then have been thought respectable. There may have been a certain romance to marrying immediately after a long journey, but it must have placed a strain on a young bride. Andrew Sardanis (2003 p.106) describes the wedding of a friend in Ndola in 1962. The bride arrived by plane from UK at 11.00 on a Saturday morning then dashed to be married before the *Boma* closed at 12.30, quickly changing into her wedding outfit at a hotel.

Of course there was premarital sex but contraception was not available to unmarried women even after the introduction of the pill. When there was still a concept of illegitimacy, accompanied by powerful social stigma, there were hurriedly arranged marriages – the DC could even waive the minimum age in an emergency. There was gossip about gin and hot baths or abortions in Moçambique, and there was banishment to "mother and baby" homes "down south", enforced adoptions and charitable European children's homes. Few single women had control of their own fertility, other than by clinging to their virginity, so the majority married young. In the government school hostels it was normal for young girls, particularly Afrikaner farmer's daughters, to be working on their trousseaus, hemming and embroidering tablecloths and pillowcases for their *kist* and thinking ahead to marriage soon after leaving school. Several were already engaged and even I knew one girl who had been promised in marriage as a baby to a friend of her father, growing up engaged and always knowing her future was as a farmer's wife. She was proud of this.

Extramarital sex was an altogether different matter and the Copperbelt, in particular, was depicted as prone to affairs and divorce, accompanied by stories of "wife-swapping" parties (I never worked out how they managed not to swap husbands too) though I suspect much of the scandal was the lurid product of small minds.

Danger

When the Independence struggle became more intense in the late 1950s and early 'sixties, fears about the safety of European women became more intense; police wives had greater awareness than most of what was going on. There are several stories in *The Donas Remember*:

I learned to shoot a .22 pistol. At one time I kept it under my pillow. Goodness knows what I would have done if anyone had come into the house! I think I would have been petrified about using it. It wasn't a very sensible thing to do because if anyone had taken it from me I would have been killed.

Another refers to the terrors of having to cross the Congo Pedicle from the Luapula province to the Copperbelt with her husband and baby when they were stationed in strife-ridden Fort Rosebery. They were stopped on the way by an armed gendarme:

He allowed us to travel on and we were relieved because there were many instances where these armed and leaderless gendarmes had been responsible for atrocities, including several murders.

(Me too, but I was on my own and the officer in charge of the border post insisted on my giving a gendarme a lift across – I locked his AK-47 in the boot.)

Politics

It should come as no surprise that most European women were politically passive, predominantly right-wing and unquestioning of the rightness of the colonial status quo. As the franchise for elections to the Federal Assembly and Northern Rhodesian LegCo was limited by an income/property/education qualification, then extended to the wives of qualified men, many single, widowed or divorced European women were denied the vote. The threshold was designed to restrict African suffrage but, unsurprisingly, there was no alliance between the excluded categories. There were never any women members of LegCo, but a few served on municipal councils.

There were, however, a few women who were supportive of the Independence movement. Pauline A wrote of her mother:

Not often discussed are the subtle strata and prejudices in white society that went beyond just black and white. My mother was different from the mothers of my friends. Not only was she a closet socialist who didn't approve of colonialism (but obviously could never say so openly due to my father's high profile), she asserted her ideas in her own way and made the shocking decision not to have black servants in the house any more and to do all her own cooking and cleaning. Such a thing was virtually unheard of and it did nothing to ameliorate the snobby attitude of other women – especially those from England who looked askance at foreign accents of any kind. Being at the height of the Cold War her Russian background wouldn't have helped either. Her few friends were in the Jewish and Greek communities as they would have identified with her situation. Yet she, in turn, looked down her nose at miners' families, especially Afrikaners, the majority of whom were pretty uncouth and uncultured by her standards.

Naomi Radunski told me about her parents supporting UNIP and their house outside Livingstone being used for meetings where, as a child she met some of the party's leading figures; her mother, Agnes ("Paddy") Radunski helped draft the

Southern Province UNIP Manifesto and took risks in providing hospitality and protection. (Kikamba, 2013) Jewish people were often marginalised in European society, thus less concerned with the opinions of the white establishment, many have a record of assisting the Independence struggle.

Perhaps the most prominent of the women supporters of UNIP was the journalist Barbara Hall, who co-owned the radical *African Mail* nationalist newspaper with her husband, Richard, and as such played an important role in the movement to Independence. Best known as "Josephine", the paper's agony aunt (a photograph of a Congolese model accompanied her byline, so few knew her identity) she had considerable influence on the mores of young urban people. Feisty is a word that doesn't begin to do justice to Barbara Hall. Then there is Grace Keith, now famous as the mother of Guy Scott, Zambia's Vice-President, but a prominent liberal who, shortly after Independence, wrote an incisive, and at times wickedly funny, book, *The Fading Colour Bar* (1966), describing the foibles of Europeans trying to adapt to the new regime. Yes, all these women are wives.

After Independence

After Independence the role of colonial wife, of course, disappeared and as time went on there were new situations to face, including an impending move. The European population was changing, with "expats" arriving, many focussed on accumulating capital. Philippa White describes the Copperbelt:

What I remember of those early married years was how lonely some of the mine wives were. Many were far from home and didn't have a mother living round the corner as they had done in England. Their husbands worked long hours and were intent on saving money to take home at the end of their contracts. We young wives had servants and pleasant homes with big gardens, but for those of us who had been born and brought up in Africa it was a lot easier than for the girls from outside. Even coping with servants was quite a challenge to many of the UK wives.

Then the Rhodesia situation impacted right down at household level:

There was quite an upheaval in the population and in the '70s a sharp downturn in the economy. Every time we went on leave we had to take cold boxes with us. Coming home from South Africa with cheese, chocolate, spices etc. in our hand luggage developed muscles we didn't know we had! ... We always managed to get meat and fresh vegetables so we coped fine even during the worst of the shortages.

Happy?

There were women in Northern Rhodesia whose horizons (literally as well as figuratively) were far wider than they could ever have been in Britain or South Africa. Someone who wanted a challenge could find plenty of scope. Patsy Rawlins told me that when her husband was posted from Mongu to Livingstone she decided to travel down alone by boat on the Zambezi with her dog – I assumed that "alone" meant "alone with half a dozen porters and boat-men", but it didn't, she meant alone with the hippos and the crocodiles.

For the majority of women, however, theirs was a dependent and often passive role. Even the châtelaine of *Shiwa Ng'andu*, Lorna Gore-Browne, was unhappy, though she was kept busy helping to run the estate. Her daughter, Angela, is quoted as saying, "I remember terrible scenes as a child. The problem was that it was always his dream, not hers." (Lamb,1999 p. 239). Stewart Gore-Browne had built his fantasy baronial hall by a remote, crocodile-infested lake in the Northern Province and filled it with the trappings of an English country house, including a much younger wife (the daughter of his first love). In this world of masculine dreams few men could understand that, however sumptuous the estate, playing a supporting role in one's husband's drama was not enough for all women.

Martin Field had been in NR/Z for seven years when he met Penny in London just after he had taken his Bar Finals on leave from Zambia in 1967. They married a few months later and flew straight out:

It was Penny's first time in Africa and, unbeknown to me, her mother had given her the airfare for a quick retreat in case it did not work out well! It could not have been that bad as when we came home on leave 2½ years later with baby, Penny still had the money to spend as extra pocket money and returned to Zambia with me for another tour.

(I know that in including Penny I am breaking my "rule" that this account is about people who lived in Northern Rhodesia – but that is one irresistible mother-in-law story!)

Despite everything, perhaps even because of the challenge of rising to the obstacles, most women say that Northern Rhodesia was a wonderful place to live and to bring up children. When it came to leaving, women were often the most reluctant, and when it came to constructing a new life elsewhere, it is women who express the greatest difficulty. If I think of my own mother, she took time to adapt to the country, but she never got over leaving it.

7. THE POLITICAL CLIMATE

This chapter is not an account of the politics of Northern Rhodesia approaching Zambian Independence, there are good histories that do this (e.g. Hall,1965; Rotberg, 1965; Roberts, 1976; and particularly Phiri, 2006), it is an impression of the political climate as remembered by people today. India's Independence had shown the way to other British colonies but, incredible as it now seems, most Europeans in Northern Rhodesia were in denial about the strength of African opposition to Federation and the viability of demands for autonomy. With poor sources of information, they dismissed nationalist aspirations as the work of a few "troublemakers" and assumed that things could continue as "normal". The politics of Northern Rhodesia is largely the politics of race

The "Big Sweep"

Richard Hall (1965) comments that the 1958 Accra All-African People's Conference strengthened nationalist aspirations across the continent saying, "The year 1959 was a watershed. From then on, until its demise, the Federation was almost continuously in a state of strife and emergency" (p.184), but locally this was interpreted as just a series of scares. In Northern Rhodesia 1959 started with the removal of nationalist leadership in a "Big Sweep" when 2,000 people were arrested and imprisoned or rusticated (Sir Arthur Benson, the Governor unhelpfully referring to them as "Murder Incorporated"). As Hall comments, security was becoming an increasingly important issue, expenditure on the Northern Rhodesia Police rose dramatically and its manpower increased from 4,200 in 1958 to 5,600 in 1960 (p.198).

In addition to the organised nationalism of the ANC and UNIP, the Government had to confront the messianic *Lumpa* church in the politically fraught Northern Province, the major locus of the nationalist *chachacha*. The *Lumpas* had been growing in strength since 1953, when Alice Lenshina experienced a vision urging Bemba people to put aside the things of this world. In 1959, as nationalist activity intensified, so too did *Lumpa* opposition to government – members were withdrawing into unauthorised villages, disregarding customary law and refusing to pay taxes. When Lenshina refused the DC's order to evict people who had flocked to Sione, her capital, the Mobile Police were drafted in, (Hudson,

1999 p.30; Wright, 2001 p.293); thus began the conflict that would rumble on until the dreadful bloodletting in the months immediately before Independence. The *Lumpas* were opposed to all secular authority and by 1964 the government that they were resisting was African nationalist, not British imperialist. In 1959 few Europeans in the towns were aware of what was going on, it seemed to be just more Bemba trouble in the Northern Province. Don Bruce, who served in the NRP, wrote a fictionalised account of his encounter with Lumpa followers, regarding it as a defining point in his career – regrettably, his novel remains unpublished. Generally, Europeans did not take the movement seriously enough – with the sangfroid one associates with long term residents Philippa Pamphilon, the wife of a police officer, combined the first *Lumpa* uprising with the problems of establishing a decent tennis court:

The Alice Lenshina saga took place when Ted and I were stationed in Chinsali. Charles, who was her solicitor, made Time Magazine as she eventually surrendered to him after the uprising of the Lumpa Church [Charles Stacey, her brother, still resident in Zambia]. *Ted and I were actually on honeymoon at Lake Nyasa when it all occurred and were unable to get a flight out. We arrived in Chinsali to find the Mobile Unit camped on our so called "golf course". There were only twelve Europeans in Chinsali in 1959 – four wives and the rest guys. In desperation, and with the help of prisoners, I managed to get some sort of tennis court laid out – measurements from Pears Encyclopedia. In retrospect, Chinsali was one of the best times of my life. No electricity, no telephones, no shops (Kasama a long way off) and, in our case, no water. Our grateful Government had built us a super house above the level of the reservoir.*

It was undeniable that resistance was growing and civil disobedience campaigns accelerating. Removing the leadership was not a clever move as a less cautious lower tier of activists emerged; in response, army reservists were called up, the police reserve attracted new volunteers, school cadet corps started to take themselves seriously, patrolling at night. Racial divisions, became more entrenched and the Reverend Colin Morris (1961) eloquently recounts how many of his white parishioners tried to resist his initiative to bring African members of the Methodist church into communion with them. After taking Isaiah Chapter 58 as his text one Sunday, his church was vandalised. It was no random act, for as well as the paint daubing and furniture throwing, the offending chapter had been slashed from the Bible on the pulpit; it contained the following lines that some members of his congregation thought inflammatory:

If you do away with the yoke of oppression, with the pointing finger and malicious talk, and if you spend yourselves on behalf of the hungry and satisfy the needs of the oppressed, then your light will rise in the darkness, and your night will become like the noonday. The Lord will guide you always; he will satisfy your needs in a sun-scorched land.

Morris was struggling with a situation in which his notion of morality clashed with that of the majority of white Christians on the Copperbelt. His opponents quite simply believed that he was preaching evil, blurring moral categories and invoking forces that would result in the destruction of civilized society.

"Wind of Change"

Some people wondered about leaving, many were arming themselves, not necessarily effectively. John Anton-Smith, an agricultural scientist comments:

I was on a research station on my own 5 miles out of Kasama. Because of the unrest of the Bemba of the N. Province ... I slept with a shotgun beside my bed, but experienced nothing."

Jim Dunning was an education officer, on leave he visited an uncle who had been in the IRA pre-war :

... my Uncle Jack gave me his Luger pistol and said, 'It might come in useful if those fellars cut up rough.' So I took it away with me. Going through the Customs at Liverpool, I was carrying Robert, aged two. The gun was in my pocket, so I pinched him to make him cry. 'Move on,' said the Customs man. Which is how I got to Africa without the gun being detected. I had no ammunition for it, but managed to get some 9 mm. from the Belgian Congo. Not being sure of it fitting, I took gun and ammo into a field, held it away from me and pulled the trigger. Fortunately, it didn't explode in my hand. I never had to use the Luger in anger or self defence, but it was a comfort when we had to go on night patrols in Lusaka in 1961-62. My mother once wrote to tell me she had seen pictures on TV of riots in Lusaka. Housed as we were in Woodlands, we were a couple of miles from the African compound affected, and didn't hear a thing!

Writing to me about the immediate pre-Independence years, many people mentioned Harold Macmillan's February 1960 speech in Cape Town. Macmillan started so lyrically and then blew a gale through the assumptions of white Southern and Central Africa with the line, "The wind of change is blowing through this continent and, whether we like it or not, this growth of national consciousness is a political fact and we must all accept it as a fact and our national policies must take account of it." Whilst some Europeans in Central Africa saw that this made sense, many were convinced that it was a betrayal.

In May 1960, residents of Northern Rhodesia were horrified by an attack mounted by a mob at Ndola – the car driven by Lillian Burton, with her two daughters as passengers was stoned and burned, Mrs Burton dying soon after. The atrocity stoked European fears, but by no means everyone accepted that there need be a further polarisation of Black and White – Lillian Burton's husband, Robert, was reported in *The Northern News* of 10th May 1960 trying to calm the resulting racial tension:

She died with no malice—with no anti-African feeling. It was not in her nature to hate—and she died without any. I wish this feeling of hers to go out to everyone—because if she did not hate why should anyone else do so? I am a simple man no one had heard of a week ago—and perhaps no one will remember me in a few months' time. But this dreadful thing must never be forgotten. It must not be used for political purposes, to stir up racial hatred, but it must be remembered as a lesson and the authorities must see that such a tragedy never happens again. My wife would not want revenge on the African people as a whole. It was not in her nature to feel like that. She would not want her death to embitter feelings between the two races—and most sincerely I appeal for no unlawful reprisals by anyone.

The next month the Congo became independent, followed immediately by Katanga's secession, civil war and atrocities – the people of Northern Rhodesia were to witness Belgian refugees streaming across the border, *en route* south, sometimes in bullet-scarred vehicles, all with horror stories to tell.

Local European volunteers gathered to provide food and other help for the convoys of Belgian refugees travelling south; petrol was donated as were clothes and toiletries. Derek Dutton told me about doing emergency repairs to refugees' vehicles. There were fears in official circles that the turmoil in the Congo would spill over into Northern Rhodesia, the situation provoking heightened racial enmity. On 15th July 1960 the Management of Nchanga Mine put out a newsletter thanking staff for their "magnificent response in rallying to help the Congo refugees" but also warning them that:

We live in a climate, charged in a manner that could lead to an explosion for the most trivial reason. At Nchanga, regardless of events taking place around us, our duty to the company and the country is to maintain production, and it is important that every employee, European or African, ensures to the best of his ability that this is done. Management is anxious that nothing should jeopardise the smooth operations and harmony of relationships enjoyed between the races at Nchanga, and particularly individual attitudes or politics. Instant dismissal may follow provocation. An instruction has been issued to heads of departments that any employee, whatever his race, who indulges in provocative talk or action on the job, or anyone who incites violence in any shape or form on Company property, may be instantly dismissed.

In less than six months, it seemed that a political earthquake had taken place – many Europeans felt that it was no longer quite so "ordinary" to be living in Central Africa. Colin Heape of the NRP and his nursing sister wife Jane were posted to Bancroft in 1960 after the first wave of Congo violence:

My duties there were in traffic patrol on a motorcycle. I witnessed the mass exodus from the Congo by the European population of Elizabethville in 1961. We had to stop and search these poor refugees as they entered Northern Rhodesia. The strange thing was that most of them went back to the Congo, when things quietened down, and came fleeing out once more when the trouble flared up again. I also remember being sent to guard the local petrol station all night when trouble was expected on our side of the border. It was the only time that I had to draw firearms from the Police Store. The Africans were starting to organise themselves for independence and we used to attend their political meetings. We recorded the ringleaders' speeches with large tape recorders, which were run off the batteries of our land rovers. If the speeches went on too long, the batteries were flat at the end of the meeting and we had to ask the Africans to push start our vehicles.

Robert Olive was posted to the Congo border and saw the conflict close up from the far side of the pedicle:

North across the Congo Pedicle to Kashiba Mwense at the time of the Katanga war… Kashiba had a white population of only six – and was 125 miles from Fort Rosebery. Life in Kashiba was quite tough – there was a State of

Emergency declared and civilian unrest threatened to upset the stability of the country. Certainly my liaison duties on the Congo border, and at times in the Congo, were difficult. There was much bloodshed across the border and the United Nations forces were useless. This was serious 'growing-up time' for a young man, and the loss of two friends in our own force underlined the reality of life in a harsh political climate.

People never stopped being wary of the proximity of the Congo, even when it became relatively calm, as Rob Wilson suggests:

Years later I took a trip with my father to the Bangweulu swamps; we drove through the Congo Pedicle as a short cut. A vivid memory is of a huge black soldier making us stop and give him a lift; he sat next to me on the back seat with his gun rather too close for comfort.

Life could, however, be fairly normal even for some in the police. Malcolm Flower-Smith was based in Ndola for three years from 1959:

Policing in NR was fun. Although we had to cope with the occasional tragedy, on the whole, murders and other unpleasant incidents were, in my recollection, few and far between. During my first 3 year tour at Ndola I think I was involved in only one case of murder, and that was an African family feud. The European population was largely law abiding; much of the African crime was theft and burglary with drunkenness and assaults being common, the latter two being handled by the native courts.

Norman Archibald highlights the adventure of the Northern Rhodesia Police for a bachelor at this time:

I had been a cartographical surveyor and travelled to NR for adventure. I was employed in the police and started as an assistant inspector, but spent most of my time in the Mobile Unit (Riot Police). In this position I visited most of NR especially the bush areas. The position of platoon commander made me grow up and realise I had the ability to take charge of any situation, and control a large number of men, become very confident in my own ability. In 1962 I spent 3 months on patrol in the north due to riots etc. and worked on occasions with the Army. It was quite a difficult time but great for me as I was in my early twenties and, like all young men, "bulletproof".

It is Arthur Fitzpatrick, another NRP officer, who puts the situation most starkly:

The period leading up to the end of my police career was stressful, to say the least. The Territory was in political turmoil and there were frequent disturbances and episodes of extremely violent, lawless behaviour. The public was aware of a lot of what was happening, but a lot more occurred behind the scenes that they were unaware of. The Police Force managed to make life seem a bit more peaceful than it really was, and to help keep the public feeling reasonably secure and calm, but generally there was considerable unease which the press highlighted at every opportunity. So, the last three years or so were increasingly difficult, whereas the previous twelve years seemed idyllic by comparison.

Radical change was under way in Northern Rhodesia; even the Chairman of RST was hedging the company's bets by secretly funding UNIP as far back as 1959, well in advance of Independence (Prain, 1981; Temple 2010). The European media went on reporting turbulent events as being stirred up by "troublemakers", declining to take seriously either the leadership and their demands or to recognize that it was an inevitable groundswell, *The Northern News* of 2nd April 1962 reported:

Sir Roy Welensky confirmed that in reply to a questioner he told a Broken Hill meeting that it might be necessary for the Federation to leave the Commonwealth when it gets independence, because of the manner in which the Commonwealth is now developing.

It is difficult to understand that many Europeans still believed that Dominion status for the Federation with a white majority government was feasible and continued to support the United Federal Party. However, the die was cast; a new Constitution introduced the most complicated franchise ever devised, but it brought in the first African majority government by the end of 1962. Federation was doomed, but limped on for another year while Northern Rhodesia moved towards Zambian Independence, most Europeans still incredulous at the speed with which their reality had shifted. Anthony Noel was present at the Marlborough House Talks and gives an insight:

Back in the UK, my leave was interrupted by a summons to attend the Zambian independence talks at Marlborough House in London as an aide. The duties were light, ensuring various politicians received the correct papers on time. The meetings were chaired by Duncan Sandys who was simultaneously sorting out problems in Aden. He was held in great awe by the British civil servants. ... The experience gave me an insight into the workings of government, it was clear the welfare of the people of Zambia was not first priority, that was how things would look in the UN, secondly in the House and way down in Zambia.

The next two accounts show how the attitudes of a teacher and an administrator shifted in the waning years of Federation and the dawning of Independence Roger Marston stayed in Zambia until 1970, having arrived from Britain just after the Congo crisis:

Like most whites I rapidly became a passive racist, largely because I did not think about the socio-economic and political grievances of the blacks and had no contact with them; Chingola High School was all white. I swiftly accepted that any racial imbalances were justifiable given the clear intellectual superiority of the whites and, to my eventual shame, actually wrote a letter to my old school magazine outlining this argument. I changed radically for three reasons. First I began teaching Africans at night school and soon realised how intelligent, abused and charming they were. Then there was a pay dispute with the Federal Government which made me realise that if I was being ripped off then the Africans were in a far worse plight. Thirdly I got married and my wife's family lived in Bulawayo where racial discrimination was shameless compared with the Copperbelt and exposed all the illogicality behind it.

I remember voting for the Rev. Colin Morris (UNIP) in the 1962 election; he lost to the UFP candidate. I was also a presiding officer in one of the voting stations in one of the townships. The Nkumbula candidate withdrew leaving a one-horse (UNIP) race, but still the voting exceeded 90%. Then at the critical time, late 1964, we returned to the UK on leave. When we came back to Zambia there was a transformation: I was the Deputy Head (so many had taken the money and run), there were Africans in the school and soccer took the place of rugby. A term later I was offered the headship at Solwezi High School ... it was a joy to be associated with 300+ ardent students on whom the future of Zambia would rest.

Hywel Griffiths took stock of his position as a member of the PA and switched into what he felt would be a more useful role:

Looking back now, with the benefit of subsequent events, and also after revisiting the history of that period it is clear that the Federal concept was based on lies and bolstered by self-deception... Before my first year in the country was out, I came to realise that the African population had a deep hatred of Federation ...

This shattering of idealistic illusions left me pretty demoralised and for a while I thought I would pack it in. Then I became involved in community development, first as a development of my role as District Officer and subsequently by transferring to the Department of Rural Development. Most of my PA colleagues thought I was downgrading. But I was happy with the work and saw my goal as contributing to the development of new political and economic structures which would ultimately create a foundation for the future development of democratic government... However as time passed the main preoccupation of the Government was security – the avoidance of riots and civil insurrection and the protection of the Native Authorities upon which the structure of indirect rule had been shakily built.

He resigned and returned to Britain in 1963.

As these transformations took place, the various fractions of the European population took stock of their position, knowing that living in the country would never be the same again. Faith Brentnall captures the worries that many had about the breakdown of order around Independence:

Northern Rhodesia became independent in 1964 and my mom and I and my youngest brother, Eric were sent to Durban South Africa as "protection" in case there was another "Congo", you see, my dad was in the Police Reserve during the Congo uprising and as such, saw the most unbelievable carnage and cruelty imaginable. He was afraid for us and hence we were relocated to Durban. When another "Congo" didn't emerge, my mom and brother came home and in 1966 I was sent to a boarding school in Pietersburg, South Africa.

Lumpa Rebellion

In May 1964, the date of Independence having been announced, armed members of the *Lumpa Church* intensified their struggle in the Northern Province. By June there was stand-off with the NRP, then the Northern Rhodesia Regiment. John Hannah was the unfortunate (and exceedingly brave) District Commissioner who had to face the appalling outcome:

I took over as "DC Chinsali" just before the balloon went up and the Lumpa supporters attacked and killed a young English Police Inspector and his sergeant. I immediately went to the village in question with a second platoon of Mobile Police to try to recover the bodies, but they were not prepared to confront the Lumpa supporters. It was becoming clear to me that I would have to ask the Government for the army to deal with what was becoming a very serious problem. This is, in fact, what happened, but I did ask the Governor, and he agreed that before attacking a Lumpa village I would have the opportunity of trying to reason with the villagers in the hope of avoiding any casualties.

The carnage continued through to August, spreading beyond Chinsali and poisoning the atmosphere surrounding Independence. The outcome rumbles on to this day as Lenshina's name is still evoked in opposition to government. At the time, the reaction of many Europeans to the horror was that the suppression of the *Lumpa* Rebellion was evidence of what a UNIP government would do to its opponents. I still find it hard to follow their logic.

As the country edged towards Independence, European people realised that they could no longer depend on the continuation of their privileged position. Though racial attitudes in Northern Rhodesia were nothing like as hard set as in South Africa or Southern Rhodesia, there was both institutionalised racism and routine bigotry. European people started to look at themselves through African eyes, realising that some covering of their tracks was in order. Prior to Independence the records in government and private officers were selectively pruned for their content and their style. Liz Dunn, who worked in Security, and Rosemary Witt of the Special Branch talk of destroying files. Liz Dunn explained this was to protect informers, who would stay behind after white police officers had left; Rosemary Witt came to realise that it was futile:

Just before and after Independence I was by now working at the Police Station in Mazabuka. This was an interesting transition as I was in Special Branch. They destroyed lots of stuff before Independence and then had to resuscitate some of it afterwards.

As we look at the impressions European people have brought away from Northern Rhodesia we see that theirs was a temporary community, thrown together from disparate elements for a mere flash in time, and yet, for these people it was a crucial period – their own histories interlocking with the history of the country on the brink of Independence.

7. WHY DID YOU LEAVE IF YOU LIKED IT SO MUCH?

I'm surprised in retrospect that saying goodbye to friends wasn't harder.
Noel Wright

Recently a young Zambian asked members of a nostalgic Facebook group why they had left if they liked the country so much. Few people replied to him and most of those who did said their parents made the decision but they had wanted to stay; generally that is futile wishing, rather than frustrated desire. The real answer is that, one after another, people came to the weary conclusion that their time was up and that there was no longer a place for them in the country. The reasons for thinking this and the timing of the realisation was not always as simple as it might appear; sometimes it turned on political ideology and refusal to identify with independent Zambia, but often it was a matter of circumstance – personal factors working in conjunction with economic, political and social situations. People have expressed their feelings sometimes resentfully, sometimes ruefully but rarely joyfully, some expressing otherwise repressed racism. There was no mass exodus even though a great many people did head south in 1963/1964, and, like Mik Wright's family:

... left with what we could get into two cars and drove to the Bechuanaland Protectorate. My dad said that we were not going to live under Kaunda.

As Roger Ridley points out, there was unease amongst working class Europeans:

During the early 60's many families left BH with Independence looming, and I lost many friends, most of whose parents worked on the Mine. There was also an exodus of personnel from the Railways in NR, and probably to a lesser extent from the Municipality and other sectors. The stronger the tie with (Southern) Rhodesia or South Africa, the earlier the migration occurred. The jobs were filled mainly by expatriate staff from the UK and I do remember quite a few Swedes who I think were civil servants or involved in developmental work. This changed the social composition among the Whites. My parents finally left Zambia for SA in 1969, by which time I was at the University of Natal, Durban.

Easy Assumptions

Writing about a nostalgic return visit in 1989, the Reverend Merfyn Temple describes meeting a Swedish man in Kabwe; this was Boria Pilblad who had come as a volunteer building instructor after Independence, married a Zambian woman and stayed on. Temple tells us that Pilblad owned:

A house on a one hundred acre farm, whose white owner had decided that life under black government was too complicated, so he sold out and went to South Africa... The chicken farm that Boria and his wife started did very well. (Temple, 1991 p. 68-9)

Such a simple story, such a cliché of white retreat, but Temple made it up, not maliciously, but because he made an easy assumption. I was, however, furious when I read those few seemingly bland lines. It was my parents' beloved smallholding that he was describing, bought in 1962 with my father's cashed-in pension when the all-white Broken Hill Municipal Council sacked him for his pro-UNIP "political sympathies". My parents built up the chicken farm so they could remain in the country and we led a semi-subsistence existence in the months before and after the first African majority government (planting 10 acres of maize by hand and eating an awful lot of omelettes) .

The new Local Government Act was drafted in the farm's sitting room by Kenneth Kaunda, Grey Zulu and my father – Dad certainly didn't cut and run to South Africa, a country whose politics he abhorred. When things didn't work out financially, he took a job in Blantyre but kept the farm, returning after Independence as Acting Town Clerk of Kabwe, training his successor. The post was Zambianised nine years after Independence – my father was 54, my mother 48; they retired to Britain, selling the farm to Boria and Gladys Pilblad and they were invited back to Zambia as official guests for the 10th anniversary of Independence the following year. Their departure was just a few months before Temple himself wrote to President Kaunda, still paternalistic:

I am fifty-four, four years older than you. I have been a missionary for thirty-one years and I am telling you that the time has come for missionaries to leave Zambia ... I have become convinced that the most effective way of freeing the churches for mission is for them to be saved from their dependence on foreign personnel and foreign funds. (Temple, 2010 p. 200-201)

My parents left when they were no longer needed in the country, just as Temple moved on when he became uncomfortable in his role in Zambia; unlike the missionary, my father had no job to go to and no chance of finding one, but still felt that his time was up. I have taken so long over this one example not just because I know it intimately, but because it motivated the research underpinning this book. A while ago I sat with Grey Zulu and, referring to my father as "my elder brother", he sadly asked why Dad had left, when he had pleaded with him to stay – I had to answer that I didn't really know.

Swart Gevaar

The atrocities immediately following Congolese Independence had done nothing to allay the old fears, nothing was ever quite the same in terms of European confidence. The Independence struggle, as we have already seen, took a violent turn and there was a general jitteriness, especially after the murder of Lillian Burton (Kalusa, 2011) George Dublon referred to both of these events as prompting his family to go to Britain in 1960, quoting his father as saying that he wanted to leave while he could still go on his own terms – having been a refugee from Nazi Germany, he had no intention ever again of being forced to flee with nothing. They did not wait for Independence.

Like Dr Dublon, Brian Robinson was heavily influenced by the Congo crisis which he had experienced directly as a member of NRP. He and his family left in 1961:

It was plain to me that career prospects in NR were very short term. If you had eyes to see, the writing was on the wall and so, with a wife and baby daughter, I took the decision not to renew my contract. It was a hard decision to take as Pat would have willingly stayed on. She had not had contact with the Belgian refugees from the Congo, heard and read reports of the unspeakable atrocities there. My OC said it would take many years to shake the dust of Africa from my boots and he was right, even to this day the odd grain or two remain ...

Bob Huntley explained making his decision to leave – he departed for the United States in 1963 and had no regrets about leaving when he did:

I started making my decision at the time of the murder of Mrs Burton – I'd been in the army in Kenya. I'd also been up in the Congo after the killing of Lumumba when Moise Tshombe was in charge in Katanga. The manager of the mine asked me if I'd drive up and take some lubricants to the mine at Lumumbashi, which I did, and I was ambushed on the road, just past Chililabombwe, on the way back. I just thought it was the time – the "winds of change" had arrived; it was a political decision more than anything. I also had a domestic problem with my first wife and we had two small children ... but the decision to leave was purely and simply the fact that I thought that the white man's tenure there was going to be somewhat obstructed.

Others made a similar decision closer to Independence – the Lumpa uprisings frightened a great many people, whether they lay the blame for the carnage on the members of the Lenshina movement or on the new government. I'm not in agreement with Catherine Strang's father's depiction of Lumpas as sweetly beatific, but I wasn't there either:

The idea of Independence made the white population very uneasy, although my parents were prepared to stay on and see how things went. The main reason they did not stay was my father's experience during Alice Lenshina's Lumpa rebellion in the Northern Province, shortly before full Independence. According to my father they were peaceable farmers, whose villages were neat and well organised ... My father went there with the Police Flight. He saw a Lumpa village which had been attacked by UNIP and burned in what amounted to a massacre before the Army arrived. He didn't tell us much, but I remember him saying that experienced Army officers had been physically sick at what they'd seen, and that although he didn't go there on foot until a few days after the event, they could still smell the burning. After that, he decided that Zambia was not where he saw a long-term future, and, because he was then in his early forties and knew his employment prospects in the UK or elsewhere were diminishing, my parents decided to leave shortly after Independence

I was 16 when I went to the Independence ceremony in Lusaka ... I don't remember a great deal about the ceremony, except that it was long and noisy. There was a lump in my throat when the old flag came down and I didn't cheer when the new one was raised.

Skatie Fourie, a former Copperbelt miner of Afrikaans descent, acknowledged that when younger he had accepted the package of beliefs upholding white supremacy but he was no longer so sure. When I met him in Cape Town he told me he felt he should have stayed on for a while to see how things developed in Zambia instead of moving down to (Southern) Rhodesia. He asked me whether I knew the Afrikaans term *swart gevaar* ("black peril"), explaining it as an ingrained horror, combined with fear of unbridled attack on Europeans, particularly on European women – it was the old myth of the *Heart of Darkness*. Experience had made him question its logic, but he remains a stalwart Rhodesian. Like many who fought in the bush war, he moved on to South Africa where he is a central figure in the Rhodesian community, remaining loyal to Ian Smith, who became a neighbour, and serving on the committee of the *Flame Lily Foundation, Cape Peninsula*, a charity that does voluntary work on behalf of pensioners in Zimbabwe. An avowed African, he's a generous man who embodies the contradictions of contemporary Southern Africa.

Though one might have assumed that the country's white population emptied out at the same time as Skatie and for the same reason, only 66 of the 632 people who communicated with me in this research left the country in 1964 and only 29 in 1963, the first full year of black majority government. This however, is not a statistically valid sample of the population. We are probably never going to know how many European people crossed into Southern Rhodesia, some to stay, others passing through, in 1963, when Federation still existed and there was no border post. Certainly the European population started draining out from early 1963.

Reluctant Colonials

It was not, however, always the anticipation of a breakdown in order that impelled people to leave Northern Rhodesia before Zambia's Independence. Disillusioned by "development" initiatives, Hywel Griffiths left before the date of Independence was announced:

Independence came the following year, but we were not to know that then. Most senior people in the government who had family responsibilities were naturally worried about their futures and more preoccupied with that than with anything else. We did not know when independence would come nor what terms we might be offered in compensation for loss of career. For me the problem was expressed in this way. Was I prepared to continue enduring a deeply frustrating experience in which I could no longer work effectively for the sake of an unspecified sum in compensation at some unspecified time in the future? I had a wife and two baby girls. I should perhaps have put up with it for their sake, but I could not face it. The alternative also, though challenging, did appear to offer opportunities. I believed that in my newly developed specialism I had acquired a professional qualification which I could carry forward as a basis for a new career. So I resigned. I had to go up to Lusaka to sign off with someone in the Secretariat. He offered no thanks, he expressed no curiosity; he just made a joke that we would probably end up in the same queue applying for a job as a carpet salesman one day. After that I turned my back on the Colonial Service completely.

Neville Price left in 1962 after one tour:

I worked through the (Northern) "Emergency" of '61, being entrusted by my DC (who decamped to Tunduma, our hyper-sensitive "Tanzam" border-post) to take day-to-day responsibility for the Boma, the Court, the Southern half of the District and the soldiery which was encamped on us for a month or so. I was subsequently commended for this work. My reason for resigning was the uncertainty regarding when and how Independence would come. I could see nothing but negativity towards it in Lusaka; it was a bad joke in Salisbury and as for London, who knew?

I loved the work (which means the people) so why did I resign? I suppose, at bottom, I felt I'd joined the Colonial Service under a false prospectus. I was bright and idealistic and went to help a people become independent. I knew it wouldn't be easy, but was given no warning of how difficult it was going to be nor that there was little political will "at the top". After two years I felt that people like me were powerless to help. I would have thought differently if I could have seen serious preparations for independence being made: rather, it was "Keep the lid on the kettle!" Colonially, it seemed we never learned!

Weighing things up

Leaving before Independence wasn't always a matter of ideology. Don Smith left at the age of twenty-eight because he had calculated the costs and benefits, weighing his age against a likely compensation package:

We departed in 1962, realised that independence was coming quickly and was unstoppable. Many of those young enough took the chance of losing any pension in exchange for job seeking earlier than the rest!

There were young police officers making the same decision, as Colin Heape indicates:

Many of the senior Police Officers had come from the Palestine Police. A number of my fellow officers went on to join the Hong Kong Police. We were very undecided about what to do at the end of my first tour of duty. Our reasons for returning to UK after only one tour were mainly because we knew by then that my career in the Colonial Police would not last forever and we wanted to start afresh in UK while I was still young enough. I was only 24 years old in 1962.

By 1964 more people were worrying about the long-term stability of the country and were estimating how long to stay, they were not panicking but they were wary. Members of HMOCS were given varyingly generous "abolition of office" lump sums (colloquially known as "lumpers") depending on their length of service and age, but in order to facilitate the transfer of power, there were inducements for remaining in post on a contract after Independence (an additional 15% above normal salary, the right to have a proportion of salary paid into a foreign bank account and a gratuity on leaving). People had to make fine calculations about the timing of their departure, taking into consideration lump sums, pension size, future employment potential and the stage of their children's education. When deciding whether and when to go, a man's age was an important factor; most people thought that forty was the watershed for finding desirable employment elsewhere – some drew the line at thirty. Staying longer built up capital for subsequent house purchase, but could reduce employment prospects.

The third volume of David Salmon's incomparable letters home sees him in 1964 musing about the most advantageous time to leave the service. A bachelor, still in his late twenties, with no children's education to consider, he was balancing his love of his work with varying severance terms at different dates, he was also considering his salary in Zambia against possible teacher training and the British Council. He resigned, then was persuaded to withdraw his resignation, but we see him becoming uneasy, having to summon up great reserves of patience, experiencing declining job satisfaction, and watching friends leave. He was sent as a Zambian representative to Malawi, staying on without staying on.

Government employees were not offered unlimited renewal of contracts and, though it was possible to spin time out through reappointment to new roles for a while, it was uncommon for former members of HMOCS to be retained much beyond the decade of Independence and, once their final post was Zambianised, few European people had the means to remain in the country.

Andrew Angus, a research botanist with the Ministry of Agriculture decided in 1964 that:

We were sorry to leave such a pleasant environment, but having a family of four children to raise and educate we felt we were doing the right thing. There were rumours of violence. We all knew about Kenya's troubles with the Mau Mau. There had been disturbances in Nyasaland which had to be put down by the Federal Army, resulting in fatalities and a few minor incidents in Northern Rhodesia, particularly on the Copperbelt. But Northern Rhodesia was generally peaceful, the path to Independence going smoothly. But there were rumours in the local press of possible Africanisation of jobs done by Europeans and that the new government would do its best to replace Europeans by indigenous Africans. We seemed to get caught up in a mini exodus of 'whites' – professional people like doctors and school teachers ... Another factor that influenced our decision to return to UK was to be once again with ageing parents, who were happy to welcome us home.

Fred Andrews, the Headmaster of Luanshya Primary School, reasoned in 1964 that it was time to get his daughter and then his son into the British education system, even though it meant separation for a while:

The writing [was] on the wall – By this time Alison was at high school and clearly had academic ability. Richard was at primary school and needed to work hard. We felt that, however well we had settled in Zambia, we would not take chances with our children's future & consequently decided to return to the UK. I still had the best part of two years' contract to honour, so Alison returned on her own to stay with ex-NR friends ... We did well to emigrate, were reluctant to return to the UK, but realised the need to do so and in the event, everything turned out well for the family.

John Orr-Ewing of the PA left in October 1965 aged forty-five, happy to take up a second career in England where his ten and eleven year-old daughters had started at boarding school a year before.

I received my 'Abolition of Office terms' – a golden handshake. At the time I was Assistant Secretary in the Office of the President in Lusaka. It became evident that the government was becoming corrupt in the months before October – and after we had gone I realised how hard it would have been to stay on – this was confirmed by friends who served after independence. I realised that we would have had to go within a year or 2 anyway – there would have been no life for me within a very short time. It wasn't a hard decision at all and I have no real regrets, although we missed the lifestyle.

Paul Bourne exemplifies the decision-making of a former member of the PA, who, like many, stayed on for a contract with the Zambian government. When he decided leave he was taking his age into consideration, he was concerned for his own future employment prospects, his children's education and the continuity of administration; the only thing he omits from his account is the fine calculation about pension and "lumpers" that usually accompanied the choice of final date of service:

I retired in 1967 to the UK. My last tour was based in Lusaka. I was then 39 years of age and I felt I ought to get into the jobs market overseas before reaching forty. Additionally my three daughters were attending school in Lusaka, where standards up to this point were very satisfactory. Teaching staff, however, were themselves pulling out and the future standard of schooling was not assured. As far as my particular job was concerned, this was ongoing but the procedures and parameters had been established and a Zambian shadow with mature experience should be able to handle the department.

Norman Williams left Zambia in 1970, realizing that another contract would make him nearly fifty thus less attractive to employers:

Why did I leave Zambia? Basically, I suppose because it was time to leave. Africanisation was naturally proceeding apace, most of my old friends had already left, and there was always the thought that now aged 44, I would find it difficult to get a job in England if I left it any later. I retain very fond memories of my time in Northern Rhodesia/Zambia and the people (local and expat) I met there. With half my time bashing around in the bush and half my time at the centre of things in Lusaka I experienced the best of both worlds.

Education is a theme that recurs over and over again – schooling after Independence was the major factor in the decision to leave for a great many people. If their children were young enough, people felt able to delay departure for a while; Martin Linnette a police officer decided to leave in 1972:

... mainly because the schools system was collapsing just as my two kids were starting primary, and again because, although a Permanent Resident, there was no long term future for me with the wrong colour face and no Zambian passport. Went, unhappily, back to UK.

Jim Dunning combined thoughts about the unavoidable Zambianisation of his post with concerns for the education of his children:

I left Zambia in 1965 because my role as Provincial Education Officer, Solwezi was being taken over by an African. This came as no surprise and in some ways was welcome since we lived on a bush station with no suitable schools for our children. Our eldest, Carolyn, was attending a convent school in Ndola as a boarder. My elder son, Robert, was limited to a correspondence course from Salisbury, so it was high time they got into suitable schools in England.

When considering worries about education, it is important to balance the misgivings European parents had about sending children away to boarding school against those involved in using local schools. Ron and Elise de Kock decided to leave:

If you had school-going children there were many weighty decisions to be made. If you were offered a further three-year contract, the decision to accept and stay meant that you now had to face decisions concerning the education of your children. Do you remain for the high pay and accept the lower level of education? Do you remain but send your children Down South to boarding school? Finally, do you move the family elsewhere to where the educational standard is better? We faced these decisions as our eldest was already in her second year, coming home from school and talking with a black African accent... You only have your children with you for a short time before they grow up and move away to start their own lives. We had no intention to lose her for some boarding school to bring up. Eventually in 1972 I gave notice to Chibuluma Mines.

At the other end of children's education, I have been told that the generous payment of British boarding school fees and children's fares back to Zambia were an inducement for older men to take another contract to see them through the sixth form.

Barbara and Richard Hall had been committed to Independence all along; their paper, the *African Mail,* was the voice of nationalism in the country, then Richard was made Editor of *The Times of Zambia,* which replaced the pro-Federation *Northern News.* With the abandonment of A-Levels in Zambia, foreign schooling became essential for families aiming at an elite university – Barbara and Richard had five sons and the cost of sending them all to school abroad and flying them home to Zambia three times a year was impossible, so they left in 1967. It was probably getting near time to go anyway – Barbara showed me a photograph of a student protest with a young man holding up a placard "Richard Hall is a crypto-neo-colonialist" – before Independence he'd been labelled a "crypto-communist".

Rose Newman commented that:

Dad retired as my younger sister, Barbara, neared high school age and my parents began to get jittery about her being in class with boys who were more like young men – because of their disadvantaged backgrounds and lack of proper education, they would have been entering Form 1 at 15 or 16 while Barbara would only have been about 13... so mid 1966 we reluctantly left to settle in Cape Town.

Phillip and Mary Lee (police and teaching) were concerned about their children's health rather than education:

I left Zambia in 1967, I was asked to stay on and offered another promotion, but alas at Ndola the health system was breaking down. The malaria was coming back, right into town and I would not risk my three young children.

But children rarely were consulted about whether they wanted to stay or go and Trevor Snyman is typical of many whose parents thought that it was time to leave by the time there was African majority government:

The irrational and mob-driven behaviour that we had seen in black people in the Congo, coupled with increasing mobilisation of the people of Northern Rhodesia to demand independence made my parents uneasy, and plans were initiated to leave Northern Rhodesia. I was devastated that we would be leaving, but the decision was with my parents. This was 1963, and I had been in High School for less than one year. I was 13 years old. The fateful day arrived on which we climbed into our car and drove away from Bancroft, heading for South Africa from where we had left 7 years earlier. Now, out of a family of 6, only I have ever returned to the place that was mine in every sense whilst I lived there.

It was not just a familiar place that was left behind, friendship networks were destroyed and affectionate ties were sundered. Geraldine Luscombe was obliged to leave in 1964 – as we have already seen, the possibilities for a young woman staying in the country on her own were slight but, aged 18, in those days she was still legally a "child", unable to decide her own fate:

I was devastated when my parents decided to return to England after Independence. I had a boyfriend that I didn't want to leave behind, and a lifestyle that I loved. I found England quite a frightening place to be.

Similarly Mike Coetzee, now in South Africa:

I have literally lived N.R. in my head daily for forty years and feel cheated that my parents immigrated to South Africa, taking me away from the country I still love so much. I left Zambia in 1968.

All these years later, someone confided:

Each school holiday that I came home there was less and less available until eventually one holiday I didn't go 'home' to Zambia as 'home' was then in Rhodesia. I have been very resentful of that – apart from my love of the country I had someone who was so very special to me – I still have that resentment and I still have not found peace.

The End of the Line

For many people there was no choice in the matter, their jobs were Zambianised and there was no alternative work. Many former members of HMOCS who stayed on contract and gratuity terms had to walk a tightrope at work, doing their old job "shadowed" by someone nominally senior; in a potentially highly charged ex-colonial situation this required considerable sensitivity on both sides. The normally patient and egalitarian DO, David Salmon frequently refers in his later letters home to the problems of transferring senior administrative posts that had hitherto been the preserve of Oxford and Cambridge graduates to people who had had formerly been clerks holding Standard Six school-leaving certificates (8 years of education) – he keeps saying that they are good men, but they lack formal education and experience. Of course, if the British Government had been serious about the task of HMOCS being to prepare the colony for Independence, there would have been rather more than one school going up to A-Level for African boys and there would also have been a continuous scale in the civil service; that said, come Independence, there was an existential problem. Salmon's earliest letters home in 1959 amply demonstrate the greenness and lack of confidence of the new recruit from Oxford, then we see him gaining stature and confidence over the five years, but it was impossible to grow a senior bureaucracy overnight. Learning the advantages of elevated status was easy enough, but learning the job itself would take a lot longer and couldn't be easy when the only available teachers were men who were worried about their own futures. Furthermore, if they enforced regulations officers could find themselves accused of racism or neo-colonialist motives.

Realising that the Director of the Zambia Youth Service was embezzling funds, in 1965 John Pitchford refused to sign a large cheque:

I was then hauled up before our Director. I remonstrated and got the reply: 'If you don't like the way we do things in Africa ... Get out!' So I did. But not until after a physical breakdown which started with malaria ... We motored down to the Cape, shipped our little Mini Traveller aboard Pretoria Castle and sailed for Southampton. About six months later two Zambian detectives visited me in the UK to get more evidence of fraud within the Zambia Youth Service. I believe that my Director was subsequently convicted... (Pitchford, 2013 Kindle edn.)

People in government service may have been advised that their job was to work themselves out of a job; older men believed that Independence would be a distant event and that they might retire in their mid-fifties, but those joining in the late 1950s and early 'sixties had few illusions that they would be long in post. This was reflected in a new practice of offering young men straight from the public schools a newly created grade, Learner District Assistant, to appeal as an alternative to university. One of these, Tim O'Hara, knew all along that the Colonial Service could be no more than a stage in his life:

At my interview in London I was cautioned that, due to 'the Winds of Change' sweeping Africa, I could only expect a career of 15 years, before NR was granted independence. In the event they were out by 10! So, joined 1959 at the age of 18 at an annual salary of £620. Independence 1964. Married the Resident Commissioner, Mongu's, daughter 1965 Left 1966.

Why did we leave when we did? Being a young expat Local Government Officer, it was made clear that there was no future for me in the Zambian service. As it transpired, my posting at Independence was at Kawambwa, Luapula Province. The Kawambwa Local Council, composed of course of active UNIP party members, believed that membership of the Council was their reward for winning the battle for independence. My job was to curb their enthusiastic excesses, so inevitably I became deeply unpopular, the subject of constant harassment. Finally, Kenneth Kaunda, himself, came up to restore discipline. My last year was spent back at the provincial HQ at Mansa, auditing the provincial local council books. But even there, local politicians were loud in their opinion that I was out to sabotage the fledgling republic. There is no doubt that I was very unlucky to be posted to Kawambwa at that time. It was never a popular station at the best of times, but the experience coloured my final memories of Zambia.

Tim was young enough to make another career, then take over the family farm in Ireland, but leaving could be traumatic for other people who had to uproot their homes, jobs, lifestyles and identities.

Throwing in the towel

Some people did not think it necessary to look for an alternative career outside Zambia expecting to live out their days there. It was home and they intended to adapt to change, but gradually most realised that there was no place for them. For many people there was a straw that broke the camel's back, a point at which they could no longer relate to the new country. Connie and Robert McChesney meant to stay, moving from government employment to partnership in a business, then work with a multinational company, but they left in 1971 because they wanted their children to grow up more British:

Southern Rhodesia's UDI in November '65 had a profound effect on all of us in Zambia. There were shortages of the most basic items in the shops and petrol, which had to be brought in via the infamous Hell Run, was strictly rationed. By the beginning of 1967 Zambianisation was creeping up on us.

Our doctor recommended that our children should have their tonsils removed. By now the hospitals were multi-racial but children's wards had been done away with all together and they were both put into separate adult medical wards which was horrifying for them. At this juncture we knew that we would have to make a move soon for the sake of the children, who were too young for boarding school. Education was also multi-racial and both children were in Primary School with Zambian and European teachers. One day our daughter came home very puzzled and showed us a picture of a ship. She said her teacher had insisted that it was a 'sheep'. Our English speaking daughter was being taught to speak English! This little incident was the one that prompted us to make that final decision, which was in fact very hard because we loved the country and the climate. It had become our home. I was apprehensive about leaving Africa entirely because I was now 43, not a good age to start seeking a new career, but Connie was adamant that we had to go for the children's sakes.

Radical Change

The 1968 Mulungushi Reforms had started a process of state ownership; this was extended to smaller enterprises in 1973. Zambianisation of posts and nationalization of companies proceeded apace, killing some people's ambitions. As time progressed more and more of the white population came to realise that they would never be in the ascendant again. Ray Critchell, who had worked as a fire officer in Northern Rhodesia and Zambia said:

It had been my hope and ambition to retire there eventually and buy a plot on the lakeside or a riverside and build and develop a game viewing lodge. Under the policy of Zambianisation this was not to be, and we left in 1974, rather sad and disappointed that I had been unable to complete the planned development of the service. I brought my family away from their homeland to make a new life in the UK.

The 1970s were a terrible time for Zambia. The Second *Chimurenga*/Bush War in Rhodesia/Zimbabwe put the country onto a virtual war footing; massive international oil price rises, the collapse in world demand for copper and rising indebtedness triggered hyperinflation and shortages of imported goods; there were strict exchange controls and yet élites seemed able to operate in a shady dollar economy. Good people who could go were leaving, even those who had wholeheartedly supported Independence. The political economist, Morris Szeftel, who had been born in the country, attended school there and was deeply committed to national Independence, was working at the University of Zambia and took study leave in 1975 to complete his Ph.D thesis in Manchester, accompanied by Carolyn, who became his wife and was also completing a Ph.D:

I left Zambia in 1975 with almost no money. I was supposed to get 6 months pay from Unza under the study leave arrangement, but none of that ever came to me and none of it was ever banked in my Lusaka account. We survived – and no more than that – by living on Carolyn's expatriate gratuity from Unza plus loans from friends in Manchester. When we set off for the US in 1978, we still intended to return to Lusaka after Carolyn got her Ph.D. However, life intervened. Carolyn's mother in California was diagnosed with terminal cancer. So we went to California and both of us worked in itinerant, temporary university jobs which friends helped us find. They were good enough for us to subsist and allow us to repay all the loans through 1979. When her mother died in late 1979, we decided it was time to go back to Lusaka.

But then another problem took over. While we were still in Zambia, Carolyn had developed an eye problem which they were unable to diagnose in Lusaka but which an optician diagnosed in 10 minutes in Manchester. It was to be a lifelong condition. So much for development and underdevelopment. Anyway, the condition made her virtually blind unless she had specially cut lenses fitted in her eyes. This needed trips to the UK twice a year for treatment. I wrote to Unza to tell them the news and to ask for them to get me special permission to fly with Carolyn twice a year (at the time, there was no forex and such trips were difficult if not impossible to arrange but I hoped that it would be agreed on compassionate grounds). I did not get a reply but a letter came from a friend to tell me that the Unza authorities felt I was making unreasonable demands and being arrogant. On the day I got that letter, there was a small item in The Times (London) reporting that the wife of a Zambian minister had flown into London to have a broken arm reset. I can't tell you how angry I was. I'd been offered a job in Leeds and when that happened, I took it and I've been there ever since. I didn't go back to Lusaka for over 12 years! Once we had the end of exchange controls and problems of movement, the question about going back arose again but by then our 2 children were established in schools in Leeds and the Zambian economy had pretty much collapsed.

So I left Zambia for accidental, negative reasons and the years from 1975 to 1981 were years of terrible financial hardship – but it turned out to be the luckiest thing that could have happened to me because we were able to make a modest living and I was able to send my children to university, where one qualified as a lawyer and the other as a doctor. I visit Zambia regularly now (less so since my wife died) and continue research there.

Richard Samson left in 1972; he had been mayor of Lusaka and in 2014 was honoured by the Zambian Government. He was Chairman of the Commercial Bank, which was nationalised, and Chairman of London based, Eagle Star insurance, but it was decreed that all Insurance had to be through Switzerland.

Samson had set up the Lusaka Medical Society with its own small hospital – private medicine was abolished. He moved to the United States in an executive position with Hospital Supply Corporation and now lives in California.

As the 1970s progressed, more and more European people who had assumed that they could adapt and stay on were beginning to question the wisdom of that decision, whether they blamed the difficult situation on the consequences of Rhodesia's Unilateral Declaration of Independence or endogenous economic and political problems. Robert Butterworth was of the latter persuasion, but he was also conscious of changing conditions in Britain:

This idyllic life began to crack in the early '70s. The Zambian government's obsession with interfering in the affairs of our neighbours, coupled with a World Bank scheme to buy-out the productive expat farmers, without ensuring that the cooperatives which took over their land were capable of so doing, led to all sorts of shortages – and these did not affect only the expat mine employees, no one who lived through those years can ever forget the tearful, hungry, local housewives sitting by the roadside hoping for deliveries of maize flour, or bread, or cooking oil, or beef, which sadly arrived sporadically, if at all... By 1975 I had reached 40, had a wife and a 5 year old daughter, and faced the fact that things were never going to improve, so, with a very heavy heart, decided to get out before I became too old ever to find another job and to return to UK, rather than trying our luck elsewhere on the feckless African continent. I had saved steadily over our years at Nchanga Mine and was able to return to Britain with about £30,000 – a small fortune by 1973-74 standards, but by 1975 inflation was raging. House prices were rising every day – clearly it was imperative to get a foot on the housing ladder before inflation priced us out of the market.

By the mid-1970s things were changing fast. Jenny Rorison explained that:

We left in 1974 having felt we'd had a 'wake-up' call with Kaunda's Mulungushi speech. We had personally not sent lots of money back to the UK, but had decided to invest in Zambia and built our own house. But after the Mulungushi speech we felt the writing was on the wall for Europeans.

Sue & Paul Hoar left in 1975:

Most of our friends were in their forties when they left Zambia and if they worked for a large company like Lever Brothers, they were able to be posted elsewhere, such as Johannesburg. However, there were many, like us, who

145

worked for themselves and it was very difficult to start from scratch somewhere else. At the Mulungushi Conference one year President Kaunda actually said that at one minute past midnight there would be no private schools, no private nursing homes and only Zambians could run businesses of any kind. Of course we could have employed a Zambian to 'front' our business, but obviously the writing was on the wall and it seemed futile to carry on in the face of growing difficulties. However, at that time bank accounts were frozen so that you couldn't move your money out except in a trickle of remittances every year. So we had a business we couldn't sell, a house to sell that wouldn't fetch much, and nowhere to go.

Dominic Fuciarelli, who left for Canada in 1979, writes of the problems of an expatriate-run family business:

My father started a construction company and I joined him as a junior partner. We also bought a small brick factory at the same time and within a short time were doing really well. Things in general were very good in Zambia, especially the five years after independence, however, conditions started to go from bad to worse from 1971 on. "Communocracy" was adopted in a big way and we ended up losing the brick factory when our employees were encouraged to take over our business without our consent and without compensation. They lasted six months as all the equipment was reduced to scrap. The construction end of it continued to do well and at our peak we were employing two hundred and fifty people, but having married in 1971, and with three small kids, my wife and I soon started fearing for their safety. As law and order started to break down, the professionals, such as doctors, nurses, teachers, etc. started to leave the country. On top of that we constantly faced shortages in foods and building materials. We started looking for a new "home", even though the thought of leaving left me very sad. I considered myself an African and dearly loved the country and the easy thing would have been to stay. In the end our children's future was more important and we opted to leave our home, business, and friends.

Penny Giorgio left twice, finally it was because there was no place for an advertising business in a centralised economy:

I came over to the UK to a college for young ladies, which was great fun in the swinging early '60s and then went down to Rhodesia to take up training as a radiographer during the beginning of the war-torn years there. This was at variance with the benign government of Zambia and well integrated society where we enjoyed a pleasant diversity both at school and socially. Post training I travelled for 3 years in Europe on a 'working holiday' and then went back to Zambia to work in the Health system there. I met up with my husband to be married in '74 and we battled through the hard times of the '70s, but had a great deal of fun along the way and made yet more friends both homebred and expatriate. In '76 we were forced to leave as the economy destroyed my husband's line of business.

The government's support for Zimbabwean nationalist parties and guerilla armies could make being white in Zambia difficult; racial attitudes were polarizing again. People like Harold Williams, a forest conservator, started to worry about increasing levels of crime and the targeting of Europeans:

Everything went quite well until the late 1960s when policing deteriorated and there were burglaries. Our sons, when on holiday with us, would be stopped and asked to hand over any cash they had and watches they were wearing. In late 1970 my wife became seriously ill and had to be brought home for major surgery. I had accumulated over a year's leave so we spent 1970-71 in our Welsh home. We decided not to return.

David Small and his wife had left once before but:

Having returned to Zambia we settled back into a very easy life style of servants and plenty of cash and would have worked out the three year contract had my wife not been caught in a riot in Kitwe when the petrol storage tanks blew up and "Rhodesians" were blamed. So, soon after that [1971] we left for Cape Town.

One experience could be enough to tip the scales when people were already becoming apprehensive. Margie Robinson remembers that:

A lady in my father's church was brutally raped, it was a very difficult time, Kaunda was almost condoning this because he said white women were wearing mini skirts so they were asking for trouble. My father then decided that my sister and I should move to South Africa, we did this in 1972.

"Overseas Experience"

It wasn't always economic or political circumstances or recognition of exclusion that made people of any racial group leave Zambia. There had always been European people who moved away for career reasons, just as today members of

147

Zambia's middle class bewail the fact that their highly educated, cosmopolitan children are lost to them. In most professions, there was, and still is, a limit to the level to which one could rise and there was virtually no scope for employment in the creative arts and many other specialist fields. John Lambert, for example, left in the mid-sixties for drama school in Britain, knowing that there could be no career for him as an actor in Zambia. Creative people had always leaked out.

We have already seen that elites had always educated their children at schools abroad – some didn't return, more were lost after university. Many young people aspired to a year or so travelling, in Europe – Northern Rhodesia/Zambia could seem very remote from international affairs, culture and fashion and the overseas trip was seen as part of becoming a sophisticated adult; some stayed away permanently for work or marriage. People who were caught between work and education at Independence had to think globally, knowing that there was little chance of building a career in the country, though several served one contract. So long as parents were there, most young people regarded the country as home – I am never sure when to say it was that I left, but my parents' departure in October 1973 seemed, until recently, to be the definitive end of my relationship with Zambia.

Graham Snow's desire to be part of the London scene in the mid-sixties was far from unusual in young people who felt that they were living in a backwater, but it was also compounded by family circumstance and the sudden limitation of opportunities for white school-leavers after Independence:

Dad was working for the civil service, so got 6 months home leave every 3 years. So we maintained contact with England. Dad set up the Lusaka Lodge of the Masons. He died aged 47 in February 1966. My mum came over to England for a 3 month holiday. I joined her in June after my A levels. When I got to Heathrow, I announced I was not going back! When mum got home to Lusaka, everything had changed. Her boss was very unfriendly to her, and most of her friends had left. She decided to sell up and come back to England with my brother and sister. They got here in October 1966. I didn't see any future for me in Z, due to the "Africanisation" of everything, and the fact that I wanted to be with the music in England.

Alan Chattaway's experience was tragic, losing his home and his mother at the time when he was just about to embark upon independent adulthood, he could not return to Zambia after graduating:

In 1966 my mother died in Luanshya hospital of lung cancer (age 62). Somehow my dad got the entire town to keep the news from reaching me in Durban in case it disturbed my exam performance the following week. As I left my final exam, Dad was there, which seemed very odd. He said, "Mom's dead, she died last Thursday." We drove to Salisbury for her cremation, then on to Luanshya where Dad (who by now was a Shift Engineer running the Power Plant control room) took early retirement and moved to Durban in January 1967 to stay with me. With no home in Zambia to return to, I give 1967 as the year I left Zambia. In mid-1967 my dad went to the UK and then Canada where he met his widowed sister-in-law, married her, and announced he would not be returning to Africa.

Having to leave

Lindy Wright gives a child's eye view of leaving, not really understanding as an eleven year-old what was going on when her family left in 1964:

We had to get out of Zambia as my Dad was in the police reserve and my brother Patrick did not take kindly to being seated next to anybody that was not white – at school they were getting close to asking him to leave, so we left with all we could fit in our car. Mom, Dad, Mik, Pat, me and our dog Suzy and off we went to Botswana We were only going to stop there to visit our uncle and ended up staying 6 years. At one stage we tried to go back to Zambia to sell the house and try and get some more of our stuff but were stopped on the Zambian side and by then Ian Smith had declared UDI and they wanted my parents to renounce Ian Smith, which they would not do, so they made us prohibited immigrants.

Deportation and prohibited immigrant status became an ever-present shadow, especially when paranoia about Rhodesian spies set in and when old scores could be settled by dressing them up as opposition to the government. In July 1966 fifteen European Special Branch Police officers were deported on suspicion of subversive activities. Frank McGovern, who was in Security at the time, tells me that it was "on a tip-off from a friendly government", that possibly not all were guilty but it was decided that it was sensible to be cautious. In October of the same year twent-five European people were deported for "promoting racial or industrial unrest to the detriment of Zambia's national unity and security" (Chongo, 2009 p. 89) and so it went on; Chief Justice Skinner forced to flee the country after stepping out of line over his response to Portuguese soldiers discovered on the wrong side of the Angolan border – there was an underlying belief among many Zambians that whites could not be loyal.

European farmers were not evicted by the State in Zambia (Heather Hunt of the Zambian Commerical Farmers Union is adamant about this) but many felt it impossible to continue when it became increasingly difficult to control squatters and to manage a politicized workforce. John Thompson talks of his father, a successful farmer, coming under attack from arsonists and eventually giving up, trying to make a living by driving a truck on the notorious "hell run" after the Rhodesian border closed, eventually forced south and dying in poverty, dependent on his children. Marion Carlin's father, Robert Moffat, one of Northern Rhodesia/Zambia's most established figures, a direct descendant of the pioneering missionary and himself a liberal politician, left for Scotland when he could no longer control rampant cattle rustling on his Mkushi farm. There was increasing murder and theft on isolated farms and yet significant numbers of farmers did hold on, particularly in the Southern Province. After 1977 land was no longer a saleable commodity, only improvements could be sold.

Farewells were so much a part of NR-Z life

Liz Price told me how her family left nineteen years after Independence because of the pull of a better job, not the push of conditions in Zambia:

Our children went to the International School and we were happy to be living in such a multiracial society. Eventually most children were sent to boarding schools in the UK and a few to South Africa. Ours were no exception. There were difficult times too, the war in Rhodesia was only 90 miles away, just over the border, security was an issue, supplies were often hard to come by and basic things like flour and toilet paper were often in short supply but the expatriate community learned to overcome these inconveniences and we became good at bartering with each other. Good meat and vegetables were readily available and many of the wives became excellent cooks with what they had available. I learnt to make bread and for a number of years made enough bread for my family and household staff.

My husband feels that managing a business during these difficult political times gave him a lot of experience that would be very useful in his later business life. In 1983 he was offered a job in the United States. His office was in New York City and our family moved to a pleasant suburban town within commuting distance of the city.

Noel Wright, the teacher to whom I owe so much, complained jokingly that I was setting him homework now; he also said something that applied to many people, but no one else expressed it. He and Anthea, his wife, came in the late 'fifties as idealistic new graduates from South Africa, seeking a less racially divided society:

We lived in Northern Rhodesia-Zambia for more than fourteen years. It was where we started married life, where our children were born, where we made lifelong friendships, where promotion was thrust upon us, and where we enjoyed a relaxed and comfortable lifestyle we couldn't have had in many other places. It should have been harder to leave, you would think. One reason it wasn't is that NR-Z set us up so well for later life, including with fair compensation for loss of career.

I'm surprised in retrospect that saying goodbye to friends wasn't harder. If we took it more or less in our stride, that had a lot to do with farewells being so much a part of NR-Z life. People were constantly moving on, and others arriving, either transferred from elsewhere in the country, or recruited from outside.

Many Europeans in Northern Rhodesia were people who made friends easily, but moved on easily too – footloose people who thought that the world was theirs. Many now yearn for deeper roots.

8. WHERE DID THEY ALL GO?

So four continents later we are still surviving *Karen Horn*

I knew one couple who, contemplating where to go when his job was about to be Zambianised, drew up a list in 1965 of the "last pink bits" worldwide. The list, of course, was short, most of the territories on it were very small and one would be hard put to find some of them on a map. He was a specialist in tropical agriculture, a calling difficult to practice at "home" – I have no idea what they finally decided.

Perhaps we should be surprised that a population of more than 74,000 British nationals and British Protected Persons could shrink down to next to nothing and there be no account of where they went. It was the end of empire, so the colonials just evaporated? More fuss was made in Britain about Banda's expulsion of Malawi's tiny Goan community in 1976 than ever greeted the matter of Northern Rhodesia's colonials, they didn't exit *en masse* and they didn't make a fuss. In July 1964 when the British Parliament passed the *Zambia Independence Act*, every European in Northern Rhodesia knew it was impossible to put off decisions about residence and employment. For many there was also the matter of nationality. How happy people were, how they fitted in socially and how they fared financially once their initial choices were made varies a great deal.

People knew that they had to work out their futures for themselves – there was no general resettlement scheme, neither were there reliable sources of global information – no effective means of assessing employment opportunities, housing availability, or costs of living in other countries. People made major life-choices on the basis of hearsay, out-of-date knowledge and their personal contacts – it is no wonder that some made bad initial decisions and moved on.

Restrictions

Then, as now, people did not have free choice about which country to settle in. People with full British passports had the advantage over others, but the *Zambia Independence Act* specifically addressed the question of nationality (subsequently repealed by the British Nationality Act of 1981). A Citizen of the United Kingdom and Colonies (CUKC) would, on Independence Day, "Cease to be such a citizen if he becomes on that day a citizen of Zambia." The same applied to British Protected Persons. Crucially, South African nationals (of whom there were many among the permanent residents of Northern Rhodesia) had ceased to be CUKC in 1962 when South Africa withdrew from the Commonwealth. People born in the Federation to South African parents remained a sort of trailing category that could not get a full British passport with residence rights. There was no obvious way for children of South Africans living in Northern Rhodesia to remedy this, unless they had a paternal grandfather born in Britain.

The assumption that all persons are "he" and the ruling that only fathers can transmit nationality is difficult to swallow fifty years later, but at the time a British woman married to a South African man could not transmit citizenship to her children born in Northern Rhodesia; there were many such. This started to matter acutely, particularly after Rhodesia's UDI. When some people refer to being "sold down the river" by Britain (as they often do) it is not always a comment about the granting of Independence, it can be a reference to the citizenship issue that mattered crucially to where one might live. In the case of Northern Rhodesia, the principle of *civis Britannicus sum*, drilled into the white children in the schools of the Empire, appeared to be a sham, but if not all of the European residents of Northern Rhodesia had automatic entitlement to residence in the United Kingdom or the Dominions, they weren't necessarily welcome in Zambia either.

Lizzy Gornall, a teacher married to a British NRP officer, found herself bereft of a UK passport in 1966 because both her parents were South Africans of long descent. Her husband and her baby daughter, however, had British nationality:

While John worked his six months notice we thought it best that we two girls should leave at once. Simple it was not! Independence had brought with it the unwelcome realization that my family and I had been made stateless. Our UK citizenship was void as residence in Zambia was not by then, a qualification. Zambia declined to confirm citizenship because I was born in South Africa. The South Africans said that my parents had severed my right to citizenship, but they would admit me and I could re-qualify after five years residence. This was not a solution. I had no valid passport and could not travel.

Eventually, the authorities at the British High Commission granted me a temporary travel permit in the form of a piece of paper with my photo on it granting me the right to travel and reside with my infant daughter who was a registered citizen of the UK. On our way to England my peculiar status caused problems at every step of the journey. I was fearful for our safety and our future, but we arrived intact – or nearly so.

Ron de Kock of long Afrikaner ancestry believed like many that:

Up to a certain date all whites in the previous Northern Rhodesia could apply for and be granted British citizenship and hence a British passport. I thought about this for a while and in the end decided not to take advantage of this offer. The reason was that prior to October 1963 and our marriage we had applied for new passports for our honeymoon trip. This was given with a five-year validity. I still remember that the cover of the passport said, 'British Passport. Northern Rhodesia.' We were then assured that when these passports expired in 1968 we would automatically be granted renewed British passports. Since our present passports still had four years validity I reasoned why bother about changing after just a year. In the light of latter events this was the wrong decision.

He was actually entitled only to a Zambian or South African one. As late as 2014 the consequences of ambiguous nationality are still being played out. The subject often comes up on Facebook groups in varying degrees of complexity.

The EU has been a boon to Europeans born in Northern Rhodesia who want to live in the UK. They may have been brought up to think of themselves as British subjects, attended annual Queen's Birthday Parades, learned British history at school and speak not a word of German, Italian or Greek – but if they can trace a grandparent's birthplace to an EU country, they can live in Britain, if they can't, they can't. To this day, there are still people born in Northern Rhodesia of European descent who are researching their genealogies to find a qualifying grandparent who might have left as an infant. Heather Chalcraft tells me that, like other Europeans living in Zambia, she is frequently asked to help people now living outside the country to find the birth, marriage and death certificates of parents and grandparents that could prove entitlement to EU citizenship and residence. She even locates gravestones and burial records to check proper names and dates of death that will facilitate finding the records leading to the desired passport. Things were a little easier in the 'sixties for non-British immigrants to the UK than they became later.

You're on your own

After exclusions on the basis of nationality had been taken into account, employment chances were the major determinant in selecting the next country of residence. The chance of gaining employment of similar status in a new country was slim for men over the age of fifty, who had to adapt to early retirement or a drop in status. Since the Dominions were already closed to retired people without existing family ties or very large amounts of capital, late middle-aged people either returned to their country of origin (frequently to the countryside or the coast, rather than their original home), or they went to Southern Rhodesia, South Africa and countries like Spain that were being promoted as low cost, sun-drenched retirement destinations.

What I have been able to piece together from the remnants of this population has no statistical validity in trying to reconstruct this exodus. Statistics are a dry way of looking at things, anyway – what I have gained is a glimpse of realised possibilities but it is indicative. There are few Afrikaans names on my list and, though the majority of the missing Afrikaners probably went to South Africa, by no means all did – for example, Gert van Niekerk became sports coach at a college in Canada (and well into his sixties was still working). For sure, not everyone who originated in Britain returned there.

Unlike colonial officers who always assumed that they would retire to Britain, "settlers" had come to Northern Rhodesia hoping for a better life and, regardless of where they had originated, many did not want to return. Retrospectively, one might wonder how the UK government could absolve itself quite so easily of concern for its colonial population – no employment advice, no assisted passages, nothing.

Where they ended up

Of the people who informed this project I know the country of residence of all but one. This is the breakdown:

UK	283	44.7%
South Africa	142	22.5%
Australia	79	12.5%
USA	34	5.4%
EU (other)	28	4.5%
Canada	26	4.4%
New Zealand	15	2.4%
Other Africa & rest of world	25	4.0%

I believe, however, that there are probably more old Northern Rhodesians in South Africa than in Britain. These figures relate to where people were when I contacted them, these are not necessarily their first destinations and they obscure the many moves that some have made.

Constantly moving

Veronica Guest exemplifies the restless nature of many former Northern Rhodesians, but also the pull of Africa and the desire to use one's life to the full. It is currently fashionable in the social sciences to think of people as always in a state of "becoming":

My love for travel and adventure continued and I did many exciting trips in my twenties and thirties. Val Lubbe, also from Mufulira happened to end up in the same South African town as me. We decided to go to Australia for a year's working holiday and spent the most wonderful year of our lives, hitch-hiking around Australia, New Zealand and Tasmania, working on and off as barmaids in all sorts of places, including the Great Barrier Reef. We then went to Namibia but eventually ended up living in Johannesburg. Val got married there and I continued doing free-lance secretarial work, travelling when I could, mostly to African countries. In 1978 I decided to emigrate to South America, as I could not abide the apartheid system any longer. I spent seven months travelling through fourteen South American countries, but concluded that there was just as much exploitation there as in South Africa. After working on a Kibbutz in Israel for a while, I eventually realised that my roots would always be in Africa so I came back and decided to do something positive. Since it did not look like I would ever marry, I began to study for a career. After doing my matriculation through correspondence at the age of 30, I studied a for BA degree and teaching diploma. I started working in black education since I believed education was the only answer to building a country with critical thinking people. In 1989 I was offered a job near Nelspruit as a principal of a matriculation college to upgrade black teachers who only had Standard 8. Twenty years on, I am still involved in education development work in black rural schools in the Mpumalanga province. During these years I continued to further my studies and eventually obtained a Masters in Education Management.

Karen Horn was born and brought up in Northern Rhodesia and left to marry a geologist who had accepted a new job in Australia. Though now settled, they have enjoyed a peripatetic life:

After Australia we lived in Brazil then to England and now in Canada. So four continents later we are still surviving. My husband is now retired and we live in Victoria, Canada, after spending 17 years in Toronto. I paint and write poetry in my spare time and my husband writes books, which hopefully will be successful. We have two sons in their early thirties who also live in the Northwest of North America.

John Hyde is another who recognizes the restlessness of so many old colonials:

I realised I needed to get some decent education behind me as I was going nowhere fast. So I went to the UK, applied to a company called IAL, who contracted out Air Traffic Controllers to underdeveloped countries. I started my training in 1973, passed the course and was posted to Bahrain. I spent 7 years there and got all my ATC qualifications, then I went to Botswana for the ODA for 5 years as a training officer at Gaborone International Airport. After that my travels took me back to the Middle East to Dubai for 3 years. Then I went to Vanuatu in the South Pacific for 4 years as Senior Air Traffic Control/Training Officer at Port Vila International Airport. Then back to Bahrain for a further 3 years. Then the UK to Bailbrook College in Bath at an aviation training institute as an ATC Instructor then finally to Luxembourg where I work as an ATC Instructor with the Institute of Air Navigation Services for Eurocontrol training ab initio students to work in the Upper Area Control Centre in Maastricht, the Netherlands. What do all these moves mean? Well for a start I get itchy feet. Then, I never really wanted to work in a cold climate, so put it off as long as possible. Finally I loved travelling at the expense of other people! Unfortunately all the different moves have meant that I feel a little bit of a refugee with no real roots anywhere. I am looking for somewhere (hot) to retire to.

Some people chose professions in the 'sixties that would allow them to work globally and keep them in the tropics. Several took employment with global corporations, the British Council or development agencies. Settling was often anathema. After a degree in geology at the Royal School of Mines, Chris Legg returned to Geological Survey of Zambia, remaining there until 1980; next he specialized in GIS working in Kenya, Sri Lanka, Cameroon, Indonesia, Nigeria, but since 2007 he has been a GIS consultant in Bristol, UK.

Crossing the Zambezi

A large number of people drifted South from late 1962 onwards, often with few assets. Many of those who had the hardest time after leaving Zambia made what then seemed to many to be the obvious move to Southern Rhodesia; most of these relocated south again. Heather Chalcraft introduced me to the derogatory term in Zambia for these people – they are "Soweto", wondering "So where to now?" constantly running from African Africa; Ann Bailey capped this with "Escape Town" (from which people leave for Australia and New Zealand).

Like many Railway employees, Cecil Frowd was transferred to Bulawayo in 1965 when he was in his late forties. He and his wife, Joan, enjoyed living there but:

The family finally left Rhodesia in 1978 as Cecil had retired and his pension was meager. Probably the main reason, was for their son John [who is disabled] *to have more security living in UK. First, they went to Rochdale where their eldest son, Tony, had opened a tyre re-treading business, in the hope that Cecil could help Tony out and earn a few shillings. Sadly though, Cecil's health was on the decline and soon they decided to go back to their native Wales. They stayed temporarily by day with fellow ex-Rhodies and lived in a hostel by night, Joan says this was a terrible experience, (she found it difficult to talk to me about their time there even after such a long time). There was a Curfew from 10 p.m. till 8 a.m. (They had to suffer this place, in order to be housed.) After a few months of hostel life, they were housed in a new-build house backing on to a railway station in Dinas Powys, Cardiff, where they have been ever since. Cecil died there in 1985.* (From Linda Frowd, writing for her mother-in-law, Joan.)

The Frowds had lived in railway housing, but even if they had owned their own home and sold it, by 1978 there were strict exchange controls and also limitations on what possessions could be brought out of Rhodesia. (Uusikakala, 2008). The Bush War was at its most vicious. Cecil Frowd had been a prominent figure in Broken Hill (Kabwe), serving on the Municipal Council and he had seniority on the railways, but after the Rhodesian experience, both he and his wife were past the age at which they could find employment in Britain. Their experience shows how easily one could find one's personal autonomy eroded, but we know that things would have been even worse for them in the long run had they stayed in Zimbabwe, where they would have become utterly destitute – with British nationality they were able to return to the UK and the provisions of the welfare state.

Things were different for the Frowd's elder son, who was young enough to carve out a business career. Linda Frowd wrote on his behalf:

Tony left NR in 1965 to go to teachers' training college in Bulawayo which didn't come to fruition, as his grant was withdrawn by the Zambian Government, insisting that he attend University in Lusaka for the 3 year course, wanting him to sign a contract to work in Zambia for a further 7yrs after that! He declined this offer. He found a job in Bulawayo ...he was offered a job by Dunlop which would include a further education course paid for by Dunlop for him to study for 3yrs and hopefully qualify as a rubber technician. In 1972 he started his own business opening a tyre re-treading plant in Bulawayo, then a second one in Salisbury, continuing with these until leaving Rhodesia finally in 1978. He decided to leave for political reasons and was only allowed to take £200 out of the country!

He went to UK Rochdale and opened another tyre re-treader business, however this business became bankrupt due to the breakdown of a business partnership. He went over to the USA and worked for a computer board manufacturer, while becoming involved with a software house who were developing a relational data base. This job enabled Tony to travel the world, including his beloved Africa promoting this product. He opened Pearl Software in Poole, Dorset. Where he lived for a few years before moving to Lanarkshire, Scotland, and eventually to Merthyr Tydfil, South Wales, where he bought a pub, "The Drovers Arms" and met me, his 2nd wife Linda, and we opened a restaurant in the village of Cefn Coed. In 2003 we sold up our pub and restaurant and came to the Costa del Sol, we lived in our mobile home for 8 months while deciding where we wanted to settle, Tony took a year off before starting a stair-lift business, of which he is still at the helm today with no talk of retiring!

I have quoted Linda Frowd at length because her husband's career captures a willingness to cut losses and switch countries that is so characteristic of many former Northern Rhodesians. What is not mentioned is that those "political reasons" for leaving Rhodesia would have included the requirement that all white young men serve in the army and fight a very bloody war, often in virtual hand-to-hand combat. Rhodesia had become a militarised society.

Moving to Southern Rhodesia was almost invariably disastrous, but for reasons of nationality and because they did not think beyond Africa, it seemed the obvious destination for many. Ron de Kock was third generation Northern Rhodesian and a descendant of *voortrekkers*. Despite believing African people incapable of government or management, high wages induced him to stay on at Chibuluma Mine until 1972 when the family moved to Rhodesia. It was difficult for him to find work as a mining ventilation engineer there and he writes of the terrible conditions and sulphur dioxide pollution when he did eventually land a job in a smelter at Inyati Copper Mine. Within months he was able to find a better job as Ventilation Officer for the Ministry of Mines:

At this time the Rhodesian Government had established various incentives for new immigrants... We were also exempt from paying tax for the first two years. We were also allowed six months rent free government accommodation. Also, I was exempt from military duty for two years.

Regardless of that exemption he joined up to fight, but in 1978 with the Lancaster House Agreement he was looking to get out of the country:

I could not stomach the thought of now having to live under one of the terr black leaders ... I had written to Mines in Australia and the many letters I wrote to American Mines just resulted in polite letters of 'Sorry no job' ... Eventually I decided to go to South Africa ... I received a job offer from Anglo American to work at Vaal Reefs Gold Mines near Orkney and also from Union Corporation to work at the new Mine called Unisel just outside Welkom in the Orange Free State ... Ironically I still said that at least I will be going to a country where the Afrikaner will fight. Boy! Was that wrong or what?

The Bush War/Second *Chimurenga* left its mark on all the young men who moved south to Rhodesia. Several have written of the toll it took on their emotional health, none more dramatically than Basil O'Connell-Jones, who suffered such terrible injuries that he believes that he was snatched from death and his survival was a miracle. As a consequence of this trauma he renounced his former life and took to religion, becoming the leader of the Grace Gospel Church in Durban and Johannesburg, a charismatic but controversial organisation (For

examples of his preaching see http://www.gracegospelchurchsa.org/videos/).
O'Connell-Jones' autobiography *Amazing Grace* (2008) depicts a dissolute and
violent youth on the Copperbelt and at boarding school in Zimbabwe. When
"born again" he expresses remorse for lying and drug taking, but none for his
part in the war.

The activities of the *Grace Gospel Church* have caused concern in South
Africa, over young people being estranged from their families, required to
accept arranged marriages, urged to quit education and careers to follow the cult
leader's revelation of a new world. (John, 2009, 2012). Its congregation seems
to be predominantly middle class white and O'Connell-Jones makes the classic
offer of otherworldly transcendence to a fraction of society that regards itself
as beleaguered. Unlike the journalist, Victoria John, my background in social
anthropology causes me to think twice before dismissing the *Grace Gospel Church*
as a money-making scam – I see O'Connell-Jones as having been fashioned by
his traumatic experiences and his church as a classic millenarian movement.
Research in psychology (Smailes et.al 2014) shows that people hearing inner
voices (auditory hallucinations) are likely to have suffered traumatic events
that make it difficult for them to distinguish external reality from imagination –
things don't get a lot more traumatic than the Bush War. We can regard him as a
prophet who believes that he came back from the dead, just like Alice Lenshina,
the other famous product of Central Africa's colonial contradictions. O'Connell-
Jones certainly has charm and eloquence – it is not difficult to understand his
appeal to people who see little future for themselves in South Africa; he replaces
their forfeited status as the master-race with that of the spiritually elect. Several
former Northern Rhodesians now living in South Africa have directed me to him
as an admired religious leader, others have been attracted to other charismatic
churches and are persuaded of the power of miracles.

That war took people in different ways. Russell Kilner wrote:

During the Rhodesian War I didn't fly in the Air Force, I did one call-up
during which time I served with Ken Jackson (from Broken Hill) that was in
1974. After that I started working for the Ministry of Internal Affairs (civil
administration) And I remained with them until 1989, so I fought my war as a
civvy, although being a civilian in those times made absolutely no difference. I
finished the war having been shot down twice and the second occasion I was

shot through the guts – oh yes! They even gave me a medal. I stayed in aviation and spent my life bush flying, including stints with MSF and the UNHCR, both in Mozambique. I finished off my flying career in float planes on Lake Kariba and that really was fun.

Médecins Sans Frontières and the *United Nations Refugee Agency* are not exactly what some people might expect of a decorated veteran of the Rhodesian Bush War, neither was staying on in Zimbabwe so long after Independence, including nine years in administration, but I knew Russell Kilner well when I was young and it did not surprise me he was still in Central Africa. What I couldn't understand was how he'd come to be living in rebel Rhodesia, so I asked him. His reply was:

A lot of the moves that I and my family made, or did not make, were not planned they just happened! But I'll give you my details when we meet in October.

I never did get that "interview". Just a week before I arrived in Harare, Russell Kilner died, far too young. His widow told me that when he retired he had declared that he wouldn't be seen dead in a suit again, so she'd insisted he be buried wearing his customary khaki shorts – a white African gesture. She told me that they came to be in post-UDI Rhodesia because his job in Lusaka with Central African Airways was made temporary when it became Zambian Airways in the late 'sixties; then the post was Zambianised. He stood to take over his father's small farm but, finding no employment in Zambia he went south to work, remaining close enough to help his parents. When his father retired and his parents moved to South Africa, he discovered that land transfer fees had become so high that he could not afford to keep the farm, neither could he sell it because of a change in the law. Meanwhile, events in Rhodesia had shifted – as he said, things "were not planned, they just happened."

Unusually for Europeans in Zimbabwe, the Kilners' house on the edge of Harare had no high walls, no burglar bars and no gate, let alone one with a guard – they lived a modest life and Russell had seen no advantage in barricading themselves in, not even during the war. Staying on in Zimbabwe, they had suffered the privations described in Godwin's *When a Crocodile Eats the Sun* – a dwindling income, short of food at times, their son's farm confiscated, ultimately suffering the consequences of poor medical facilities, "But this is home". The easy stereotypes don't always work.

Steve Birchall had also worked for Central African Airways, moving to Salisbury in 1967. She married a police officer and, with an interval in South Africa, remained in Zimbabwe until 2003. Two of her husband's brothers were murdered and her life was constantly on a knife-edge. With magnificent understatement she says: *We have no regrets about moving to England when we see the way things are working out in Zimbabwe.*

After refusing to submit to the regime of a Rhodesian boarding school Hans Dielissen needed a job:

I worked for a firm fitting auto-glass, met my wife Linda and we had three daughters. We were really young when we got married and struggled along but were very happy. The war came along and I was called up into the army, first a year and then call-ups from six weeks to three months, I enjoyed army life but didn't see my family much. I was blown up in a landmine in '72 [aged 21], my brother-in-law was shot and injured in '73 and my second brother-in-law was also blown up in a landmine a year or so later. Luckily we were all still alive, my wife and I spoke about moving to Holland for a better future for the kids and ourselves but we just didn't have the means. We cashed in my pension, which was enough to pay for our tickets and sold everything we had for next to nothing in 1978. I flew to Amsterdam three weeks before Linda and the kids, they were 3, 5 and 7 years old. It was the same as my parents had done 22 years earlier, but in reverse. With no job or money I stood shaking at the airport; a friend of my dad's picked me up and took me to his house, from there I found a job in an aluminium plant in the province of Zeeland. Linda and the kids joined me and we rented a house, the company I worked for gave us moving allowance and we slowly built up a new life. It was very hard in the beginning, as I only knew a little Dutch and Linda none at all.

My dad and mom also came back to Holland a year later. He had to wait to go on pension as then you could take more foreign currency out of Rhodesia; we found a house for him around the corner from us and a little later one of my brothers also moved back to Holland and he also just lived down the road so we were a bit of a family again.

In 1972 Richard and Vi Brooklyn also initially considered Rhodesia a good place. He was an electrician and found it easy to get work:

The schooling was becoming so bad [in Zambia] *that people were sending very young children to boarding school, we decided that we did not want this for our two sons so we wound up and moved South. We lived in Sinoia and Que Que and were very happy in Rhodesia and fitted in very well, soon making lots of friends. There were problems with exchange control and it was very difficult to take money to Rhodesia from Zambia.*

I decided we should move again and we ended up in Pinetown, west of Durban; it is quite industrialised so it was easy for me to get a job. In retrospect I made all the wrong decisions, we should have left the African continent when we left Kitwe. The schools were very good here and the boys got a good education, however, we have always found the people here unfriendly and we have made very few friends. Financially, moving has been a disaster, as we lost money with each move. There are quite a few Copperbelt folk in S.A. and when we meet them it is great to remember the good old days. Neither of us ever really settled here.

Eveline Kriel is still in Zimbabwe, running a milling company in Chinhoyi, but like all Europeans in Zimbabwe she and her husband have a plan – in their case a house in Australia:

I don't think I could live without tight security here in Zimbabwe. We have lots of security here at the factory and yet we still have theft etc. I don't think one can be careful enough these days. No, things are not good at all and now we are facing the threat of our company being taken over by the Indigenisation people! As if it wasn't enough having two farms taken already – the farms are now derelict and now they are looking at the lucrative businesses. I suppose everyone thinks that money grows on trees and you don't have to work for it. Well we are not going to entertain having to give 51% to partners, not of our choice, and to wait for them to tell us when to open the safe! We will just pack up and go.

In the meantime our business is good and the private school for our little grandees is good, so we will enjoy it until they close us. Apparently they are having an emergency meeting (the Politburo) to see if they are going to go ahead immediately with the Indigenisation. There are at least five families here in Chinhoyi that are ex-Northern Rhodesians.

Like Eve Kriel, Ian MacKenzie, an accountant, has adjusted to life in Zimbabwe. His family thought of themselves as Southern Rhodesian, but his father had been transferred by Rhodesia Railways to Ndola and Livingstone. Ian remains firmly committed to Africa and feels that those who left have done it a disservice:

I have found living here most fulfilling in spite of all the problems. I am constantly amazed whenever I leave Zimbabwe how shallow and parochial the majority of people are elsewhere. Their troubles tend to be so minor as to not even come up on our radar screens as issues! Zimbabweans are, by and large, very good people. The structure of society here has changed almost as much as it has stayed the same, which is perhaps a good thing, as traditions have been kept while cultural differences have blurred (to some extent) and become far more accepted and understood. Society is after all always in flux. Those who left very often have perceptions of this part of the world that are founded on the past and places them in a time warp.

Graduating from the University College of Rhodesia and Nyasaland, Ron Sayer, with South African citizenship saw no future in Zambia, did not want to go to South Africa for political reasons, but neither did he wish to stay in Rhodesia:

On writing finals and listening to UDI, I had to overcome my principles and followed my father to Cape Town. I studied at UCT and became a Chartered Accountant and was conscripted into the SA Army. This was a bleak period in my life and I loathed the military experience. The Nats had discrimination fine tuned and made my life a misery most times. During this unhappy interlude I married and we had two children. However I was keen to leave SA. Henry Kissinger felt he had a deal to solve the Rhodesian crisis, a peace deal was announced and all sorts of good things were going to happen; this coincided with an offer by Mobil Oil to manage the Accounting and Finance for Rhodesia and Malawi. I went up to Rhodesia with one condition, that if I was called up to serve in the Rhodesian armed forces I was out of there. So I passed a few years experiencing the conflict on some wonderful people and left Rhodesia with great sadness. Our return to RSA was brief, as my ex wife was now convinced there was no future for us in Africa. So we applied to Canada, got in, struggled for a while and settled in Vancouver. I had to re-qualify as a CA and have had various jobs in the commercial sector. Now retired, I am having a wonderful time investing and working for small start-up companies. I walk around wondering how the hell I did it and why I did not come to Canada sooner.

John Thompson walked away from school in Kabwe, having turned on a teacher who'd caned him once too often in his final term in 1962 – a university place and professional qualifications were forfeited in one day. After working for a while on his father's farm, he took a job as a tobacco buyer in Southern Rhodesia shortly before the Federation was dissolved. He'd thought of applying to an American college, *"I did try and get a grant from the US Consulate in Lusaka right after leaving school, only to be told after standing in line for over 3 hours that I was the wrong colour. The grants were only for the under privileged."* His South African nationality certainly didn't help and he talks ruefully of the times he was treated badly at border posts in various countries.

A few years later, after some scary cross-border sanctions-busting transactions, arson and sabotage driving his parents to abandon their farm, a failing marriage and growing anxiety about the situation in Rhodesia he was delighted to be offered a job by an American tobacco company, on condition he was willing to work anywhere in the world. Willing? All he wanted was to get out:

I was required to do back-to-back [military] *call-ups before I could emigrate. The first one of the most disturbing. We were assigned to follow-up and tracking operations, following the Elim Mission Massacre – 12 missionaries were slaughtered – the men horribly beaten first and then they had to watch while the woman-folk were tortured and raped – not before having to watch a 12 month old infant being decapitated and the head impaled on a stake. We followed the bastards for two days, gaining all the time – then the rain came and the trail went cold!!!! It is not a pretty sight watching grown men cry, including myself, in pure frustration that we never caught up with the murderous scum of the earth…. The second stint was also very depressing. SA in their infinite wisdom cut off our fuel and ammo supply – the war was over for the territorial forces. All we did for the rest of that call up was try and stay alive.*

His company had had him working weekdays in Zambia, returning to Rhodesia; neither his Rhodesian nor South African passport made leaving the country easy, other than to visit South Africa:

If I was ever to get out of Africa and advance my career I needed another passport – Brit, Irish – whatever I could lay my hands on …. It was my mother who was able to shed some light on acquiring a Brit passport. I had been several times to the British High Commission – no joy. Mom, however, had a friend who worked there. She advised me to go to the Federal Registry Office in Salisbury and get a certificate from them confirming I had been registered as a Federal

Citizen as a minor and she would see if she could pull some strings .... Returned to Lusaka and I had the passport issued in two days. I owe that lady a huge thank you for making it possible. It was information they were withholding from whites. On my visits there it had been obvious they were handing out passports indiscriminately, passports to the blacks with no Brit connections!!! I was euphoric – I could now travel at any time without too much hindrance almost anywhere in the world.

It is obvious that the British passport was issued as a result of turning a blind eye to the South African one and was building on CUKC, but as Thompson informed me later:

... it did not give me the right to live in the UK as there was a proviso stamped stating "Right of abode not established" which made me madder than hell as our source at the embassy confirmed black Zambians with no ties to England whatsoever, were being given rights to live in the UK.

Those comments about African Zambians being given full UK passports with residence rights can only be a twist of memory, probably drawing on the granting of visas to the many Zambians who followed courses in Britain after Independence; they do, however, illustrate the terrible angst about citizenship. After years of war, marital breakdown, a turbulent life of constant travelling, seeing his father dispossessed and broken in South Africa, it is little wonder John feels discriminated against on grounds of race and has become a recruit to American libertarian politics. He fulminates at "liberalism" and "political correctness", loathes any hint of welfarism. I rarely agree with him, but I know where he's coming from.

South Africa

Many who had been raised in Africa went to South Africa without thinking about the options, others had no options. At that time few believed that the *apartheid* regime would come to an end in their lifetime, but they did not always find the country welcoming. David Small, a computer programmer specialising in accounting systems, found work in Johannesburg but the death of his baby son made the family take stock of living there:

I will always remember standing in the foyer of a hospital with my son while the reception checked our credit rating to see if we were in a position to pay for his first operation. It was successful, but he needed follow-up surgery the best chances of success were at Groote Schur, where Dr Barnard was the principal coronary surgeon. Unfortunately the operation was not a success and our son died in Groote Schur, which was devastating to all the family. Medical Aid in South Africa at that time was generally provided as an insurance cover by your employer and, to add to the stress of losing a child, there was a limit on the amount of medical costs that you could claim in a period and we had run out of cover on his first operation. We then went through a period where we had to sell our house to pay some of the bills...

Soon after the birth of our third child the Soweto riots happened and we decided South Africa was not the place to bring up our children. I realised that while my qualifications were fine in South Africa, I needed more if I were going to the UK and completed the Chartered Institute of Management Accounting exams in 18 months.

They moved to Britain and then on to Australia where things have gone well for them professionally and as a family. He and his wife have fostered children and adopted Kristie, a baby with Downs Syndrome who was not expected to live, now a young woman they are proud of.

Though South Africa was an attractive holiday destination for Copperbelt workers, living there was nothing like as enjoyable, as Rose Newman recounts:

I absolutely hated Cape Town – missed my friends, my horse, the riding fraternity and the life in Zambia ... and the Cape south easter! I loathed it! However, I made a couple of good friends, worked for the Southern Life in Newlands, had a boyfriend and plodded on until June 1969, when I went to England to do some travelling and see a bit of the world.

On that fateful trip Rose met and married a roadie with a rock group and they led a 'seventies lifestyle, eventually returning to South Africa, running a venue at Sun City. Widowed young, she started making wedding dresses and now lives in Johannesburg and has, *"Recently started a new little business, making church vestments for bishops, ministers, priests, etc. I love it!"*

Plenty of people did take to life in South Africa. Tony Sparks was one:

I had a ball at varsity – I attempted a BA (Drama) as I eventually wanted to get into broadcasting, but between doing drama, playing around campus and in restaurants and taking up my dancing again, I didn't get my degree after 4 years!

I spent a while in Bulawayo, then went back to Cape Town, where I landed up working in a music shop for 4 years, then back to UCT full-time, supported by my band-work, and finished my degree with much better results! I moved to Jo'burg and completed a post-grad diploma in Librarianship, then worked for the Johannesburg Public Library for 11 years, from JPL I moved to Wits, as I'd always wanted to work in a University Library ... I was appointed Performing Arts Librarian, a job I absolutely loved. However, I was promoted to run their Biological & Physical Sciences Library, then I went on a training programme, moved into admin and landed up as the Registrar, Faculty of Science.

Whilst at Wits, my partner and I visited my sister in Brisbane and spent a week in a gay-owned B&B in Sydney. I decided that was what I eventually wanted to do. It took 5 years before we had enough money to take the plunge, found the right place at the right price. I resigned from Wits at the end of '96 and we opened in March '97. My partner left his job after a few years and is now a qualified tour guide – so between the two us we have a pretty good life-style and enjoy what we do. We've been together for 25 years.

Several former Northern Rhodesians have opened guest houses in South Africa (all that I've been to are excellent). Andrew Thom, the son of early settlers, after teaching in Swaziland, opened *Die Lang Huis* in Barrydale and Trevor Turnball-Jackson has *Beachcomer Bay* in Margate.

Mark Tanner is one of several police officers who moved to the Cape:

My NRP experience was the best three years of my life (unless someone waves a magic wand pretty soon!) After Police service I moved to Bulawayo and worked for a petrol company which I hated. After less than a year I moved to Durban and returned to the world of civil engineering which was my training prior to the NRP, though I am not a qualified engineer. From there I moved to the Cape to try and save a bad marriage – rough times – especially as it did not work out, but at all times my NR experiences and memories put me in a position of strength and confidence in myself. When I first came to Franschhoek in 1981 I often referred to the village as 'Choma', at last I had found a similar lifestyle. I now run my own business from home exporting quality wines to the UK.

There are people in a wide range of professions in South Africa, many had always regarded the country as their home and it was always a popular retirement destination. To some extent they cluster in Johannesburg, Cape Town and Pietermaritzburg, often reflecting sites of their schooling or university, but they are scattered throughout the country. Many, but not all, find the new South Africa difficult to adjust to and have encouraged their own children to seek residence elsewhere; they talk wistfully about grandchildren they rarely see who are growing up American or Australian and they wonder whether they will make another move themselves. On the other hand, there are people who, having worked in Britain, are satisfying their Africa cravings with retirement to the Cape.

The Old Commonwealth

It is not surprising that people who had been happy in Northern Rhodesia would consider the Old Commonwealth, often winding up there after earlier moves. Australia seemed most likely to offer something similar to the Northern Rhodesian lifestyle – wide open spaces, a mostly good climate and a sense of newness. Several arrived in Australia after becoming disillusioned with their first choice.

Robin Vaughan-Johnson is an NRP officer who went to Australia after a global career. His final profession is something of a surprise after the previous excitement:

I resigned in 1962 to go flying and returned to UK. I obtained Air Line Transport licences for fixed wing and Helicopters and concentrated on helicopters gaining ALTP licences for UK, Canada ,Pakistan, India, United Arab Emirates, East Africa (Uganda – where I lived – Kenya and Tanzania) and Australia where I became a citizen and still live in Perth WA. In 1983 I was awarded the Australian Bravery Medal for a major rescue. After flying I went to University and took a degree in Podiatry and was in private practice for ten years retiring at the age of seventy, ten years ago.

Kevin Lee, like many who went to university in Southern Rhodesia, stayed on after qualifying even though by then UDI had been declared:

After medical school, I worked in Bulawayo and Salisbury and started pathology training at Harare hospital. After a couple of years, I was offered a job at Guy's in London, where I got a couple of diplomas, and returned to Salisbury for three years or so. By this stage, the war was getting a bit much, but it provided me with a fantastic knowledge of firearm and explosive injuries.

I then returned to Guy's for a further five years. Much as I love visiting London, I hated living there, and when an opportunity to move to Australia presented itself, off I went to Darwin.

Norman Archibald of the NRP took a while getting there:

I left after my contract expired and with a friend travelled overland in African buses to Mombasa, the journey took 2 weeks. Then by ship to India Bombay, a train to Madras then ship to Penang, train and bus to Singapore, then finally a small tramp ship to Sydney. The whole journey took 5 months. I decided to stay and work in Sydney, my friend left in 1964 and we did not meet again until 2006 in South Africa.

Barbara A is another person who has travelled widely but settled in Australia. Her father joined her there after finding it difficult to establish himself elsewhere:

After getting my qualifications in England, I enjoyed many years travelling and working in different countries. I had circled the globe before I was 21. I spent time in California and several years alternating between the UK and Canada. I saw much of Europe and also ventured into Soviet Russia to see my mother's birthplace. I met my future husband in Mexico. I even returned to Salisbury for a while, but never had interest in revisiting Zambia. I married in Perth, had my children in Sydney and Canberra, and now live near Melbourne. Although after all these years I still don't really feel Australian, I do know I couldn't live anywhere else. Maybe I was always destined to be an outsider no matter where I was born – probably genetic, given my parents' history and peripatetic lifestyle. I've worn many interesting and varied career hats – legal secretary, BBC TV production assistant, travel agent, published author, small business owner. But, best of all, I have been blessed with the stability of a happy marriage that has produced two smart daughters who have been given far wider choice and opportunities in education and careers than I could ever have dreamed of.

When my father was voted out of office [he was an MLA] *and Independence changed everything for many white administrators and business people, he sold his accounting practice and began years of wandering. From England he went to Canada, where he was lucky to get a job, being close to 60 by then. After forced retirement, it was back to England, but money was a major issue. He had limited savings and no state pension from any of the many countries in which he had lived. Britain now had a cold attitude to its old "empire" men like him and refused him a pension. So there seemed to be nowhere else to go but back to Africa. He found work as a menial bookkeeper in Rhodesia while the Bush War was growing with intensity. After my mother died, he again returned to British Columbia where he relied on an old friend for a time, before finally being allowed entry into Australia to live with us and he was extremely fortunate that the Australian Government gave him an old age pension which helped to ease the financial strain of his remaining years.*

Val Foster returned to Britain but after marrying she moved to Australia then South East Asia:

I adapted easily to life in Australia, Singapore, Indonesia, etc., but I found great difficulty adapting to life in England. I envied people with life long friendships ... I was never able to say "Do you remember when..." to anyone.

Julie Swenson is another who moved about a great deal but settled in Australia:

My parents & I left Zambia in 1969, headed to the UK to visit relatives then picked up a camper van and toured Europe for the next 9 months – France, Germany, Italy, Yugoslavia, Greece – ending up in Spain which we loved. We stayed in Spain for 18 months but eventually my dad had to look for work as there was nothing much going in Spain and as a foreigner you could only get a job in the tourist industry. I went to the UK 1970-71, where I took up computer programming – almost a pioneer!

My dad got a job on the iron ore mines in Sierra Leone and my mom and I joined him...there I got married to an Englishman in 1972. I had 2 children in Sierra Leone, Guy and Kerith. They were born in a bush hospital and I always joke that there was no chance of them being switched at birth as they were the only white children ever born there – most expats went to the UK to have their kids, I wanted mine born in Africa. Late 1975 the mine closed down. My husband and I went to the UK, my parents went to Spain.

Julie then went to South Africa, divorced and remarried an Australian. Disillusioned by Black Economic Empowerment, they moved to Australia:

It upsets me to see how Africa has been raped and pillaged by black Africans – I hate how badly they treat their own people and saw it in Zambia, Sierra Leone and South Africa. Africa will always, always be home and I miss it all the time, although we have done really well here and are settled.... My parents were

173

rolling stones as was my husband, I have moved about a fair bit as well but did try to give my kids a stable childhood. I went to 9 schools in my youth.

Derek Dutton, now in Perth said:

Actually I miss all the moving and I am sure my wife does too. There was nothing she liked better than a new home, new curtains to make, walls to paint, and furniture to buy. Life seems a bit bleak now, with the knowledge this is where we STAY! Like we are in God's waiting room. In Africa, after Independence, there was always the background knowledge you would have to move someday. So each day had a vague feeling, how long, when and where?

He and his wife had done a lot of travelling before settling down in the Perth hills:

We settled here, though not in my heart, that stays in Africa. Coming to Australia was a long drawn out affair, starting in 1968. Our ex-Chingola friends were in Townsville, Australia and asked us to join them. I sent my wife off, with three huge packing cases. I thought the children ought to go as well. They got there after a bit of a nightmare journey. They caught a cyclone in the Indian Ocean for a lot of the way. Most of the passengers were ten pound British migrants to Aus.

I was still in Kitwe, I sold the house and the new owners, Swiss, took my Great Dane. The time came to fly out but I could not leave my dog and went and got him back. It was fortunate I did, as the Swiss engineer was deported for "racialism" – telling someone to get on with his job. I flew the family back and we stayed until we moved to Rhodesia. After six months there, we went back to Zambia, where I joined Anglo-American's Engineering Training School in Kitwe.

Later in 1975 we moved to South Africa. I went from there to South West Africa [Namibia] Like all the other women, Bet hated it. It was so cold, the melting ice from the Benguela current produced freezing cold weather and a thick mist nearly every day. It was like a piece of Germany that had been deported in 1800 and told never to come back. We left there to go back to South Africa.

Eventually we came here [Australia] again in 1978. We waited for my son, who had gone to England from Jo'burg, being told it would be the best place to apply from. He phoned to say they said he must work for two years in England as he only had South African trade papers. We sent the furniture off and booked to go back to South Africa. Four days after our furniture went, we got a letter saying he could come any time. He went back to South Africa and I sent him money. We also went back to South Africa. Later he came here and we followed in 1980. It was hell saying goodbye to my grandchildren. It made me realise how, today, with families all over the world, how sad it was many grandparents never see their grandchildren and the kids don't know one.

Returning to Britain after all those years never crossed his mind.

Dominic Fuciarelli who left because the changing economic regime in Zambia made his business unworkable went straight to Canada:

We left Zambia in July of 1979, unable to take our hard earned money and scared to death of what awaited us. We arrived in Toronto and immediately set about starting a new life. It was very tough at first but once we got going we managed to buy a house, start a business, and over the years have grown very successful. While living in NR I often felt guilty *about our "wealth" because I was comparing it to the natives' earning power. It was quite an eye opener to find out that in fact people in Canada doing my kind of work were actually earning far greater amounts than we ever earned in Africa. In Zambia we built many houses and my father had been involved in building a great portion of the town. Had he come to Canada instead of Africa and had we been involved in the same volume of business as in Zambia, we would have amassed far greater wealth and, more importantly, would have been admired for it by society at large and not looked upon as parasites and racists.*

The fact that we always faced shortages of building materials and equipment in Zambia did pay off in my new life. It made me very ingenious in getting the work done by using whatever substitutes were available. This has helped me tremendously in Canada. Whereas I only put up new buildings in Zambia, I started out by doing renovations in Canada, mainly because I didn't have the money required for financing new buildings. I then discovered how easy it was for me to solve the many problems one encountered when adding to or remodelling older buildings, thanks to the Zambian experience!

The last Pink Bits

The British Empire was shrinking fast, but a few people from Northern Rhodesia were able to continue to find employment as the "last pink bits" made the transition to Independence. Harold Williams and his wife, who came back to

Wales on leave in 1970 and decided not to return to Zambia spent the next nine years in Fiji. He ended his career as Permanent Secretary to the Ministry of Forests there:

Looking back on things, we thoroughly enjoyed our life and work in NR/ Zambia and were sorry that we had to leave. We were lucky to be posted to Fiji and settled in there quite quickly. We were offered Resident Status by the Prime Minister, but Wales has always called its sons and daughters, so we 'came home'. The retirement age in the overseas service was 60, so we settled down here and I took part in the local activities (still do) and for some years did voluntary forest work for the National Trust. Apart from the last few months there, we enjoyed our life in NR and we still have a reunion of the Forestry Department Officers every two years.

John Holloway of the NRP applied to the Solomon Islands and rose to Commissioner of the Royal British Solomon Islands Police, then Commissioner of the Vanuatu Police before retiring to Australia. Hilary and Jamie Broughton also went to the Solomon Islands after a few years in Britain, she as a nursing sister, he as an administrator. Hilary had been born in Northern Rhodesia and, unlike many PA children, was educated in Northern Rhodesia, though she did her nursing training in London. When they returned to Britain, she felt frustrated by the pettiness of it all and was delighted when her husband took up the post in the Solomon Islands. She was once again to take on a challenging nursing role: *We went out there and it was like a release, I was like a lion let out of my cage.*

Several of the NRP joined the Hong Kong Police; probably the best known is Ron Clibborn-Dyer who wrote:

I retired in 1996 a year before the handover of HK to China, and as Veronica was born in the middle of Africa and I was born in UK and our three children were born here in HK – we decided to stay here until anything better occurred to us. We had lived for the last 20-odd years in a house with a wonderful uninterrupted view of the sunrise every day over the hills and the water. When we retired we discovered quite by chance the place where we now live, an old nunnery / Chinese Temple, and we were asked to be the guardians of it by the family most concerned with it, who had lived in the UK as long as we had lived in HK. We have electricity and telephone, and inside toilets, most of which need a bucket to flush. We have no mains water and rely on water piped and channeled from a mountain stream.

We have a little house down in South Africa in the Cape as a civilized home for Veronica, and a cottage in Surrey for when one of our families is over there. Our eldest son lives in Cape Town, the second lives in Bangkok and our daughter has recently emigrated from UK to Perth in Oz. My sister and all her family live in Colombia, South America, and Veronica's brother and sister live in South Africa. So we are very spread out across the globe.

The very last serving member of HMOCS anywhere in the world was David Browning, who had been a Learner District Officer in Northern Rhodesia. He stayed on in the Ministry of Local Government in Zambia, then worked for a while with the Tobacco Marketing Board in Malawi before returning to Britain. He was delighted to be appointed once again as a district officer, this time in Vanuatu, then Hong Kong. (He tells me he didn't actually turn the lights out.) David and his wife, Coco, now live in the hills of Alpes-Côte d'Azur, where he introduced me to Pére Claude Galmich, who still wishes he hadn't had to return from Zambia to a White Fathers retirement monastery.

The Land of Begin-Again

It is surprising, given that we'd all been brought up on Hollywood movies, that more people didn't try their luck in America after leaving. Though there are some who struggled to make good there, most do seem to have been happy with their decision. Bob Huntley arrived with no contacts:

Wanting to arrive in America the old fashioned way I took the Queen Mary from Southampton and sailed into New York past the Statue of Liberty and docked in Manhattan. I was thrilled to be in a country where I knew that this was the land of begin-again. Before I left Africa I bought a Greyhound bus ticket for $99 to get me from New York to San Francisco. I had no idea what I was getting into. Fortunately, I played squash racquets with a fellow passenger on the ship who invited me to help him drive his car across country. I arrived in Los Angeles at the right time...

Liz and John Price moved to New York in the 'eighties when Lonrho offered him promotion. Richard Sampson's move into the American Medical Supply Corporation was logical after his Zambian experience in medical insurance and a private hospital – he retired to California. John Thompson's work with a tobacco company located him in North Carolina and Neville Isdell's international career with Coca-Cola naturally took him to its headquarters in Atlanta. Stanley Fischer, having been Chief Economist at the World Bank and President of the Bank of Israel, is now Vice Chair of the US Federal Reserve System. Then we have Mik Wright, settled with *Those Shoes* in West Virginia.

Back to Blighty

Britain often seemed the natural choice to those who had started out there – it was familiar territory and many had been revisiting throughout their time in Africa. The pull of family was often important – ageing parents could make the move "home" seem inevitable, as could children who had moved there for lack of opportunities in Zambia. The British National Health Service was an important consideration for people looking ahead to old age and many had sensibly maintained their National Insurance contributions to provide a minimal pension.

Some first weighed up their chances elsewhere. Dudley Brown was the son of a District Commissioner who joined the PA as an LDA and Mary Brown was a teacher who came from an old South African family. Regarding Zambia as their long term home, he took a position with Shell Zambia at Independence and they built up a smallholding and brickworks. When they decided to leave the country in 1973, following major economic changes, they considered five countries:

It would have been easy to cross the border into Rhodesia, but we could see what was coming there. I was offered a job in South Africa, where we saw a future for ourselves but not for our children. Australia and New Zealand would have accepted us but they were far away from our English and South African families. I followed my career in Shell UK and Mary continued to teach.

Mary, who had visited England only once before, settled down almost immediately. I spent the next ten years regretting my decision to leave Zambia. After a life threatening illness in 1996 we both retired and bought a ruin in Portugal where we became aware of the influence the Portuguese had had on Africa and the influence that Africa still has on the Portuguese. Spending half the year in each country has allowed me now to feel completely at home in both.

Similarly, Connie and Robert McChesney decided returning to Britain was the best bet:

GEC/AEI said they would give me introductory letters to their branches in Salisbury and Johannesburg. Although it is easy to talk with hindsight, we did feel that sooner or later the rest of southern Africa would become independent and we couldn't live through a repeat of such an unsettling experience. Reluctantly, the decision was made to leave Africa. Now we faced the obstacles with the banks and Exchange Control; we were only allowed to take a limited amount out of Zambia and that included the value of the car and its contents. The rest of our money was frozen and would be allowed out on an annual basis. With high hopes we left Kitwe on 11th April 1971 en route for Cape Town and the Union Castle's S.A. Vaal with our car and all our worldly goods inside and on the roof. On the way down we met several families from Kitwe making the same journey.

For many others, like Paul Wheeler, once the decision to leave had been made in 1968, the choice was straightforward – back to Britain:

I retired to England largely because we felt it was in the best interests of our four children, for schooling and safety, and we had already sent our 2 sons home to Gordonstoun as boarders.

Some who came to Britain used it as a base, setting off again on contracts. Tommy Tomkins took up senior posts in the Gulf and then the Caribbean, whilst Lizzie, his wife took up a teaching post and maintained a home for their daughters. Born in Zambia, she took a while to adjust to living outside Africa, but she was joined by her mother who had initially settled in Cape Town; her sister, Judy Bobolski was already in Manchester. (Their mother is known to ex-Rennie girls as Mrs Anderson.)

Most of the PA finished up in Britain, even though some were able to work abroad for a while, many of those maintaining a house in Britain at the same time. As we have already seen, HMOCS conditions of service had always prepared its personnel for returning "home".

Scatterlings

There is a thin scattering of people elsewhere. Aviva Ron told me of numbers in Israel, maintaining contact with each other and with members of the Jewish Central African diaspora in other countries. There are a few in various African countries and some who retired to the Mediterranean sun – Cyprus attracted several as did Spain. Others moved to work or marry in Belgium, France, Luxemburg, Switzerland, Sweden …

Members of the next generation were not necessarily tied by their parents' decision – they came from families with a tradition of looking abroad and a new round of migration is taking place, whereby ageing former Northern Rhodesians are pulling up sticks again to be close to their children and grandchildren.

So there we are, dispersed around the globe – some deeply attached to a time in the past in a place that is far away, some having moved on but remaining affectionate, some bitter and resentful about what they have lost, others more or less indifferent – but invariably the colonial experience made some mark on subsequent lives. It could be a springboard to success or a hindrance and it could also be the cause of great insecurity and anxiety, but at the end of empire few European people were able to sit back and just follow a predetermined trajectory.

9. AN AFTERLIFE

Where people went and what became of them obviously overlap, so this chapter and the previous one are separated by orientation rather than content. People not only uprooted themselves, they had to make new lives and this was easier if there was a financial cushion to depend on whilst they found a new home and new employment.

Members of the Overseas Civil Service were a special case. Having been employed from Britain they were (very properly) awarded index-linked pensions and compensated for loss of office on the basis of age and years of service. Costs of repatriation were paid and most returned, though not always immediately, to Britain. In July 1964 the British Government extended "a long-term loan of £3 million to enable the territory to provide its share of the compensation for overseas officials in Her Majesty's Overseas Civil Service." (Hansard 20th July 1964). This lump-sum compensation ("lumpers") of up to £12,000 would be paid immediately into overseas bank accounts, but officers were encouraged to stay in Zambia for a while on contract and gratuity terms to facilitate the transfer of the administration.

When the *Zambia Independence Bill* was debated considerable attention was paid (in both Houses of Parliament) to the pension terms of civil servants. The situation was clear for the 1,200 members of HMOCS, but 400 locally recruited pensionable staff were classified as "non-designated" officers, not directly employed by HMG. This might seem rather arcane now but it mattered a great deal, as their pensions and "lumpers" were calculated less generously and were to be paid in Zambia by the Zambian Government. Non-designated officers, being "local", were not entitled to relocation costs. There was a further category of about 2,000 European ex-Federal Government officers in Northern Rhodesia who were transferred to NRG when administrative functions were divided on dissolution of the Federation. Although some had originally been recruited in Britain to NRG pre-Federation, technically they became "locally recruited" thus "non-designated". The complicated arguments for enhanced pension terms can be followed in the *Second Reading of the Zambia Independence Bill, Hansard 7th July 1964*. Individual British MPs of both major parties argued the case of the non-designated officers, but to no avail. Robin Turton (Conservative) expressed the view that:

To make a difference between the two categories based on whether the officer was recruited in Britain or in the Federation is quite ridiculous ... as these countries become independent Britain has a continuing obligation to the men who served them and got them ready for independence.

In 1966 provision for non-designated officers was brought more closely into line with those for designated officers, largely as a consequence of advocacy on the part of the Overseas Service Pensioners' Association, but the case demonstrates that Britain was keen to wash its hands of its colonies as cheaply as possible.

No questions, however, were ever asked in either House about pensions for local government officers, all of whom were directly recruited by the separate municipal councils, often in the UK using British local authorities as agents. Nor were people employed in the private sector given any thought. Northern Rhodesia as a colony had more than paid its way and, arguably, the high copper revenues repatriated to the UK in both taxes and profits were less the product of the work of the HMOCS officers out in the rural areas than of the people who maintained the urban infrastructure or the railwaymen and miners. As Zambianisation of posts took place, severance terms for European employees varied enormously across different employments, from none at all to very generous. Pension issues, like questions of nationality, haunt former colonials, several of whom are close to destitution.

European mineworkers (but not "staff"), despite their fabled high bonuses, were always employed on daily contracts. When their posts were Zambianised they were awarded six months basic (i.e. non-bonus) pay, plus an additional month for every two years worked – the "Copper Chopper". To receive a year's pay (or what he'd get in a good bonus) at severance, a man would have had to have worked for the mines for twelve years. This was a sum that would easily be eaten up relocating a family and finding work. Shortly after Independence the *Zambian Mines Local Pension Fund (Dissolution) Act* of 1966 wound up miners' pensions – employee and employer contributions to the funds were paid out in eight instalments and anticipated retirement pensions were wiped out. People who moved over onto contract and gratuity terms could then earn enticing salaries, but they had no security of tenure and with each contract their employability elsewhere became more uncertain.

"What Sort of Employment can a Surplus DC Get?"

Things were fairly straightforward for those with a good education, a British passport and not regarded as "too old", but everyone had misgivings. There was a satirical song, *My Old Man's a DC* (written by Gavin Barr, DC Mbala) that ruefully caught the mood in the Provincial Administration as Independence drew near – it contains the following verse:

He came here straight from Oxbridge, thought he was here to stay,
But there's no doubt he'll be thrown out on Independence Day.
He hasn't saved a penny since he was a Cadet,
And what sort of employment can a surplus DC get?

The retired colonial servant, tediously reminiscing about the good old days, had long been a stock figure in English novels and theatre – E.M.Forster snidely comments in *A Passage to India* that, "At Chandrapore the Turtons were little gods; soon they would retire to some suburban villa, and die exiled from glory" (2005 p. 25), but Turton, the Collector, would have been fifty-five – until the 1960s there was little precedent for retired officers to be in their twenties, thirties or forties and the number of colonies to which they could be recycled was fast diminishing.

Humorous it may have been, but the song caught the prevailing mood as Independence drew near – what on earth *could* a retired District Officer do outside the colonial context that was of equal status? They had entered a profession guaranteeing enduring connections with the UK and the built-in assumption that, after retirement they would return "home" to a generous pension. Independence, however, meant that retirement was coming early for many We have already seen that the immediate solution for many in HMOCS was to stay on in Zambia for a few years to do transitional work, enjoy a last few years in a beautiful country, accumulate funds, and take stock of their future.

The British government set up the Overseas Service Resettlement Bureau (OSRB) as an employment agency for officers of HMOCS. Questions were repeatedly asked in Westminster as to whether non-designated Northern Rhodesian Government and former Federal Government staff might be permitted to consult it as well, but this was refused. The Bureau did not guarantee placement but introduced retiring officers to prospective employers who knew that they would be recruiting highly qualified men with proven leadership qualities and great adaptability. By and large, it seems to have been a fairly successful initiative, often its clients were British local authorities, government departments or institutions like the British Council and popular wisdom has it that the rapidly expanding new universities and polytechnics drew their bursars from this source. Kirk-Green (2006), writing of the African District Officer in general, cites the Bureau's director (formerly a DO in Tanganyika) as warning that DOs were not necessarily easy to place, but many officers, "… were grateful for the help they received, none more so than T. Gardner who, on his way home from NR in 1964, found a cable waiting for him when the ship berthed at Port Said, informing him of a vacancy as Deputy Treasurer of Cambridge University." (Kirk-Greene, 2006 p.227).

John Orr-Ewing was one of several who finished up in university administration:

I did think of going to New Zealand or elsewhere, but on account of our families we came back to the UK. I went to the Overseas Resettlement Bureau in London who put me in touch with jobs being advertised – primarily within University administration. I think I would have been happy to go anywhere.

I nearly got a job at Aston University – but am happy I didn't! I was disappointed not to get a job at Lancaster University. There were two of us they would have employed but the other chap could start immediately, whereas I had taken up a temporary job teaching at a prep school in Rugby for one term while job-hunting. I then got the job of Registrar at Wye College – the Agricultural Faculty of London University, based in Wye, Kent, and started there July/August 1966. I knew five or six other ex-colonials who were Registrars, Bursars or Administrators at universities.

He had no difficulty settling back into Britain once he had arranged employment:

The Christian community we became part of, wherever we were, helped us to feel settled very quickly. We both have very close and good family ties and that helped. My wife was/is utterly loyal – she is very practical – and faces everything and gets on with contributing to wherever we are. Her family helped us to settle too.

Barbara Mackinson told me that, although she and her husband Ian spent many years abroad (Swaziland, Seychelles, Tuvalu …) after leaving Zambia in

1971, she did not find settling in in Hampshire at all difficult, "It was just like coming home on leave." This, of course, was the intention of the policy of long and frequent "home" leave – a familiar base one could retire to.

Occasionally the OSRB brought men into really unexpected new careers, perhaps most famously the appointment of Colin Rawlins, formerly Resident Commissioner of Barotseland, to the post of *Director of Zoos and Chief Executive of the Zoological Society of London*. He wrote in some notes reflecting on his career that:

I had a well-paid and prestigious second career, in which the need to mix with and manage an assorted bunch of both professional and 'blue collar' employees was similar to that of a colonial administrator. I cannot say which of the two groups could be the most difficult to deal with!

Jonathan Lawley, who had been DC Gwembe at Independence, had mixed feelings about the advice given by the OSRB when he came to Britain, particularly about his consultant:

Whose main aim, rather than boost your confidence at a difficult time, seemed to be to pull you down a peg or two and convince you that, even though you might have had huge responsibilities in the colonies, you were of little potential use to commerce and industry.

(Lawley, 2010. p.99)

After a few false starts, he took up the offer of the post of Personnel Manager Designate with Anglo-American in the Congo, with all the attendant problems of living in that country, but this started him on a lifetime of overseas development work, with which he is involved to this day.

Don Smith put his African experience to some use when he returned to Britain:

I pushed a pen in the South Eastern Gas Board for 6 months before becoming Deputy Head of the Commonwealth Department at the CBI – there were only 2 of us! Then, five years later African Group Coordinator with Vickers. After a year I was asked to move to Paris and do Europe from there. We then started our own company, now run by our daughter. We never thought of settling elsewhere – fairly short of funds and two young children, I suppose we stuck with what we knew. But will never forget the years of colonialism which gave us unforgettable experiences that cannot be repeated.

As Jonathan Lawley's consultant warned, moving into industry wasn't invariably congenial to a former District Officer. Adrian Forrest found it a culture shock:

Settling into a new career was quite problematic. My service in NR had all been in the districts. They never sent me to work in the Secretariat or the new ministries, which were created at the time of independence. My last year at Serenje was not always easy, frankly, we in the PA were the ones the new politicians most wished to be rid of as we represented the old regime. As a new career I was keen to continue working abroad, but I could not find anything really suitable and finally found employment in ICI as a Personnel Officer in a factory in my native Northern Ireland.

This was one of Britain's prime companies and I entered it thinking that it might be like the Overseas Civil Service in that it was a great and famous company, offering the best conditions of employment and that the employees would be loyal to the company and proud to be of its number…There was none of the loyalty which we knew in the Overseas Civil Service. Forty seven years have passed since leaving NR but I still attend reunions of staff. Such a thing in industry would be unthinkable. I was shocked at first by the indiscipline of industry as I saw it.

Tim O'Hara was another PA man who adapted to the world of industry, but it was not really what he wanted:

On return to the UK, I was lucky to be offered several jobs. I had done a CIS course by correspondence – which helped. I joined a Tube Investments graduate trainee scheme, and finished up assistant company secretary to a company building steel rolling mills, based near Bournemouth. Not a bad place to be if you are in industry in the UK. But I found the workplace environment to be so completely foreign to my experience in the Provincial Administration. After two years, the company was taken over, and it was every man for himself. I survived the change, but when the chance came to return here [to Ireland] to farm it was an easy choice.

Hywel Griffith's movement from the PA to Rural Development and his resignation before Independence figured in the previous chapter, as a consequence he left without a "lumpers":

Returning to the UK I had no job, no home and 4 months leave-pay to tide me over. I looked in vain for a job that looked like community development. In NR we were exposed to international currents of thinking on social development but, to my surprise, I found the UK was insular and very behind the times, although that did not prevent some bureaucrats from expressing contempt for new ideas. I became very depressed. I missed both the African environment, particularly Africans themselves, and also working in my field of expertise. Eventually I decided to go back to Africa via an appointment with the British Council to be Director of the BC Centre in Port Harcourt. I enjoyed the experience in Nigeria, but it was not my kind of Africa and I was always in tension with my head office who wanted me to focus on cultural events like Blake's illustrations to the Old Testament, whereas I wanted to focus on adult education.

I was offered the job of Lecturer in Community Development at the Adult Education Department of Manchester University ... Then in 1970 the ODA asked me to evaluate the progress of community development in 5 countries, extending from Ethiopia to Zambia and lasting 6 weeks. It was very exciting to visit or revisit these countries and to be once again amongst African people in an African environment. (Do you remember the smell of dust after the first rains?) I enjoyed my visit a lot and learned a great deal. But it was also disappointing. African politicians were in thrall to the idea that national development was best achieved by large scale expensive development and that to accept that something like community development was needed was to imply that African people were in some way inferior ... Aid departments of donor countries had begun to syphon their aid through charitable aid agencies who acted as their proxies and offered accountability in the management of funds... In due course these would become crypto-colonial in the way they operated.

David Salmon may have been youngest ever District Commissioner in Zambia, having been promoted shortly before Independence at a time when many senior staff were already leaving. His three volumes of letters home are essential reading, but they stop in Zambia. In the final volume he had been thinking about a teaching diploma and perhaps the British Council, but in the event:

It was plain that there was no long term future for Europeans in the civil service and in mid 1968 I resigned and returned home. I had no real idea what I wanted to do and after a few months drifted via a graduate entry scheme into Post Office management in London. It soon became apparent that that was something I definitely did not want to do and I resigned again. I decided that I would try to qualify as a solicitor and for financial reasons went back to live with my parents in Stoke. I was lucky enough to get articles with a long established firm; I qualified in 1973, became a partner in 1974 and married in 1975.

I became a family law specialist and head of the family department. At the end of 1989 I decided to leave as I disagreed with the policy of reducing legal aid – potentially a disastrous decision as I had two young daughters at the time. Luckily my partners treated me generously and allowed me to take the family law department to set up my own firm which grew fairly quickly to a four partner practice. I also became a part-time immigration judge until I had to retire on age grounds at 72. I had been back to Zambia on holiday with my wife in 1982 but in 1991 I was fortunate to get on a four-man Law Society team to monitor the election which saw the advent of the third republic.

Wendy and Mick Bond had arrived in Northern Rhodesia just before Independence; they were newly married and in their early twenties, Mick was recruited as one of the very last of the PA, but they stayed on in Zambia until 1973, enthusiastic about the new nation. Wendy obtained her PGCE at the University of Zambia, then started a children's magazine called *Orbit* and Mick moved over into academic administration at the Zambia Institute of Technology. Their Zambian experiences formed the basis of their later lives as Wendy went into teaching in England and Mick into University administration, retiring as the Deputy Registrar of Newcastle University:

While the whole family was very sad indeed to leave Zambia, we have all become inveterate travellers, with a lively curiosity about people the world over and an appreciation of and respect for their cultures and ways of thinking – an excellent gift that we took away with us from our wonderful eleven years in the country.

We left after working ourselves out of a job – as we had always known we would do. We came, after all, to help bring about Independence in as helpful a way as possible, knowing full well what was coming. Returning to UK was the obvious choice as we had friends and family here, but we knew we would have to avoid the city and even suburbia for the sake of bush-raised children whose sense of space and freedom was different! We were lucky to find a house in a village on Hadrian's Wall and naturally felt that a 40-mile drive to work was perfectly normal! Inevitably adjustments had to be made, especially for schooling, but in contrast to all those house moves in Zambia (15 or so!), we still have our home in the village. It was a sensible time to leave as far as finding a new career was concerned – where Mick would find himself a small cog in a large machine at first, in contrast to knowing absolutely everyone in Zambia. We left with the very best of memories, all intact.

Several people thought that teaching could be a stimulating and useful profession, so we find former District Officers enrolling for teaching qualifications. John Hannah recounts the frustrations of routine teaching:

I stayed on for four years after Independence, then returned to England where I spent the first year back at Oxford University studying for a Dip.Ed. I then taught at a comprehensive in Oxford, but it was not my scene, so I decided to put my name down at the Foreign Office in the hope that I might be offered any vacancy comparable to the level I had reached in NR/Z.

Meanwhile, I was offered a job at a Catholic Prep School teaching French. It was a complete contrast to the comprehensive as it seemed to cater for the sons of the catholic nobility – I have never come across so many belted earls as in each classroom. Although I was only there for two terms, I enjoyed the teaching ... When I announced that I intended leaving, the headmaster offered to teach my son, aged 6 for free but I was beginning to feel that the work was repetitive and that I was young enough (42) to start another career.

I was offered the post of Assistant Administrator on the Turks and Caicos Islands and was told that on completion of the 2 year contract there was a strong possibility of another appointment as Senior Assistant Secretary in the New Hebrides – a condominium run at the time by England and France jointly. As I am half French and bi-lingual, having spent the first 10 years of my life in the French speaking part of Switzerland, it was a prospect that appealed very much. When it definitely looked as if this post in the New Hebrides would materialise I said "Yes! Yes!" and my wife said "Oh dear, Oh dear – we have two small children aged 5 and 7, they need a settled home and an education in England". My wife was the daughter and granddaughter of colonial judges and had a young life trailing round the Empire, finishing up in NR where her father was Chief Justice (Sir John Griffin).

I therefore decided to see if I could become a Queen's Messenger, for that way I would be based in England, the children would be at schools here and I would be able to travel… I was fortunate to be accepted as I was told that there were over 400 on the waiting list. Retiring in 1990 at the age of 65, I completed a TEFL course at Oxford and started teaching at one of the language schools there, but I found the 40 mile journey from Burford time consuming and tiring. So my wife and I started having students living with us, but only one at a time …

Brian Heathcote's father had finished his Northern Rhodesia career as PC Central Province and continued in HMOCS when he returned to Britain:

Father was given a job in the Overseas office in Victoria, part of it was selecting candidates for foreign postings. He was offered the post of Falkland islands Governor, but I think my Mum did not relish the thought and liked seeing more of us kids and being in Europe. My Dad, having been in Africa since 1935, found it a bit difficult to settle back in UK. Also, having lived in government housing for so many years, we did not have a house in UK and not much savings, so life was not that easy. He retired in January 1973 but by April was diagnosed with cancer and died in the November. Very unfair such a short retirement and life, aged 60.

Age could make finding suitable employment in Britain difficult; it was too late for retraining and few employers wanted new high level staff. Roland Hill stayed on as long as he could in Zambia:

When I left I was 50. One might say I was unemployable anywhere else! I had contemplated a post in the Congo with Anglo-American and involvement in a development scheme in Angola, but for family reasons I decided to return to England. The first people to feel the cut off from NR were my two boys, aged 18 and 16. As to myself, my life's work really finished when I left Zambia. Nothing would ever replace it and even so long after leaving NR I still have dreams about Africans.

When we returned to the UK we quickly realised that people were not the slightest bit interested in what you had done. I was advised to apply for jobs even if I did not want them – to gain experience! I made the decision to buy a house in Pershore which my wife had chosen and where we have stayed to this day. I had commuted half my colonial pension and used the final 3 years of my contract in Zambia for house purchase. Leaving Zambia in May 1975, I took a post at the Medical School in Birmingham in February 1976, 32 miles each way – as DC Samfya my office was at the bottom of my garden!

This was my first employment as a civilian in the UK. The world of academia is very different from anything I had ever experienced – it took some five years to readapt my thinking ... pettiness, narrow-minded individual rights were paramount ... To leave one's career aged 50 needs greater adjustment. I had reached my ambition in the colonial service and afterwards in Zambian Service. Others who left under 45 had the opportunity to sit exams for the foreign and UK government service with pension prospects.

Roland Hill had made a list of the post-Zambia careers of his immediate contemporaries in the PA, he gave it to me, saying: *When I joined we were a band of brothers, hardly anyone ever resigned, we looked after each other*

University Administration	(6)
Bursar	(4)
Teaching	(4)
Solicitor	(3)
Management/Industry	(3)
Stockbroker	(3)
UK Civil Service	(3)
British Council	(3)
British Gas Board	(3)
Barrister/Judge	(2)
Land Agent	(2)
Colonial Service, Western Pacific	(2)
United Nations	(2)
Head of Lands Department Cambridge University	(1)
Ambassador to Liberia	(1)
Hotel management	(1)
Colonial Service Hong Kong	(1)
Broadcasting Regional TV	(1)
Queen's Messenger	(1)
Inland Revenue	(1)
Irish Office	(1)
Hospital Administration	(1)
Administration Island of Sark	(1)
Living in South Africa	(1)

It could be a struggle

Rhodesia Railways solved the problem of Zambianised employees by transferring them to Southern Rhodesia and we have already seen the example of Cyril Frowd. Other firms with their head offices in the south, including banks and building societies, also transferred staff, who usually went willingly. When these employees reached retirement age, their normal pensions would be paid in Rhodesia – but we know what subsequently happened to these (I have multi-billion $ Zim notes framed on my lavatory wall).

Sandra Fann refers to the plight of her father:

My parents left Rhodesia in the '70s to live with my brother in the UK. Needless to say, my father never got a bank pension – the London office citing the fact that he went to Bulawayo and was there when UDI was declared, thus severing his connection with the British operation. He had worked for Barclays Bank DCO for 40 years when he retired aged 58!

A great many people who had spent substantial parts of their working lives in Northern Rhodesia and paid regular superannuation contributions found themselves without incomes in old age. My father received his last bi-annual pension payment from the Zambian Local Government Pension Fund in the late 'seventies – inflation had been so rampant that there were more Kwacha on the stamp on the envelope than on the cheque it contained. There was a letter saying no more would be sent. When he returned to work after Independence he'd paid back the amount drawn down to buy the farm and, though the bulk of the contributions had been made in sterling, the pension itself was not underwritten in any way by the British Government. Part of the lump-sum component of the pension had been repatriated and annually a dribble of savings could come out – with this my parents had bought a derelict cottage on a remote Scottish croft, building it with their own hands into a decent house. Once again they were living a semi-subsistence lifestyle, with goats and a vegetable patch, letting out both their bedrooms to tourists in the summer. They were not unique.

For those who left with no compensation for loss of office, the consequences could be dire. Stuart Mclean ended up in a career he would never have anticipated:

Getting work in the UK was difficult as I was naïve in modern business methods, unskilled and could not prove my past work record. I almost got a couple of jobs which subsequently fell through when the employer found out that my references were to be found in the "illegal" regime of Rhodesia. By chance, I found out about the Prison Service and the opportunities it offered, so I joined as a Prison Officer. Being a single man, I was sent to London and started at HMP Brixton. I met and dealt with a huge range of people from the notorious to the mad to the pathetic… Had I come to the UK after I left NR, I think that I would have probably got further up the ladder. On retirement I quickly moved to Spain, possibly as it was as close as I could get to the African lifestyle that I so loved, without the risk of being outside Europe.

Liz Dunn had a small government pension but not enough capital to buy a house; her husband had a business in Zambia that floundered with the new economic policy. They rented in Cyprus where she remained for several years after his death, eventually coming back to Britain where she lives in the rather splendid Morden College in Blackheath, a 17th century merchant's charity set up for "such as have lost their estates by accidents, dangers and perils of the seas or by any other accidents ways or means in their honest endeavours to get their living".

More people than we know about have sunk right to the bottom and others fear it, but these don't usually join reunion societies or Facebook groups; they just disappear. In New Zealand I met a man, then in his late fifties, who lived in a garden hut. He had come with his parents and sister from the Copperbelt, where he'd had a job as a shop assistant – he never worked again and was virtually derelict, living on small grants from his widowed mother. Unable to get things together, he wanted to talk about the golden life in Northern Rhodesia. We also know that Zimbabwe has many stranded elderly Europeans living in dire poverty (McNally, undated) and the plight of the poor whites in South Africa is increasingly being reported internationally (O'Reilly, 2010); there must be several from Northern Rhodesia among them.

Early in his memoir/diary *Hamba Gashle* Ian Hassall refers affectionately to the family he boarded with as a child in Luanshya when his parents were divorcing; he has changed their names, but assures me that they were real people. Towards the end of his book, writing about 1968 Hassall says:

"Dad tells me that Auntie Elsie has divorced Uncle Oscar because of his drinking. I am shocked, they seemed the perfect family, warm, easy going, a safe haven, how could this happen? After they left Luanshya he couldn't settle,

getting odd jobs, nothing regular, too many refugees from the north in the same position. He's always been a drinker and it just deteriorated. Apparently now he's begging on Durban beach. Some pages later in 1970, *"Uncle Oscar's died, another tramp on Durban beach. But not for me, I grieve as I would for a father."* (Hassall, 2012 Kindle edn)

Stuart Goodwin recognized that there were deep problems for many of the people he knew:

It must have been so hard for the adults to pack up and go and make another life, whether down south or overseas. Even youngsters battled and I have known of alcoholism and suicide among my age group, I'm sad to say. The diaspora happened in a short space of time and I reckon the mid-to end '60s saw most whiteys leave and then the rest in the early '70s. The shock and sadness – from a "perfect" life to uprooting and starting again. I was, and am still, particularly sad that I lost touch with friends I had and I wish I knew what happened to them. We seemed to leave NR in a bit of a rush, not thinking that you wouldn't see your mates again. Thankfully I am in touch with some of my friends that I grew up with and am on a bit of a mission to try and track others down. But some I know have died.

Canada seemed the obvious destination for Alan Chattaway when his father moved there, but often people who grew up in Northern Rhodesia had to fend for themselves very young:

I arrived in Canada in the spring and learned at once that I could not stay in my dad's home as my new stepmom had not gotten along with my mom. I had no money and no possessions and no job, but had to leave their home within 2 weeks of arriving. At the end of the 1st week I visited a church that was becoming well-known in Vancouver and there I recognized the organist as a man who had visited University of Natal as part of a visiting mission team and through that church I found a place to stay and, several weeks later, my first job in Canada.

I found Vancouver very hard to adjust to after Durban. It's considered a jewel but in 1967 I found it ugly, cramped, old, and unfriendly, I think I would have disliked any place that wasn't Durban and didn't have my good friends living within driving distance. My experience of life since 1966 had been one of regularly losing everything, I lost my country (first Zambia and then South Africa), my family (first my mother, then very close friends from Christchurch in

Durban who are still like surrogate parents to me, then my father when I couldn't stay with him), my studies, my home, and my girlfriend. I arrived in Vancouver with $23 and one small suitcase containing all my possessions. Inside the lid of the suitcase I had written a Bible verse, Hebrews chapter 13 verse 14, "Here we have no continuing city, but we seek one to come." It seemed to describe my wanderings well.

Meeting the young woman who became my wife in 1969 changed the picture for me. Home is anywhere she or our children are! I made one trip back to Zambia and South Africa in 1997. I went to every place that held an unhappy memory for me, to remind myself that those places no longer have any power over me. It was a very healing experience.

Ruth Spindler was married to a former NRP officer. She remains in the USA where her grandchildren are and she owns a small antiques business:

We left in 1961 and went back to UK to settle in with relatives until my husband could find a position with the Police there. He had to start all over again (his tour of duty in NR did not count). It was quite a let-down – no servants, gloomy, rainy England and a toddler and new baby. What a struggle it was! I don't think my husband was too happy with the Police in UK ... so different of course. In 1963 we emigrated to the United States, first to his Mormon sisters in Utah, and when we couldn't stand that, we moved to California. In 1971 we divorced and in 1974 I remarried. After 20 years my 2nd husband died and my first husband also died in 2004. He suffered a stroke when he was released from a Federal prison in Utah after 8 years; a 2nd stroke killed him. He didn't do very well in the way of work in the U.S., couldn't be in the Police because he had to be a US Citizen and had to be in the country 5 years before he could apply. I never really wanted to go to the U.S. at all.

Britain seemed so strange

Northern Rhodesia's Europeans had been encouraged to think of Britain as the homeland, but when they arrived many did not receive much of a homecoming. Although young people had often hankered for the overseas experience, the circumscribed, small-town life of NR/Z left rather a lot of them feeling like fishes out of water in British cities. Geraldine Luscome felt lost:

I found England quite a frightening place to be. All the long haired hippy types, the drugs that were apparently being taken and everything looked so drab and grey! Like with most things I eventually got used to it, but never lost my hankering for Africa. In 1973 with my (then) husband, and three month old baby I emigrated to East London in SA where we spent nearly five years. Two more sons were born to me in East London. Returned to England in 1977, and have never been back.

Catherine Strang also had problems in coming to terms with "swinging" London:

I joined the lower sixth form at a local grammar school, where I was once again the New Girl, seeking acceptance among classmates who had well-established groups. Most of them were politically left-leaning and socially much more mature and "trendy" than I was....

This was London in the mid 1960s, and I was initially shocked by and disapproving of the freedom and attitudes which were emerging. On the other hand, I always felt that I had a much broader view of the world than most of my classmates, who seemed to have lived rather parochial lives in their London suburb, despite their view of themselves as sophisticated metropolitans.

Graham Snow was 17 when he arrived in Britain in 1966:

It was very hard to adjust. Not only the density of housing/population, but attitudes. How can I explain? My colonial upbringing had bred in a feeling of superiority, maybe arrogance? I found it hard to relate to everyday people. I think I was a generation behind everyone I met, especially when I went to college. The Swinging '60s completely passed me by, because I was living, and thinking in the '50s.

Roger Ridley also did not think much of British society on his first encounter and has shuttled back and forth to South Africa, currently living in London:

Coming to the UK was a bit of a culture shock. I found the attitude of the British most insular – having little interest in matters outside the UK, in contrast to those from Southern Africa who were interested in what was going on in the rest of the world. Not only were the British disinterested, they were profoundly ignorant (and still are) ... Dare I say that even back in the early '70s the educational system in the UK was inferior to that in SA? ... I also found the British men to be ill-mannered – maybe it was just the way I was brought up, but we were courteous towards women – e.g. allowing them to precede men through doors.

Jane Schillig never really became accustomed to the British in Britain – her views echo those of a great many women brought up in Central Africa, but she also refers to the problems faced by her parents in 1966:

My father was due to return "home" about June. His job, Permanent Secretary to the Ministry of Education, was being taken over by an African and my father was spending his last few months in Zambia training him for the job. My mother returned in March because she had to find accommodation for the family. We had no idea where we were going to live and as my father did not have a job to come to, it made little difference where we were so we rented a house in Farnham. This was probably the saddest and most difficult time of our family lives. My father was depressed at not finding a job, my mother had to do all the housework and her social life had gone completely, my sister hated her school and I had not got sufficiently high grades at A level to go to a decent university. We were all miserable and naturally our economic circumstances had also changed.

My mother perhaps suffered the most. She had had a very full life in Lusaka. She was Director of Red Cross for Northern Rhodesia. She was part of a circle of women who went to the local township every week to teach the women how to sew. She was a great hostess and there were always people coming to stay, mainly in connection with my father's work, people like district commissioners, education officers from other parts of the country. We even had Doris Lessing to stay when she was invited to attend the celebrations to mark independence. My mother's days were always packed with so much to do that we mocked her for her most frequent expression "I'll never get round".

Back in England, we eventually bought a house in Maidenhead but my mother had no friends close by and few means to make any. My father had got a job in London so he left early in the morning and returned late at night. We were away at various educational institutions. There was little opportunity to meet people, living as we were in the commuter belt. My mother tried to get involved with charities such as Red Cross and Oxfam, but she was looking for a challenge and it seemed that these organisations spent too much time on bureaucracy and she felt she did not fit in. Her days now revolved around housework and her health suffered. My father was not happy either as he hated commuting every day. And in addition, there was the inevitable drop in income level and the rise in cost of living compared to our life in N.R.

My sister was settled in a new school and was due to go to Art School, I was to spend a year at a college in Oxford to try to improve my grades. But I hated Oxford. My self esteem was at rock bottom. I knew no one and had little in common with the other English girls. They were all being groomed for the London "scene", spoke with a different accent to me and all seemed to be connected to one another in some way ... I never knew how to dress. I always felt awkward whatever the weather. I was always too hot or too cold, and usually dressed like a Michelin man struggling under the weight of sweaters and coats.

Lynne Morze-Langan tried settling down in Britain, despite citizenship problems, then went back to Zambia in response to Chiluba's encouragement of Europeans to return and invest in the 1990s. After building and running a lodge on the Zambezi she came back to Britain:

Britain, well firstly I abhor the weather, I can't get used to it, my home is heated like a sauna and I dress up like an Eskimo when I have to put out the wheelie bins. I honestly consider it debilitating and aging and escape at every opportunity. What I miss most is, in Africa there is no generation gap when it comes to social occasions, everyone parties together and we do 'unsafe' adventure activities, like off road biking, quad trailing, jet skiing, etc. Here I am expected to learn to knit for my grandchildren, and discuss dull safe topics. I miss being surrounded by people who are outspoken, open, love debating and are generally informed.

Lynne moved on to Australia. That coldness wasn't just a matter of climate, Judy Rawlinson attended Liverpool University where:

Some of my fellow students branded me a neo-colonialist fascist so I learned to avoid political arguments...

I married in 1965 and soon found myself in Zambia once more as my husband, an engineer, worked in the mining industry. I was able to continue in my career as a town planner, although I was paid considerably less than I had been in the UK. My two children were born in 1967 and 1969 and we finally left in 1975... In the mid-70s property prices were soaring and so were mortgage rates. Luckily, Bob managed our limited finances brilliantly. Most of our savings went into buying a cottage in a pretty Hampshire village: small but perfectly formed, all we could afford. My elder son thought that this was just somewhere we were spending our leave. I found him crying in his bedroom one day because he missed his dogs. The two boys went to our small village school and were initially regarded with some suspicion by the locals. This was strange to them as there had been such a shifting population in Chingola that there were always new pupils at their school. Being friendly, open-minded boys, they soon settled in. I found it more difficult but, remembering how hard my parents had found things, I was determined to make a go of becoming a returning Brit. Some of the villagers were friendly, others less so – in fact, some were downright snooty. I think they found it hard to slot us into a particular social category. What I did find hard was having a husband who went off at 7.00am to catch the train to his office in London and then not seeing him until 8.00pm at night!

Jim Dunning had served in a senior role in the NR/Z Department of Education, but it was back to the chalk-face:

Life back in England was difficult at first. I obtained a teaching post in a tough secondary modern school in Birkenhead, on roughly half the salary I'd received in Zambia. We used to joke that the kids played tick with hatchets, but there was an element of truth in it. During my first stint of playground duty I was called to the phone regarding a message from an estate agent, and returned to find one of the pupils had been slashed across the face with a knife .... A year later I landed an administrative job in the Birkenhead Education Office.

The people I felt sorry for were District Commissioners and District Officers in the Provincial Administration whose only qualifications were degrees. Some of them had great difficulty finding employment in the U.K., though a fair number seemed to end up as bursars in universities.

Peter and Maddy Kellett came to Britain after initially going to Rhodesia where he managed cattle ranches:

The big culture shock, for me at any rate, came when we arrived in Britain. Maddy was in her mid twenties when she came to N.R. from England, whereas I had become totally Rhodesianised. I knew, of course, that 1974 Britain would be nothing like the post-war deprivation country I had left. Initially we were staying with my mother-in-law in a village in the New Forest. I travelled to Brixham one day to meet a contact in the fishing industry. The weather must have been good, because it seemed to me that all 60 million Brits were in Brixham that day. I couldn't believe it! One evening we were watching the T.V. when a program on Northern Scotland was presented. Its opening dialogue featured the information that, "You can sometimes walk all day without meeting another human". We said, "Let's go!" bought a caravan and ended up in Ullapool, where I discovered that a fishing boat I had admired was for sale. We lived in that 10 foot caravan for the first few months, even after I had started fishing for langoustine, etc. So, that was the motivation for the move to Scotland. The move from Rhodesia to Britain was for a variety of reasons, a significant one being our estimation of the probable future for our 4 sons, aged 6 to 11 years old at the time. Being in a police anti-terrorist unit, a paramilitary arm of the police reserve, I was not happy at having to leave my family on a farm while I was away on police duties. Having had some marine experience, I was pretty sure I could make a living fishing here, which turned out to be the case, initially with a creel boat and subsequently a trawler.

I don't think I ever settled in completely. People here have been good to me, but I still feel as though I don't quite belong, but I suppose the life-style I chose here made settling in easier than it might otherwise have been. I still find this livid green colour of the country extravagant, even after 37 years! And if I pick up a rock or a log I still have a nagging feeling there may be a puff-adder under it. When I went to Zaire in the mid 1980s I felt so much in tune with the place and people. It felt like home, in spite of the post-independence degradation and I enjoyed mixing with Africans again.

Britain could be depressing to people who had become accustomed to the easy-going friendships of Northern Rhodesia, so many set off again. Dennis Pigrum and his family headed to Australia:

After a year of life in the Wirral and its surrounds we knew that our personal ambitions and my career aspirations would not be realised in the constraining environment of England. We had changed too much for life in the old country.

Recognising that Africa was no longer a continent where we could make a home for our children and desirous of seeking a climate akin to that of Northern Rhodesia we placed a ruler across a world map along Mufulira's line of latitude. Townsville in Queensland, Australia was where we decided to make our future. We needed a sponsor and since my existing employer was not supportive of our proposed move, I wrote to the Mayor of Townsville telling him of our intentions and seeking his assistance. He replied promptly telling me that as he was negotiating to purchase a computer system from my existing employer's local subsidiary he'd passed my letter on to the Queensland Manager who would be contacting me shortly. Six weeks later we were on a Boeing 707 on our way to Brisbane.

John and Lizzie Gornall had problems with an "idyllic" English village while he was following a degree course at the University of Kent at Canterbury:

John: *We rented a little cottage at Fordwich on the Stour River ... Lizzie had fallen in love with it the moment she saw it. It fitted her African childhood romancing of an English Country Cottage...The darling cottage became a prison of misery and depression during the winters.*

Lizzie: *It was obvious that there was no room for study in our confined home with a growing baby in residence. John would have to work in the University Library but it left me alone all day. I enrolled with the child care services, and attended the clinic fortnightly with Diana, anticipating getting to know other young mothers and making friends. It proved a vain hope; people were strange, unresponsive and reserved. In their own groups they clustered together and ignored my overtures.*

It was the same in the village. When I pushed the pram along the lanes, people would turn away, or gather in groups at corners and stare, offering no friendly faces. The young men were the worst. I was afraid of them. They would stand in a phalanx and stare, creating a barrier across the footpath. They did not respond to polite requests to allow me passage, so I would have to manoeuvre the pram off the footpath into the road to by-pass them.

I began to spend more time indoors, as much to avoid the peculiar, menacing people, as to escape the weather. On a freezing day in early December, as I was stoking the fire in the living room, light from the only window was blocked off suddenly. Startled, I looked around and saw three women, hands cupped about their faces pressed to the glass to give them a clear view. Maybe they wanted to be friends? By the time I got the door open, they were half way down the footpath and running. Being confined, out of place and the object of staring strangers, was mortifying – even sinister.

People could be shut out. The winter could not. Rain soaked into the bricks. The wallpaper rolled itself down from the ceilings as the paste dissolved. Green mould grew on the clothes in the wardrobes. I feared that Diana's health would suffer.

They took out a mortgage and settled into a new home but in Cambridge she encountered further horrors of English society:

Cambridge was a set-back. We lived in the middle of a row of terraced houses. Our neighbours on either side were elderly. They gossiped together across my garden, but when I emerged to hang washing on my line, they withdrew, only to reappear the moment I went in again.

After qualifying as a teacher John found comprehensive schools dispiriting, there was nothing to keep then in England and when they saw a sign in the window of New Zealand House they were off on a new life:

With income and housing confirmed, we spent the remainder of our savings on a month long visit to my parents in Southern Rhodesia before flying to New Zealand in September of 1971.

That was the last time Lizzie would see her mother, who was murdered in the farm store where she worked after she and her husband, denied British citizenship, had relocated to a precarious existence in Rhodesia. Her father eventually came to join them in New Zealand, bereft of everything. (An account of Lizzie Gornall's parents is available in John Gornall's autobiography, 2008. p 343-356.)

Chris Lyon was another NRP officer who had thought it sensible to get into the job market in Britain before he turned 30, leaving in 1963:

We drove from Southampton to my parents' (and my childhood) home in West Wickham, an outer suburb of London, in Kent. As Frances and our little boy walked up the path to the front door I turned to close the gate, looked round at the neighbouring houses and felt a sudden overwhelming depression. I had been half-way round the world, followed an exciting and relatively successful career and here I was back in front of this small house where I would have to start all over again; the previous six years had vanished to nothing.

Obviously the first thing to do was find a job and in Britain in 1963 work was plentiful, even for an ex-colonial police officer with no qualifications and 28 years old. Having attended interviews I was offered posts at the Portman Building Society and Barclays Bank Trustee Department and both institutions seemed eager to employ me. However the starting salaries were too low for a family man who would have to live within daily travelling distance of the City; as for the cost of such housing, it was just as impossible as it is today. I did not for a moment think of joining a U.K. police force.

I found myself drawn to the job as one of Her Majesty's Inspectors of Taxes... In order to be considered for the selection process candidates had to have either a 1st or 2nd class honours degree or have held a regular commission in the armed forces or have been in the Overseas Civil Service ... I knew I had got lucky and made the right choice of career.

We found a small fairly modern house in a village outside Wolverhampton and moved in in November, 1963. It was then that the reality of winter in England struck home. The house did not have central heating and Frances, who was by then expecting our second child, suffered at home from the cold, whereas I could warm up at the office. The days were short and dark and where was the sky and where the distant horizon? Everything was small and our neighbours' lives seemed so circumscribed; our time in Africa was a not very interesting oddity, their idea of a party was an aunt coming to tea. Frances sent me out to buy a red pepper from the local greengrocer and they had not the faintest idea what I was talking about. They offered a box of white pepper which I declined and as I walked out of the door the woman owner of the shop shouted, "And you won't find one anywhere else!" It was the weather that got us down most until we became sufficiently British again to treat it with weary resignation.

Chris Lyon is a central figure in the NRPA and has been invaluable in circulating members on my behalf.

As several people say, it could be hard for women coming back to Britain, though most eventually settled in – after a fashion. Catherine Strang has commented on her own marginalisation, but realised it was difficult for her mother too:

My mother had the hardest time when we came back to the UK. My father had his job; my sister and I were at school, but she, who had had a wide range of friends and interests and an active social life, was left alone in a north London suburb where the neighbours were not particularly friendly and she had nothing to do. She was unhappy and could have succumbed to serious depression at that stage, but being a strong-minded woman she got herself a part time job in the local grocers shop, where she worked for the next few years. Later, she joined the WRVS and did meals on wheels, but never enjoyed living in London.

A former member of the PA also thought that the move to Britain was always hardest on wives with small children. His wife had gone ahead whilst he completed his contract:

Renting a house in Sussex which we found in The Lady *magazine, my wife left for the UK with the four children. Given that she had had little experience of life in the UK, to land there with a young family on her own was an ordeal. To make matters worse, the rented house was a disaster and she had to move into a B&B. This was a difficult time to put it mildly, finding schools for the girls and coping with an infant son... Eventually she found a more suitable house to rent and she was able to get some sort of routine going. But she was far from well. There were further twists and turns in this difficult period including a trip to Australia and New Zealand as possible places to which to relocate. We eventually settled in Kent but it was difficult and my wife never really fully recovered. She died prematurely. I always felt that her illness was hastened by the worries and difficulties of settling into a new life.*

There was more anguish, I think, than people would admit to. It was an enormous adjustment and the benefits (being near a doctor for instance) somehow didn't add up – the trouble was partly Africa made such inroads into your soul that there was an enormous void. Even now, going back there as I have just done seems to resonate. I wonder whether women didn't anguish more. In my case I was enormously lucky with the various jobs I had and found much fulfillment in them, but the women folk, tied down at home, didn't have that to compensate. I had several years in Algeria and though the job was tough, the living was great and my wife used to say, "Take me to where the vines grow and I shall be happy", and she was!

Starting up again wasn't easy

People who had been self employed in Zambia had to face the radical changes of the 1970s when companies were Zambianised. Some tried to keep things going with a Zambian partner, others gave up.

Joe Behrens whom we have met earlier as a successful electrical contractor and cinema owner in NR/Z carried on for as long as he could in Zambia, but left in 1973 when it was becoming impossible to get supplies as a consequence of Rhodesia's blockade. He was fifty-two when he arrived in Britain. He had assets here, but decided not to try to set up another company as he had no useful contacts and realized that he would be lost without them in an alien business environment.

Sue and Paul Hoar recount their story of a continuing fragile connection to Zambia:

We came over to England in 1975, as by then the local schools left a lot to be desired. We found a wonderful flat in Palace Gate, near Kensington Gardens and again we all had a very happy time – except for Paul of course who struggled to get used to London and who also had to find a means of earning money. By this time he had his own wine business so managed to carry on selling in Africa, thanks to his contacts there. The children went to a little private school as we could get money out of Zambia for school fees, and nothing else.

At one stage we opened a wine shop in Pimlico, but it didn't really make a profit. Paul eventually got involved in supplying the new Government duty free shop in Lusaka, and so had to go over there to set it all up. This all came to an end in the early 'nineties when Paul's partner in the business screwed him (there's no other word for it). He then had to start from scratch again and try and build up another business with no money, just his contacts. Because of his expertise in the wine trade he was able to buy wine "en primeur" from the Bordeaux brokers, and this is virtually like a trading commodity these days as so little wine is available from the top growths. He has been doing this ever since as he can't afford to give up working! Luckily it can all be done on the computer so we can move anywhere.

About ten years ago my father died and left me and my sister his house in Cyprus, where my parents had retired after leaving Zambia. I have sent a lot of equipment out there so I can do pottery in the garden and for a few years now I have been teaching ceramics to the local expats – not particularly lucrative but a pleasant way to meet people. We usually spend a couple of months in Spring and Autumn there when the weather has cooled down a bit.

Sue and Paul have now moved from London and live between Cyprus and Andorra.

"You're too old feller"

Though there were exceptions, forty was usually seen as the cut-off age for starting a new career – finding any work at all was a challenge. Robert

McChesney the former PWD electrical engineer; found it difficult to interest employers during the recession of the mid '70s:

... I had a couple of good interviews which went well but once they noticed my age, now 45, things went distinctly flat. I even wrote to the Union Castle line as we had travelled with them frequently on home leave and I was impressed by their vessels, especially the engineering aspect, they replied saying that times had moved on since my days with Cunard ... the main point was that my age was against me. This was put very kindly but, like other sympathetic replies I received, the answer was in the negative. No one actually wanted to say, 'You're too old, feller.'

We travelled extensively, following up leads and considering business propositions. It was all time consuming and was eating into our savings. Some ex-Zambia friends had made the best of things and settled but others had a hard time. We all felt we had been uprooted. Our other worry was the children. Although in school and apparently coping, they were bewildered and aware of how unsettled we were. In spite of being spoilt by their grandparents they were clearly affected by not having their own home and their toys and playthings were all still in unopened trunks.

So I continued through the summer of 1971, sometimes applying for jobs that were well out of my field. The impression grew on me that employers didn't want ex-colonials. But Africa still called us back and I was beginning to realise I may have made the wrong decision in returning to U.K.

We were living on our savings and it was a balancing act, having to be careful and hold some back in case we decided to return to Africa or even try Australia where many of our friends had gone. It is now 40 years since this all took place ... we were finding life in Britain very difficult. What we do remember is the anxiety and apprehension of that time. It was now November and a hard winter was setting in. We were longing for the African sunshine... I made the first move for our return. I went to the Union Castle offices to arrange our passages. The first date they could offer me was 7th January 1972. I paid the deposit of £50.

At the eleventh hour he was offered a senior post at a new company specialising in alarm systems; it was set up by a retired admiral who actually wanted a suitable older man. This is a lengthy extract because Robert McChesney's problems are so typical of those faced by people without local contacts or experience during a recession. The global economic problems that were driving people out of Zambia were hitting the UK too.

Judy Rawlinson tells of her parents, who decided to return to Zambia after a year in Britain:

My parents left in 1964, prior to Independence, along with many others in the civil service whose jobs were being Africanised... they tried hard to settle back in England but within a year had returned to the Copperbelt, first to Ndola then to Mufulira where my father worked for the Town Council in both places. He was told at a British Labour Exchange that he would 'never find a job in this country at his age'! Poor Dad was so disillusioned.... His meagre colonial pension had to be supplement somehow. They had sold their house in London in the late '50s and property prices had risen so much they couldn't buy anything there. Before they went back to Zambia for the second time my father briefly worked for the Royal Aircraft Establishment in Farnborough, where they bought a small house: tiny in comparison to houses they had lived in while abroad but it had a large garden, which my father loved.

Rose Hesom found her father demoralized by the move to South Africa:

In Cape Town, Dad got a job as a bookkeeper at Table Top, the frozen food people, in Woodstock. Because of his age (60) it was pretty much all he could find and I know that the years he sat in his dingy office in that grimy building were not his happiest. Nor was life easy for Mum in Cape Town – she was having to do all the housework and cooking on a daily basis for the first time in her grown-up life and, not being a driver, she had to catch a bus to do her grocery shopping. It was a very different life indeed.

Things sorted themselves out for most of the people we've looked at and there are plenty of contented people – but as Tolstoy said, "All happy families are alike, but an unhappy family is unhappy after its own fashion."

Doing well

Perhaps more Northern Rhodesian Europeans than one might have expected from such a small population have been very successful and there is a strong feeling amongst many of them that the colonial experience made them confident and adaptable. I am afraid that I cannot find many women amongst them (this is more a matter of time than place, it is the young women of the late 'seventies who were able to forge ahead) but I know from my own experience that Britain was better than Central Africa for a woman with career ambitions in the 1960s. Kate Smith, a mechanical engineer recognizes this:

I went to school in Kitwe and took a job as a trainee Tracer/Draughtsman. I loved my work and was sorry to leave what had now become Zambia but, as my father worked on the copper mine and his job was being Zambianised, the whole family was uprooted and brought back to UK.

Finding a job along similar lines proved very difficult, but eventually I was taken on as an apprentice with a local engineering firm. I was left to fathom out what I needed to do college-wise so enrolled at a technical college to do a course in basic engineering. As I passed this with flying colours, the firm took a little more interest in me and put me on course for an ONC and subsequently HND in Mechanical Engineering. Again, I passed with good marks and considered an MSc. in Fluid Mechanics. However, I had recently married and decided to forego this and work to earn some money... Whether I would have achieved status as an engineer in Zambia is dubious, but in UK I was able to do this and hold down a responsible position as MD for an engineering company.

When Barbara and Richard Hall returned to Britain they already had international reputations as journalists and a wealth of contacts, settling back into London was not a problem. Barbara became the Crossword Puzzles editor for the *Sunday Times* as well as compiling the *Sunday Times* books of crossword puzzles and writing freelance. Richard became editor of the *Observer Colour Magazine*, the *Observer's* Foreign and Commonwealth editor and also wrote for the *Financial Times*. The Halls knew "everybody" (they even had *Roxy Music* rehearsing in their basement in the days before we'd all heard of them) but they maintained a close relationship with Zambia, Barbara bringing out the unforgettable *Tell me Josephine* collection, based on her agony aunt column in the *African Mail* and Richard publishing several important books on the country.

Of course, there are many kinds of success and I'm taking the rather narrow view that excludes wonderful grandparents and patient teachers. After early responsibility in interesting jobs in Zambia, many found their first new employment limiting and struck out again. Going from the NRP to banking was stultifying for a man still in his twenties, as Colin Heape discovered:

I joined Westminster Bank mainly because of the perks they offered. I could buy a house with a mortgage at 2%. The Bank had an excellent sailing club and the prospect for promotion was good. I became disillusioned with the bank after the merger of Westminster Bank and the National Provincial Bank. That ruined my chances of becoming a manager. I was lucky to be offered the chance to train as a Land Agent by the Factor of Locheil Estates in Fort William. We moved to Scotland in 1969 and have remained in the Highlands ever since. I have enjoyed a good life working for three large Estates as a Resident Agent and have now retired to live on the Black Isle near Inverness.

The law attracted a good number of younger NRP and PA, who had become familiar with court work and fascinated by the intricacies of justice. In the years before their departure, many studied in their spare time to take their exams on return to Britain, others waited until they could devote their attention to it full-time, investing part of their "lumpers" and subsisting on small pensions. Not a few have become successful, I think particularly of Paul Wheeler a former NRP officer and *aide de camp* to the Governor who came back to Britain, specialising in company law.

John Haddon summed up the choice of a legal career: "*In a sense the breadth and variety of work undertaken by a DO led seamlessly to work in law...*", but one had to be young enough to retrain. Martin Field, who arrived in Northern Rhodesia in 1960 as an LDA at the age of 19 took an unusual route:

After independence I started to study law by correspondence and in 1965 I was sent to London with Zambian law students to complete Bar Finals course and was called to the Bar in 1966. On return to Zambia in 1967 I was appointed Resident Magistrate Kitwe, after which there followed a number of other legal appointments (on contract).

He then practiced as a barrister in England after returning in 1970.

Members of the NRP were some of the most proactive in establishing new careers and several acknowledged that the responsibility expected of them whilst still young men made them attractive in the business world. Jeremy Hawkins moved successfully into international recruitment with the Anglo-American group including senior management in the Congo/Zaire, Angola and finally de Beers.

John and Hester Cribb, having been right at the centre of things in Zambia, had to start afresh with no immediate leads and no home in Britain. John had prepared for civilian life by completing a business management course by correspondence whilst still in Zambia and, drawing on his pre-African service in the navy as well as his huge responsibilities in Zambia, approached companies in the newly developing hovercraft industry, eventually being asked to set up a hovercraft ferry service in Jamaica. After a year they moved back to Britain, once again looking for a suitable position. Hester worked as a secretary and took in foreign language students, but John was soon offered a post at Plessey, writing technical manuals. From Plessey he was head-hunted by an American computer company and finally set up his own company, with Hester now employed as marketing/publicity manager. They have had to work hard but have been very successful and, living on the waterfront at Sandbanks, must have one of the pleasantest homes on the South coast.

The Methodist minister, Colin Morris was a prominent figure in Zambia who bore the brunt of considerable resentment from white supremacists before Independence. He was a close friend of Kenneth Kaunda and after Independence was four times elected President of the United Church of Zambia. He left for Britain in 1970 to serve as minister of Wesley's Chapel in London, but after a few years his career took a turn:

I happened to be on the Copperbelt when television first came to the Territory and made enough appearances in Zambia and in Britain to learn the tricks of the trade, so that when my time with the Missionary Society was over, the BBC appointed me Head of Religious Broadcasting.

He retired as Controller of BBC Northern Ireland and maintained his links with Zambia throughout, visiting frequently.

A major success story with its roots in Zambia is that of Neville Isdell, the son of an NRP officer, who had all his schooling in Northern Rhodesia. After taking a degree at University of Cape Town, he returned to Independent Zambia and took up what wouldn't on the face of it seem like a particularly promising job with Coca-Cola:

My first job was at a two-truck depot in a small copper-mining town called Mufulira. Cokes were sold to supermarkets, bars and restaurants. My salary was $1,100 a year. Noting that one of the two trucks was often idle because there was only one salesman on the staff, I asked if the company would hire another salesman. They wouldn't, so I offered to get my commercial driver's licence and *was soon driving a ten-ton truck, 'throwing cases' on every stop and adding new Coke customers. I doubled sales within a year. A fringe benefit of the physical labour was that I kept fit for rugby, and I was soon playing for the Zambian team.* (Isdell & Beasley, 2011 p. 27-8)

Soon Isdell was in charge of the Kitwe depot, faced with the problem of distribution in the light of the fuel shortages resulting from Rhodesia's UDI, which he solved by driving to the Congo border to buy diesel illegally. Then, realizing there was sales potential in the informal truckers' stops springing up along the notorious "Hell Run" transporting fuel and other goods to Zambia via Dar-es-Salaam, he and a co-worker worked the run themselves. After a career working for the company in many countries, he was made Chairman and CEO of Coca-Cola International in 2000. Throughout his autobiography he harks back to his formative years, acknowledging that Zambia gave him the opportunity to run with his ideas whilst still very young.

As mentioned in the previous chapter, Bob Huntley did not stay to see Independence, leaving on his own for America in 1963 to seek his fortune. He had no contacts and at the time few formal qualifications, though he had received an English school education, was very personable, and played a good game of golf. A golfing partner introduced him to a stock-broker who engaged him. He took an MBA and built up a distinguished client list, including Hollywood stars and major businessmen. He's aware of the part that luck played, but is convinced that, *"Anyone that cannot make it in America cannot have tried very hard."* Bob Huntley gave me breakfast at his house outside Carmell – he's a member of the Pebble Beach Golf Club and an enthusiastic American with a pukka English accent, but no yearning at all for class-ridden, dreary England.

Philippa & Patrick White remained in Zambia, running their own company until 2000, their successful afterlife is a contented retirement:

We retired and came to live in Knysna on the Cape coast. Never in our wildest dreams had we expected to be able to retire to South Africa. When our children were at boarding school in SA I kept quiet about it because the country was such a pariah politically. Having lived for years in an independent multi-racial society the last thing we wanted was to take steps backwards to anything like a colonial environment…. Then Nelson Mandela was set free and eventually South Africa had its first free elections. We found ourselves in beautiful Knysna and are very happy here. It's amazing how many people we have met who are ex Zambia or ex Zimbabwe and so we feel totally at home. As well as these new people we have several old friends who shared our early life in Chingola living in Cape Town and we often meet.

We always knew that Zambia was not a country for older European people and that we would be leaving when we stopped working ... and quite frankly we were getting tired of always being the oldest people at the party! Here in Knysna we live in an estate with mostly retired people, all of whom have come from elsewhere and we have made some valuable friendships. It is still a novelty too to live by the sea after all those years inland!

Mik Wright is no one's idea of an old colonial but he is an unconventional success living in rural West Virginia after a chequered career – he is a shoemaker and a free spirit. He seems remarkably contented:

I'm still here, living a good life still with the momentum of "Those Shoes". I never even got a school leaving certificate, just made it through standard 8 I think – it's a long story, many adventures, enough details to make a good book. It's sleeting and cold today and I have to go to our friend's place 60 miles away to fetch two goats and a sheep to butcher. Tomorrow my wife, Barb, and I will butcher two deer that we have had hanging for four days. We grow our own food and only eat the meat that we kill or raise ourselves. Anyway....

10. WHAT REMAINS?

There is a kind of cultural watershed; if you stay on past it you will always have a sense of exile. *Colin Morris*

When the time came to go, people made a final round of goodbyes and reappraised their possessions, selling or giving away some things, packing others, not really knowing what they would want later. Frank McGovern, who came into Lusaka from the rural North Western Province just before Independence, remarked of meeting his government colleagues there:

I thought we'd developed a nation of amateur carpenters, they were all making wooden boxes to put their katundu in to go.

As time went on and the Rhodesia situation worsened, goods transport became a problem. Anyone going to Europe had to airfreight their property, so people abandoned more and packed less. Government and some other employers paid for repatriation of personnel and property but many people had to evaluate every item they owned against its transport cost. As exchange controls tightened, limits were placed on the value of goods that could be taken out of the country – this was because of money laundering scams such as buying and selling back oriental rugs, but it impacted on genuine personal possessions.

This sorting and packing determined the stock of material souvenirs of the British colonial era in Northern Rhodesia. I have learned not to be surprised at the ephemera, such as amateur dramatics programmes, menu cards and old school magazines that made it into some people's baggage. Alistair Smart lent me his copy of the Northern Rhodesia Government Staff List for 1963 so that I could check the final composition of departments – I was delighted to have it, but what prompted him to bring it with him when he returned to Britain in 1967? Were people already laying down memories when these things were still just mundane "stuff", or were they packing in a daze? Furniture and everyday utensils rarely survived and most households had little that was distinctively Zambian anyway – a few copper items, carved elephants and some paintings, but most of those came from the Congo and were made for the European market. There had never been a vogue for collecting African artifacts (except amongst anthropologists and the like) so the collection is sparse. Alan Chattaway, among others, mentioned starting up in a new country with all his possessions in just one suitcase – I don't think many us cared much at the time, we were not a particularly materialistic community and there was always a lot of packing and moving anyway. Yet now we want to remember, to trace back to a fixed point. Whatever the reason for the survival of things, stuff that made it through has acquired sentimental value. There are now dealers in memorabilia.

It is not just distinctively colonial things that were lost – when they came to the country people brought their wedding presents, books, a few souvenirs of childhood, but not all of these survived the cull. As they age, they start to regret that they have lost many of the traces of their own history. Judy Rawlinson refers to the enforced pruning and the way she felt when her packing cases arrived in Britain:

As our personal possessions were included in the cash we were allowed to externalise, I had been obliged to sell some of my precious reference books, paintings, all my beautiful Danish furniture. I'd had to leave my lush, beautiful garden, where I knew every plant, every tree and give away my precious pots with their prize specimens. I had said goodbye to beloved staff, dear friends, some of whom were about to make new homes on the other side of the world. It was heartbreaking stuff.

The crates bearing our bits and pieces finally arrived. I sank my face into something I had been allowed to pack, my lovely sun-filter curtains, smelled the dust of Africa and wept. How would we survive? But survive we did. They say the first year is the worst.... We still keep in touch with our old friends from those days. And we returned to Africa, to work and play, time after time. Like a tsetse fly, it gets in the blood.

Photographs nearly always make the journey through time as well as space. Geraldine Mackey remarks on a reaction to a picture of the farm her family had once owned:

... when we had settled in Australia, I was framing a photo of the farm house in Abercorn when my youngest daughter said, "Was this the house you lived in before you were born?" [sic]. This made me realise the power of family stories, and the exotic, never-to-be-repeated experience of living on a farm in the middle of Africa in the late 1940s, early '50s.

But often we realise how few photographs were taken in those days of expensive film and processing and how they now seem to be of the wrong things – the Kariba Dam, the Victoria Falls (again), an elephant in the distance (partially obscured by a tree). I sent Alan Heathcote, some pictures of Kabwe as it is now and this was part of his response:

One photo I find very emotional to look at, as my father worked in the Boma. His office was the one on the right in the picture which only shows half of the window.

I knew what he meant and I didn't even get the whole window in. I'd taken photographs of my father's old office the same day, but they were pictures of now, not then, there is no picture of him there in office garb: long shorts, long socks, white shirt, dark tie.

People fear that the traces of their history and themselves will disappear through simple lack of interest in the colonial era. Pauline A contemplates this, writing from Australia:

I am sure my father always missed Northern Rhodesia to some degree – after all it represented the most successful and fulfilling part of his own life – but he was also pragmatic that it could never have lasted, with the weight of the world challenging the old-fashioned ideas of white supremacy. He was a landscape artist of considerable merit and I still have many of his paintings of the Northern Rhodesian bush. Some show forest scenes that will have now disappeared forever. They mean nothing to my own children and it would be good to donate them eventually to some appropriate archive of colonial art or memorabilia – that is if I can find one.

Marion Carlin had given her mother's wedding dress to the British Empire and Commonwealth Museum in Bristol and was distressed at its controversial closure in 2009, as are many others who donated items that now seem to have been "lost".

The things that remind us of our time in Northern Rhodesia do not always have to have been there with us, many people have started collecting books and artifacts since they left. Roland Hill articulates the way an involvement with the country can be an ongoing process:

My hobby is the lives of Africanists, African trade, the slave trade, colonial history. The research of orders and medals to former colonial administrators from Victorian times, distinguished Africans and soldiers ... I have collected an extensive library of Africana and I have African art from West Africa and Central. I have a portrait of an African District Messenger in my study and the medals of Robert Codrington of NR, Alfred Sharpe of Nyasaland & Hole of Zimbabwe, who all at one time administered part of NR. So I have Africa in my house, from study to bedroom via sitting and dining room. I am never away from Africa!

Jenny Hill, Roland's wife painted the portrait of the District Messenger (it is reproduced in Ian Mackinson's book) and she is an artist of some note, often painting Northern Rhodesian scenes in a style evocative of African art. Many ex-Northern Rhodesians have a print of former NRP officer John le Roux's painting, *Lusaka Station*. George Dublon is another who scours the second-hand bookshops and online sellers for the memoirs and scientific observations of the colonial era. The prices now commanded by the classics like Sampson's *They came to Northern Rhodesia* or Bradley's *Dearest Priscilla* indicate that there is fierce demand.

Cascading memories

An object, a sensation or a story can trigger memory, then one memory starts a cascade. Often people have told me that they had not intended writing as much as they did but, once they started, it was as if they had been dragged back to their youth in Northern Rhodesia. Rose Hesom started her account like this:

I have wanted to write something for a long time. My dear old Dad had wonderful stories to tell of his childhood and early life on farms in Natal and around the diamond fields of Kimberley where his Dad was a minor prospector … I always meant to record it, but alas never did .... Mum too had some interesting tales to tell and I don't remember half of it, more's the pity. One of my daughters-in-law has been trying for a long time to have an evening of 'question and answer time' with her parents and me just so that the family can discover a little more than they already know about us. I will continue to dig into the old memory, it seems like the more you remember, the more you remember ...

Mik Wright also realized that memory is unstoppable once it starts to flow:

Wow! What flashbacks this has brought on. I know there is a lot but the more I wrote, the more came back to me. How did this experience affect the person and life as I live it now? I'm not too sure. I still look for and enjoy the wilderness, live almost as a hermit. I hate what has become of the wonderful wild places. I think I pretend that I still live in Africa. Most folks who come to my home call it Little Africa. We say that we are going to America when we have to go to town. I have no trust of government, no faith in owning land ... Ndola, on the Copperbelt, even stranger names, Lusaka, Mufulira, Chingola, Kitwe – sometimes when I'm driving, long distance mostly, here in the States, I say those names out loud, the Zulu ones as well, and all the names of towns in Swaziland where I lived later as a young man.

Several years ago I was expounding to young researchers about the fact that people didn't really understand the nuances of colonial communities and a young man (now an eminent professor) said, "You know, Pam, you really ought to publish all this before ..." then he stopped, blushing copiously. The only possible comment was, "Before I die, or before I loose my marbles?" With all the charm of youth he replied, "Well, either, really!" I stashed that away and am doing it now. Fortunately, other people are writing too and self-publishing is addressing the problem of commercial publishers' insistence that there is no interest in colonial memoirs. There isn't space to do justice to the books that have appeared in the past few years, but there is a list of those I know in the bibliography – the trouble is that it is dominated by the PA and the Police – reinforcing that old assumption that they *were* the Empire. I wish there were more from miners, railwaymen, farmers and traders. The memories are there, but they are fading fast.

Pulled back by the senses

Many who wrote to me expressed the conviction that in some way the country had worked its way deep down inside them, often drawing on the familiar metaphor of its dust still circulating in their blood. Others say that their heart, like Livingstone's, was left there – Merfyn Temple actually entitled his memoirs *Zambia Stole my Heart*. In an email Colin Morris put it succinctly:

I have a theory that one can go out to Africa for a limited number of years and settle back into another society, but there is a kind of cultural watershed; if you stay on past it you will always have a sense of exile. That's how I felt anyway.

Alan Heathcote's memory is to do with orientation – he's certainly got a point about feeling the right way up south of the Equator:

Yes I have had a good life here in the UK, however there is always a part of me that is missing. First of all, I always function better in the southern hemisphere and secondly, a part of my heart is always in Africa. As soon as I land anywhere in Africa I have arrived home for Africa, especially Central Africa, is my home and will always be so. You see, the problem that I have living in the UK is that I have no roots ... I believe that to make one's loved ones understand, one has to take them to Africa so that they can experience it for themselves.

Skatie Fourrie expresses a complex attachment:

Nkana still resonates deep within me, if you grew up on the copper mines, you would take this country deep inside. It's a passion that you will only appreciate by having been there, it played such an important part in our upbringing, running around barefoot, where our unique winter months blend into our summer months. Profound memories have stored a picture in my mind. Can you remember that welcome rumble in the distance, it's the North-Wester from the Congo bringing a sigh of relief, it was a sign that our 'felo de se', a period during our suicide months in October through to November, was over. The rumble cast a blessing over our fertile soil for a near as perfect rainy season, where the smell of the earth wafts in the brisk mornings after each shower.

David Gray's memory is also highly sensuous:

I yearn for that period of my life which has gone for ever, a period when the musty damp overcast rainy season ended and that magic period of crisp Autumn, Winter and Spring days came round. I am not so fond of the swirling dusty whirlwinds of early Summer and the brazen skies and oppressive heat of October, but even then there were special things that I recall – the singing cicadas in the trees, the wonderful colours of dormant trees bursting into leaf ahead of the rainy season, the flying ants and the smell of those first drops of rain on the parched earth. I long for that stable world where everything appeared to be under control. I can do without the social climbing of small mining town life though! It was a wonderful experience growing up in Central Africa. Where else could I have watched my Uncle Wyn making wagons in his blacksmith shop in 1948 and a mere 20 years later listen to the radio broadcast of the moon landing?

Stuart Maclean has mentioned that the flowers of his Spanish garden remind him of Central Africa making him feel at home there, Aviva Ron decorated the cake for her mother's 90th birthday in Israel with sunflowers that remind her of their farm outside Ndola. Scent, not just that of flowers, is particularly evocative. It is to do with the immediacy of the limbic system making smell-cued memories more emotional than others. (Fernyhough, 2012 p.55). A waft can take one back with a shudder, seizing one unexpectedly.

Fort Jameson where I started school ... was beautiful – high in the hills, with jacaranda trees. The smells of those trees and rain on dry earth – and the tar when they did our main street – stay with me to this day. Rob Wilson

The smell of the charcoal burners and the way the smoke used to be in three layers through the bush... the smell of the earth after the first rains, we used to get in the car and drive the dirt roads then. The smell was like the earth being reborn, no other smell will ever be as good. Derek Dutton

How will I ever forget the sweet smell of dagga ...? George Tokarczyk

Vapourising petrol, meat grilling in the open air, acacia pods, frangipani and, over and over again, rain on baked earth ... But the scents that take one zooming back to one's youth are not all conventional:

The smell of paraffin, will always remind me of the tiny fridges that were placed in all the mine houses. The smell of sulphur, brings back vivid memories of the slag being poured on the dump and its stark beauty at night as it ran in red rivers down the dump. John Tyne

The smell I remember from those years is "Formalin". Gosh, when my dad came home at the end of the day he smelt of formalin from preparing corpses for burial. We even had our family car sprayed black so that it could double as a mourning car for the bereaved families. Faith Bentnall

Prompts to sensuous memory can also be vicarious. Shaun Marcus wrote from Israel:

Last night watching oldies on TV I saw "Out of Africa" – again, far more times than I have hair on my head. Although it is not NR/Zambia, it is the closest I have ever come to seeing a movie that reverberates so strongly and wakens my African past.

He is not the only person who mentioned the effect that film can have. Few who have lived in Africa remain dry-eyed during the soliloquy, "If I know a song of Africa ... does Africa know a song of me?" In the book the passage occurs when Blixen is musing about the fate of a hand-reared bushbuck that sometimes appears in her dreams – she is acknowledging that Africa could haunt her back in Denmark. Few of us are like this all the time, it would be pathological if we were immersed in longing for former times, but occasional remembering helps us reflect upon our previous incarnations and where we are now. Rod Madocks, the son of a senior member of PA, is now a full-time writer:

There is nothing outwardly to connect me to Africa now. I am middle-aged, settled, living a suburban life in the English East Midlands. I rarely shift from my habitual round. I have not left the country in fifteen years. Speaking to my neighbours, I am culturally and linguistically indistinguishable from them. But in reality, internally, Africa continues to beat within. I still dream sometimes of red earth, hot sun and the black shapes of animals moving in the tall yellow grass. I still hear the insistent three beats of the hoopoe's call. That sound was an insistent motif right through the long hot afternoons of my childhood. How I used to dream then of growing up to be a game ranger – tough, self-complete, at one with nature and armed to the teeth!

Africa seems to have given me an independence of spirit. I tend to sort things out with little recourse to others. I assume that the police or the law will not help me and if I am threatened my first reaction is to fight it out myself. I am alert for predators. I do not see the world as essentially beneficent. I am observant and watchful of strangers and judge people by their actions rather than by received ideas. Africa taught me that life could be short. As a child I had seen how people could die quickly by animal's tooth or by the hand of man. My first memory is of running away through long grass while my dog stood up to a marauding leopard. My second memory is of being stoned by a crowd of Africans while in my parents' car.

When I was young the turmoil of leaving Africa was more apparent. I fought my peers at school. If I had weapons to hand I would use them. I had no time for elaborate English game playing. I said "ja" instead of "yes" – it took 5 years to lose that accent or to have it beaten out of me! In my teens and twenties, I remained restless. I travelled to the Mediterranean seeking hotter landscapes that reminded me of home. I went to live in Texas, USA for a while for the same reason. Eventually the restlessness died down. Time and circumstances mired me in one area of England or maybe I just decided that one place was as good as any. I remained adventurous and self-reliant though. I sought adventure in a

smaller way, took life risks, lived a rackety life, rode motorcycles and hung out
in Caribbean neighbourhoods because I felt at ease with black people.

Reminiscing and reuniting

Memories are crafted and few modern theorists believe that they are like things
wrapped in tissue paper, stored in a trunk, waiting to be unpacked by posterity,
not even if posterity is oneself grown old. Unless memories are maintained
they crumble and become useless, but they do not resist transformation – they
are embroidered, pruned and polished as they are adapted to current needs. As
Fernyhough (2012) insists, memory is narrative – our memories are just a lot of
random bits until they are used to tell a story.

Whilst reminiscing is not quite the same thing as remembering, it is closely
related. Whereas remembering can be painful or emotionally neutral and may
come unbidden, reminiscence is a deliberate interaction with the stuff of the
past; it has some kinship with the idea of evocation and is always prompted by
the sentiments of the present. An element of loss and yearning is often involved,
some wondering about what might have happened if circumstances had been
different, or alternative choices made. People have always turned over their
stories together, quibbling about some events, nodding in agreement over others
but, as we have seen, moving to a new place involves an absence of people who
care about one's past – to tell strangers a story one needs to explain too much
background and, even when one has done that, there is no leap of recognition.
Jan Knott put it very well:

I went to University of Oregon to study architecture and worked summers in
the local cannery. The people who worked there said I was the biggest liar they
had ever met. I was only reminiscing about my youth and it was all true.

So, to avoid being thought a bore or a fantasist, people learn to keep quiet,
but that doesn't mean that they are integrated. Val Kenning, who had often been
unhappy at boarding school in UK, told me that avoiding mentioning Northern
Rhodesia meant keeping her memories of her parents and her home locked away
inside her. So it isn't surprising that people form associations and hold reunions
to remedy this sense of alienation. It is also not surprising that colleagues and
neighbours are not interested in hearing about the glories of Central Africa –
their only role could be that of audience, hence the common accusation that old

colonials are old bores! But one is never accused of being a Whenwe at a reunion.

The Northern Rhodesia Police have maintained their distinctive identity and never allowed their networks to erode. Martin Linnette's enthusiasm for the NRPA is characteristic:

We have a very active Association in the UK, in South Africa where I am, and indeed right across the world, almost 50 years after NR became independent. Although ex-police guys spread all over the world, many in other police forces, the military, law and security functions, their huge experiences and responsibilities at an early age in NR made an unforgettable impression on all of us, and has left us with a tremendous camaraderie after all these years.

Unlike almost any other similar ex-colonial association, we still have an excellent rapport with the current Zambia Police, whose Commissioner and various other high ranking officers have been honoured guests at the UK annual reunions. Many ex-NRP members and families were treated royally by the ZP when they returned to Zambia in 2004 for the 40th celebration. We have an on-going fund to provide educational grants to the children of ZP officers killed on duty, and a good relationship with the Zambian Ambassador in London, who will attend the 50th celebration at the UK Arboretum where the NRP recently erected a memorial. The bi-annual NRPA magazine 'Nkhwazi' has a fund of information and stories about life in NR with many photographs, as does the British & Commonwealth Museum in Bristol, which holds a great deal of ' stuff ' from NRP members...

Africa's in my blood – after early retirement at 55 and then 10 years running a B&B in Cornwall, numerous holidays in South Africa to see a sister-in-law and friends, I fell in love with Somerset West, emigrated at age 67. Met up with many old ex-NR coppers down here, regular lunches and a support group. I hope to return to Zambia for the first time for the 50th celebrations if funds permit. The time in NR/Zambia was by far the best time of my life – it was amazing in many ways, the country, lovely people of all colours, the wildlife, the adventures, incredible responsibility at a ludicrous young age, the sport, the weather, the travel – not everyone was a nice person, but there were no BORING people!

Mark Tanner, another member of NRPA who has been rather longer in the Cape agrees:

We meet only a few times a year, yet after over 40 years we still enjoy a communal sense of being. Our shared experiences bring us together – an 'esprit de corps' if you will, and this incredible bond grows ever stronger as time passes .... My time in NR will always be for me a time of magical learning about life and death, people and problems etc. I grew up very quickly there! While it is a pleasure to reminisce, we happily moved on with our lives, keeping up with all the developments around us. It was a good feeling to have experienced the 'last of colonialism' and to share experiences with new friends. It was a good feeling to have worn a police uniform and to have been a member of Her Majesty's Overseas Colonial Police Force!

When he was editor of *Nkhwazi* Malcolm Flower-Smith became particularly aware of the desire of former NRP officers to ensure that they retain not only their identity but also their cohesion, though the "Valete" list gets longer with every issue of the newsletter:

Since retiring from the Army I edited the Northern Rhodesia Police Association's bi-annual newsletter for 7 years and was struck by the fact that even after almost 50 years there is a great nostalgia for the country and the life we all led in those far off days of our youth. It is amazing, too, the friendships that have endured. The letters recounting incidents of our lives in NR and the present interest in the activities and achievements of old colleagues and friends all demonstrate the enormous esprit de corps and comradeship that was developed and built up in the Northern Rhodesia Police. There is, too, always a good turn out to funerals of former colleagues. It was a Force you can be proud to say you served in.

When members of the NRPA went to Zambia for the 40th Anniversary of Independence, they were hosted by the Zambia Police at the Training College at Lilayi, where they all would have received their initial induction into the service. They took with them the gift of reconditioned instruments for the Zambian Police Band; members also make regular donations to charities, support Sakeji School and have personal friendships with the current officers. Paul and Gill Wheeler "adopted" a senior officer as an honorary granddaughter. Beyond this, the NRPA is concerned with the current standing of the police in colonial history; they know that many forces have a far from uncontroversial record, hence the memorial to the force at the National Memorial Arboretum in Staffordshire. Members of the NRPA often refer to each other as "a band of brothers" and there is considerable affection and solidarity between them as well as recognition that their shared past constitutes the basis of an enduring identity.

Former District Officers do not have an association as such, but all belong to the *Overseas Service Pensioners Association*, which holds regular events and publishes a newsletter, and most also belong to the *Zambia Society Trust*. In the 1960s, former Northern Rhodesians in the United Kingdom set up the *Zambia Society* with the purpose of keeping in touch with developments in the country. In 1991 this became the *Zambia Society Trust* to raise funds for poverty relief, health care and children's charities, circulating news from Zambia and maintaining contact with the Zambian High Commission in London, where it holds its meetings. A peripheral benefit is that it keeps like-minded people together in fund-raising activities such as the annual golf tournament run by Frank McGovern – a former committee member (and DO) slyly confided that, in his opinion, its major function was to allow retired District Officers to go on feeling they were still doing something useful.

Additionally, the PA are the backbone of a reunion group that organises luncheons in UK and formerly published a newsletter. As years go by and members dwindle, these various groups are becoming less exclusive – so OSPA is now happy to recruit Associate Members who merely have an "interest" in the colonial service and the reunion luncheons are becoming less PA dominated, attended by a wider range of people with connection to Northern Rhodesia/ Zambia than in the past. When a return trip to Zambia to celebrate 50 years of Independence was mooted by Hugh Bown, a former District Commissioner, there was considerable enthusiasm. When elderly people contemplated the logistics of the journey (especially in the light of BA's recent withdrawal of the only direct flight from London) numbers dwindled and in the end only a few were there to represent the past.

Many of the Northern Rhodesians in South Africa reunite in pan-Rhodesian groups, focusing on the plight of white pensioners in Zimbabwe; Skatie Fourie, a former Copperbelt miner, is a leading figure in the *Flame Lily Foundation, Cape Peninsula*, which does charitable work, particularly relief for pensioners in Zimbabwe, but also organises social gatherings.

Then there are informal reunions. Brian Townsend gives a flavour of these:

If you meet a friend from Lusaka or Ndola, no matter how many years later, the reaction is always the same. It is as if you haven't seen them for only a couple of months. The greeting usually goes: "Hey! How have you been? What've you been doing? Do you fancy a beer?" ... Even better is the strange feeling that nothing has changed in our relationships for 50 years! Naturally there is a lot of, "Do you remember?".... "When we were ten feet tall and bullet-proof." Phil Edwards started it all in 1987. We had just made contact with each other in Johannesburg and he invited me to his fortieth birthday party, slyly suggesting that there might be a few people there that I knew. He was not kidding! 75% of our Form 2 Gilbert Rennie class, 75% of the school band, plus a number of the girls from Jean Rennie. Somehow, from then on, we have managed to stay in contact with most of those people and have added many more to the list.

Aviva Ron refers to the reunions of the globally distributed NR/Z Jewish community, mentioning both informal gatherings and a *Zim-Zam Ndaba* in Israel:

We are in contact with many members of the Jewish community of the Copperbelt – Michael Galaun is still in Lusaka, but Prof Mark Lowenthal from Ndola (his father Abe Lowenthal was mayor of Ndola) now lives in Beersheba and we see them frequently. I am in very close contact with Belle Zemack (now Amoils) from Luanshya, Ndola and then Lusaka – she lives in Jerusalem. Also in touch with Leon Favish from Mufulira – his son lives in my building...

Virtual reunion

Reunion groups have been joined by their virtual counterpart – groups that never meet in person but interact constantly. *The Great North Road* was an early site that recruited a large number of members globally, it's main function was to reunite people, but it was also a repository of stories and photographs – it closed down when its interactive section became acrimonious. To some extent it has been replaced by the smaller site, *Northern Rhodesians and Zambians Worldwide.*

Social media, in the form of *Facebook* groups, have gained greater significance as sites of reunion activity – their obvious advantage is their interactivity and immediacy, but their disadvantage is their ephemeral nature; comments slide into history, difficult to find again. The *Northern Rhodesia and Zambia Group* is the largest of these (with a current membership of over 4,000) but towns and schools have their own smaller Facebook groups constructed from dispersed European populations, together with a sprinkling of current residents of all races. Joining the group of a town one has lived in can be a strange experience, one literally re-encounters people one once knew – it is not a question of catching up with the old people they have become, the way one might at a physical reunion, but rather of meeting again the young people that they once were. Names of teachers are traded, old photographs are displayed and people rarely write about the present, other than to bewail instances of decay. Relics are scanned and posted on these websites, becoming exhibits in a virtual museum, serving as prompts for shared reminiscence. A trivial thing sparks an international conversation, but one set in a tiny town long ago.

The cliché often employed by new recruits to these town and school sites is that to scroll down through comments is to "walk down memory lane"; it is not rare to find entries saying that people had sat up into the small hours of the morning transfixed by the names of people they thought they had forgotten. An outsider, however, would find little with which to reconstruct the towns of the past – disloyal I may be, but the Broken Hill/Kabwe site tells me what I did not fully appreciate – that, though we may have had a lot of friends and parties, we led spatially confined and culturally restricted lives. We simply don't have a lot to remember! There are few mementoes from that time and when pictures are shared, sometimes recognition comes hard, even of oneself. We borrow the recollections and mementoes of others and gradually an authorised version emerges – this applies everywhere, but in the case of a diaspora the museums and archives are few, as are the junk shops and attics.

Going Back

Though many enjoy recreating these virtual communities that go back in time, there is less enthusiasm for physical return to the country. When I asked people whether they had been back recently or had any thoughts of doing so many would not countenance the thought of a return, saying that they wanted to remember the country the way that it was before Independence. But in the course of my research other people have asked about the practicalities of revisiting Zambia; they are not just worrying about safety and logistics but whether, as former colonials, they will be welcome. I think there is also the question of what one can do on a day-to-day basis in a place where one once lived and worked – once one has severed ties and has no purpose, a formerly familiar place can seem more alien than a tourist destination.

People are, however, going back and owners of guest houses in Zambia tell me they have noticed an increase over the past few years in the number of elderly tourists making a sentimental return "home", often bringing their spouses and adult children in the hope that these may better understand not only the emotional pull of the country but also who one is. For some, a casual decision to holiday in Zambia can change the direction of life at home. Margaret de Lange says:

In 1966 we came to Canada and got on with the job of settling into a new country and raising a family. We never really dealt with the whole issue of why we were here, sort of shut it out of our minds. Then in 2003 we went to Northern Rhodesia [sic] mainly because the GNR had planned a reunion in Livingstone. My younger son and his wife came with us. It was a turning point in our lives, as though once again we were able to embrace all that we were and had been. In the past five years we have become more 'Rhodesian' than we have ever been. It was as though going back opened the flood gates to a part of us that had been shut away and hidden for so long. I have developed a passion for history and have built up an extensive library of Rhodesiana, books and magazines etc. Trying to find out the 'why', maybe.

After making the trip to the Victoria Falls and taking in a game reserve (if they are very wealthy), many people have a-typical itineraries. They are strange tourists who include visits to government offices, schools and suburban houses – perhaps we might think of them as secular pilgrims. Roger Marston mentions his reactions on returning to an unusual holiday destination:

I did the nostalgia trip in 1998 when I took the "kids" back; they had little memory of Zambia and were stunned to see Solwezi. They thought it was primitive, whilst I was astonished at the progress made: electricity, TV, Supermarket with in-store bakery, tarred roads, copper mine working again and so on.

Rose Heesom was delighted with her return in 2014:

My sister, Barbara, her husband Paddy and I have just returned from the most amazing two week visit to Zambia – the first time back in 48 years! We had the best time and loved every second of it. Yes, of course much was in a state of disrepair, the urban roads were a nightmare, but that was made up for by the marvellous spirit of the Zambian people – friendly, welcoming, obliging, gentle, polite.

We stayed in Ndola from where we visited Luanshya, Kitwe, Chingola, Mufulira. We visited the hospitals where we were born, were invited into two of our old homes, were given guided tours around the schools we attended, welcomed at our churches, even visited the police stations where Dad was stationed. Nothing has changed in all the above, most of the buildings exactly the same, except it was plain to see that there is no money for repairs, the hospitals were spotless though.

The return can be very emotional but it is hard to put one's finger exactly on what is making grown men cry when they eventually return to the land of their youth. Mike Coetzee living in South Africa wrote:

I remarried in 1998 and although I tried to surprise my bride with a honeymoon on some far off exotic island, she had already made all the plans and reservations for us to spend our honeymoon in Zambia. My first trip back home was so nostalgic after years of pining and fretting. We drove there and when we pulled out of Broken Hill, heading towards Ndola, emotions got the better of me and I wept. Will anybody ever understand that feeling of coming home? We spent a whole week in and around Kitwe and all I could do was reminisce about better times. My new wife, Wendy, knew what N.R. meant to me and gave me the most beautiful honeymoon gift ever.

Trevor Snyman:

In June of 2007 I found myself standing outside the gate of number 29 Luapula Avenue, Chililabombwe. I entered the property, walked the 10 metres and the years rolled back. The lady of the house was taken aback by the appearance of a white man at the door, the back door through which I had entered and exited so many times. I explained that I had lived in the house 44 years ago, and asked to be allowed to have a look around. It seemed so familiar, as if it were only yesterday that I stood in the lounge. My bedroom, with the cupboard where I once hid from my parents and the call to dinner, the window through which I used to climb, now sadly barred with burglar guards. Outside the mango grove still stood, now as a few single, large trees... The view over the road to the main north-south road to the Congo, the bush, all so familiar that I ached to have the happy times all over again.

... the Kamenza Koppie seemed smaller, the distance from the shopping centre to Luapula Avenue, from Luapula Avenue to the grounds of the Bancroft Primary

School, shorter. The school itself, now the Kamenza Basic School, had hardly changed in 44 years... I visited the school and the Headmaster, Mr. Mwinga, was delighted that a pupil from more than 40 years before, had returned.

But no single experience has stayed with me as vividly, and with such a persistent longing in my heart, as has the simple visit to number 29 Luapula Avenue, Chililabombwe. I cannot shake off how I felt when I stood in my old bedroom. It was as if everything that I had done in my life, as if what I have become, had all led to that point, as if it was a place where I could take stock. It has proven to be one from which I am having difficulty moving on. This is what the little town in the little, insignificant African country means to me.

Johnny Holden says:

My wife (from Zimbabwe) and I find we are drawn back more and more to Africa as we age. At first we couldn't get away far enough with all the political strife and roamed the world trying to find somewhere we could belong and feel at home. We tried the UK, Australia, the USA, Kenya, and now realise that we are stateless. We don't fit into Africa anymore and can't identify with American or UK values. In Kenya the headmaster at the International School in Nairobi had a term for the kids of parents like us constantly on the move; he called them "third culture kids" defined by not identifying with a country, national anthem or sense of belonging. He came back to the USA to set up a school catering specifically for these kids. So here we sit in California, where the weather is about as close as we can get to that in Zambia, along with the same plants, hankering after Zambia but knowing we could never settle back there!

Diana Greyvenstein now living in South Africa wrote:

I once again spent 3 weeks with my daughter and son-in-law who reside in Ndola. Nigel, my son-in-law works for First Quantum, Ndola. To me Zambia is as beautiful as ever, albeit very African in the little towns and very run down. We travelled down to Livingstone passing through all the little towns on the way. [Diana then went on to describe horrified encounters with large insects to conclude] *... We gathered for breakfast and definitely decided that the bush life was not for us. I had always longed for a home right in the middle of the bush, miles away from anywhere ... that was definitely cleared from my wish list. We all had a wonderful time in Livingstone and had accommodation at the Zambezi Sun. The atmosphere reminding me of the days in Luanshya, being waited on hand and* *foot most of the time! I certainly had and still have great affection for Zambia. It took me 15 years to get settled here. I am perfectly happy here now but just love to go back to Zambia and absorb the energy that I always feel so strongly there.*

Others take a more organized return visit, staying at game lodges and flying internally. Elizabeth and Jeremy Hawkins took the luxurious *Rovos Rail* trip from Dar es Salaam to Cape Town with stops in Zambia, but many like John Hyde stray briefly from the conventional itinerary. After a tourist view of Livingstone:

We spent the last three days of our trip in Lusaka; we walked a lot and visited my old school, Lusaka Boys, and walked up Birdcage Walk to Independence Avenue and visited Min. of Fin. where my wife used to work. I was very impressed with all the verges as they were well kept with no rubbish lying around. We also went to the Theatre Club (I think they still had the same furniture from 1972!) On the Monday I managed to rent a car and we did a lot of driving. Cairo Road was one big traffic jam. We drove to my old house that my dad built in 1955 and he would have been so proud as the house is now a British High Commission residence. It really was a trip down memory lane for us and in hindsight I wish we'd spent more time in Lusaka. To sum everything up I still have Africa in my blood but I don't think I will ever live there again.

Many people left family graves in Zambia and visiting these can be poignant reminder of loss and abandonment. Graham Snow:

Went back to Lusaka in 1994. Visited my dad's grave (I cried!). Went to Kabulonga School. Kids were lovely! Lively, bit cheeky, but turned out in their uniforms better than any English school! I met the deputy head, Mr Mtewe. He was very suspicious when I entered his office, but when I explained my background he said, "You are a Zambian, an old boy, and you have come back!!!" It was strange getting back to Africa in 1994. The smell of the wood smoke, the air, the blue sky, I felt I had come home! Once an African, always an African!....even though I was born in Twickenham.

But there are those who have visited only to have their sense of exclusion reinforced. Ron de Kock drove up from Johannesburg:

I went back in July 2005. It was sad to see the deterioration of the streets between the houses in Nkana and the shoddy condition of the houses as well. The streets were better suited to driving in a 4 by 4 vehicle to negotiate the dongas. The worst sight was to see how the lovely Northern Rhodesian bush is being decimated for charcoal. It nearly broke my heart. My sister and I did manage to find our Grandparents farm and stand by our Oupa de Lange's grave to reflect on the lovely life we had there.

John Thompson warned one should not try going back to Kabwe:

Do not visit. I went back in 2006 ... You would not believe the state of disrepair and how filthy that quaint town has become. I don't believe any of the buildings have ever had a coat of paint for the last 40 years. You needed a 4x4 vehicle to navigate around the pot holes. Vendors everywhere, blocking the streets. When parking you had to pay the louts on the street to look after your car or it would be vandalized. It depressed me no end. The street to KGVI was barely passable. My heart would not let me take a look at the school, I had to turn back!

I was there on my own sentimental first return the year after John Thompson and found the same town clean and quiet. It had lost its *raison d'etre* now that the mine was closed, but I thought the road to the school much as it had always been and the school itself full of enthusiastic youngsters. I even bought a T-shirt commemorating its 50th Anniversary, bearing its colonial name as well as the new one. Perception is everything – we see what we are looking for.

Alex Morrison feels that a visit has made him immune to the longing:

My wife took me back to Kitwe for my 60th birthday last year – the first time since 1971. Glad and sad I went – at least the 'I wonder what it is like now' is out of my system. Met up with a few old (now elderly) friends at the Jozi Jol this August and came away with the feeling that the story of NR/Z should not be lost.

There are many who toy with the idea of returning sometime, but usually confess it is probably just a dream. So we find, a woman who lives in London, combining wanting to revisit the place with wanting to go back to how things were in the past:

I would love to go back to Zambia (Livingstone to be exact) where I grew up – I have spent the past 40 years (since leaving Zambia at 15 years old) pining for a time of my life I will never have again... Livingstone instilled in me something that I have never been able to experience anywhere else... I have met with some special friends from those days, thanks to internet, and they all feel the same – we just want to go back to how things were then. None of us were from privileged backgrounds or families – we were just ordinary run of the mill kids – but oh how Zambia moulded our lives. We all felt the 'unfinished' part of our lives come back to life when we spoke of 'those days'.

Finally, a great many people would never go to Zambia on any account, for them any attachment is to dispersed friends and to past times; Northern Rhodesia has irretrievably gone and Zambia is no replacement. Their resentment about this is often very raw, even fifty years later. Robert Plain is outspoken:

Would I visit again? Never! I prefer to have good memories of Northern Rhodesia. Zambia is not the same and can never be. What we had was so special but it could never last. We were all just pawns used to enrich people abroad with serious money to make more money for themselves. In 1964 they and others in power abroad decided that handing power over to people who, a hundred years before, were a few locals roaming the bush, living a simple life, was a good idea. The natives were illiterate, hungry, had no use for money and did no real harm until explorers and missionaries came along to exploit the mineral resources and convert locals to Christianity.

So, that "sense of exile" that Colin Morris refers to can mean desire for contact, but it can also result in terrible rejection. Those who wouldn't countenance setting foot in Zambia are convinced that all change in the country is a matter of disorder and decay and they are ready with examples to prove their point. But wanting it to be as it was translates to wanting a return to a colour bar and a limited franchise. Facebook is the place to find unabashed comment about the inevitability of corruption in independent Africa; a lot of frustration is displaced into hating an order that excludes one. Of course things are not the same in Zambia as they were in Northern Rhodesia – that is what Independence was about.

Wanting to repay

By way of contrast with that outright rejection, there is the sense of indebtedness one finds in others. Liz Price is one of many who supports charities in Zambia:

It was a country that was very good to us as a family and we all have a soft spot in our hearts for the Zambian people. Yes, we were among the rich and privileged who lived there and we are well aware of that and today, in a small attempt to repay in some way all that we got from the experience, my husband and I are actively involved in fund-raising for a small children's home near Lusaka, and we hope that we can make a difference for a few Zambian children by our efforts.

Aviva Ron and other members of the Elkaim family visit Zambia regularly and feel a strong attachment to the country:

We don't want to be anonymous, we are too proud of our late father Hanania Elkaim and what he did for Zambia – he received the Order of Distinguished Service First Division from President Kaunda in 1990 ... He cared deeply about the country that gave a haven to Jews before the State of Israel was created and enabled him to financially help his family after they lost all when the Jews fled from Gaza in 1929.

We are going to visit the project we started in our father's memory in 2000. This is part of the Chisankano Barefoot School project in the campus of the Fatima Secondary School at Bwana Mkubwa, run by the Dominican Convent. Our project provides training in carpentry for boys and dressmaking and soft toys (sent to Switzerland) for the girls. The initial funding came entirely from our family, we added more in 2003, a WHO colleague gave a nice donation recently for the expansion to an agricultural school, and we will give more on our next visit for the agricultural school.

Shortly after his appointment in 2013 as Chairman of the Board of the WWF United States, Neville Isdell ensured that the needs of Zambia were firmly on the agenda. He and his wife Pamela donated $2million for wildlife conservation and tourism development in the country, Neville saying:

"This is not just about the money. It is a very emotional statement of what Zambia means to us. We both arrived in Lusaka with our parents in 1954, aged 10 and 8 respectively. We were educated in Zambia, married in Zambia. I played rugby for Zambia. Not only did we start businesses here but this is where I started my long career with The Coca-Cola Company. Zambia moulded us. This gift reflects that, plus our determination to help the people and wildlife live together in harmony for the benefit of all of Zambia." http://worldwildlife.org/stories/wwf-board-chairman-neville-isdell-brings-it-back-home

This is a sentiment many will recognise, though few can give so much. The protection of Zambia's wildlife gains a great deal of support, for example there are strong PA links into the Kasanka Trust, which manages the Kasanka National Park and the Bangeulu wetlands. Martin Field has been particularly involved with fund raising and is going back for the 50th Anniversary of Independence Others, like Allisdair Macdonald, who works for Western Cape Nature Conservation

Board; work in a private capacity in Zambia:

My brother Neil returned to Zambia about 12 years ago and I have visited Zambia 11 times since 1997, the reason always being to get into the Zambian bush. I have been in Nature Conservation all my life, having worked in special places in Namibia and South Africa, but there is nothing to beat the Zambian bush with its smells, aura etc. For the past 7 years I have been assisting my brother with the establishment and maintenance of a conservancy between Kasempa and Kaoma, and I am proud to say that our hard work has paid off, with the wildlife bouncing back, after being subjected to heavy poaching over the years, an activity which we have largely brought under control.

Going back for good

Only time will tell whether it is a pipe-dream or a real strategy, but increasingly people are talking about returning to live out their retirement in Zambia. A lengthy thread unwound on a Facebook site about the feasibility of setting up a retirement village and members speculated about medical care and property prices. We are looking at a fantasy of there being a "real" home one can return to in the place where one was young – the "myth of return" is a common theme in immigration studies. A few former European residents have gone back to Zambia, but so far it has been to work, rather than to see out their old age, among them is Priscilla d'Elbee who returned from France to take over her family farm at Chisamba and set up a chocolate making business

Things in common

There is an undoubted affinity between the people who once lived in the country. Christine Gird gives an example of the dispersal and the pulling back together:

Now we're Africa's scatterlings. In our family, I married a South African but now live in England with my son in Germany (and he has an American girlfriend). My sister married a Belgian from the Congo and lives in Durban, and my brother married a New Zealand girl and lives there, with his children born in Singapore and Australia. At family get-togethers it's a veritable United Nations!

It's amazing how many people you randomly meet who have their roots there – in a lift at Heathrow recently I had a brief conversation with an unknown man

who, it transpired, had been at Gilbert Rennie in Lusaka whilst I was at Jean Rennie – we had somehow instantly known we had a common background. In Newmarket's Waitrose I was pondering what sausages to choose and there was a black man next to me – we struck up a conversation and he instantly asked me if I had lived in Africa, and I knew straightaway he was Zambian. Across the races, the spirit of Africa never leaves you and you recognise it in others.

Chris Lyon of the NRP says:

Northern Rhodesia continued to resonate with us throughout our lives. To the mystification of our friends we would ask each other before going out "Have you got some ndalama?" or "Where is the PK?" We were always alerted by any mention of Northern Rhodesia/Zambia and if some new acquaintance at a party mentioned that he had been there then we would monopolise them for the rest of the evening. I was only in Northern Rhodesia for 6 years but Africa is in my blood.

In the end, what people really miss is not anything in particular but the life in general – we are people who often forget to put on our shoes, who don't show a great deal of surprise when there are power cuts, who think little of driving long distances. After leaving, some people contrive to find similar opportunities wherever it is they settle, others embark on a lifetime of looking backwards and recrimination. Noel Wright now settled in Perth, Western Australia, after remembering the importance of amateur dramatics he wrote:

Another thing on that list would be the bush, which we'd often head for when we wanted a break. Game parks became favourite haunts, and wild life photography a hobby. We took up camping again after we got here and found the WA bush interesting in its own way, but tame by comparison. The coast was more fun. We could fish from a dinghy. Then we discovered coral reefs and snorkelling, and that brought back the excitement of entering a world of exotic and colourful creatures where all sorts of discoveries were waiting to be made and where you had to be alert and observant to make them, just as in a game park. The underwater realm may seem a universe away from land-locked Zambia, but I believe the delight it gives us stems from the interest in the natural world that Zambia fostered. For that and the other good things in my life I can trace back to Zambia I'll be for ever grateful.

A person can probably only be an exile from one place at a time but "home" isn't necessarily the place one started out from, it's the place that has insinuated itself into one's very being; there is no rule that one has to love it, just to have the feeling that something is adrift.

The best writers with a colonial background catch this sense of being exiled from a place that they cannot definitively claim as their own, even if they were born there. Albert Camus' uneasy love for Algeria pervaded much that he wrote, though he is referring to Algeria, his description of sunlight and dryness transport me straight back to Zambia and when I feel confined in dreary Britain I easily relate to his stark statement that, "... one can yearn for space and the beating of wings". But Camus is in trouble in critical circles (Carroll, 2007) for the same reason as former Northern Rhodesians sometimes find themselves in trouble – the colonial heritage is an uneasy one, demanding constant apology, but we are not always ready to give it. I am not at all sure that many of us really want to wash that African dust out of our blood.

11. TOWARDS THE END

In September 2013 I received an email from Heather Hunt who lived on a farm south of Kabwe, she'd been told about my project by her sister, Noreen Emslie, in Australia, who had been informed about it by another former resident of Kabwe. Heather was born in the Broken Hill Mine Hospital in 1939 and introduced herself saying:

I now have the dubious honour of being the oldest (white) woman born in Broken Hill!

She told me that a few "old timers" were putting together a collection of stories and that she was contributing to it, although she was hoping to come to live in Britain soon. It came as a surprise to me that someone of her age, who had lived her whole life in the country, was planning to leave – I had assumed that all the leaving had been done a long time ago and that any Europeans from the colonial era who were still in Zambia were there for good. I kept thinking about her, wondering how she could possibly adjust to life in Britain. After a few days I wrote and asked whether, if I came to Zambia, I could interview her. It would be a unique opportunity to talk to someone who was on the cusp of a new life.

People in Britain don't usually just pop over to Zambia to chat to someone they have never met and I knew it sounded like a bizarre request, but fortunately, Heather was enthusiastic and asked me to come and stay at the farm. I pointed out that she might not like me, so I'd better come for just one night, but we got on just fine and she suggested I stay longer to meet some more of Kabwe's non-African community – not newcomer NGO personnel but long term residents, mostly in farming or trading, mostly settled but some wondering how to move on.

Heather's husband, Des, came from a farming family and he had been granted the land in 1941. When they married in 1957 they built the farmhouse and other buildings (making the bricks first), they dammed a stream to create a reservoir and were some of the most progressive farmers in the area, changing their main crop between tobacco, wheat and coffee according to demand. Unlike most farmers around Kabwe, they had no thought of selling up at Independence, they took Zambian citizenship and tackled emerging labour problems by working with the local branch of UNIP. Heather was Chair of the Kabwe Farmers' Association and in that capacity became the only woman member of the national

Commercial Farmers Bureau. A few years ago, with Des' health failing and a run of bad luck – a dam wall giving way at a time when water was scarce and a poor coffee harvest – they decided it was time to sell to a Zambian company and join their daughters in the UK. The purchasers gave them the right to live in the farmhouse for as long as they wished and Heather was still there, two years later – waiting for the final settlement on the purchase price of the farm. She says that the delay was in many ways a good thing as Des never wanted to leave the farm – he died there and is buried there; thousands of people attended his funeral and five villages sent choirs to sing for a good man who had stayed true to his farm and his country.

Heather was absolutely adamant that more white commercial farmers could have stayed, that there was a place for them, saying "They will tell you their farms were taken away from them, they were not taken away from them." She acknowledged that unrealistic expectations had made many people look longingly at the European-owned farms, prompting attacks on property and stock that caused owners to give up, but she argued that a way could be found through. For Heather the crunch came with her husband's illness. Born in Zambia, citizenship was an issue, but eventually she traced a link that gave her an Irish passport and new nationality.

The farm was beautiful and I couldn't begin to imagine how difficult I would have found it to leave after a lifetime there. Behind the house were rock outcrops with bushman paintings and the scene was dominated by the man-made lake (and how rarely one knows who the man was when that is said). It was Zambia as one dreams about it, but Heather was looking forward to leaving, delayed only by the fact that the purchaser had not yet paid in full and there was a legal case pending. She felt that she was living in waiting, there was no farm work to do, Des was gone, her daughters were in Britain and her sisters in Cape Town and Australia – it was her time to move.

A few weeks after I met Heather her house was broken into, she was violently attacked and left tied up; everything of value stolen. Still incredibly strong, she refused to be panicked into leaving, pursued her case for settlement of payment for the farm, put the assault and burglary into the hands of the police. People of all races in Kabwe were outraged, but, though there was good evidence who had perpetrated the attack, the suspect was released. It was the final straw, there is always a final straw – Heather came to Britain in July 2014.

As I write Heather has been in Britain for two weeks and is about to embark upon finding a home of her own. She left behind the place where she was born, where she was married, where her children were born and grew up. She leaves the farm that she and her husband built up and where there were heartbreaks as well as successes. She leaves the family graves too but she is one of the least sentimental people I have ever met and she has no regrets.

12. CONCLUSION

This book has been about the European relics of a country that was governed (indirectly) from Britain for just forty years but has been Independent for fifty. Currently rather a lot of histories of the British Empire, the end of empire and the post-colonial era are being published in the United Kingdom but, time after time, Northern Rhodesia does not figure, or it just gets a paragraph or two in relation to Federation. When I pitched to academic publishers in Britain and America regarding this project, I invariably was told they could not see a market for a book about Northern Rhodesia and its European population. (I'd never had a book proposal rejected before.) We need to confront why Northern Rhodesia's remnants are not "interesting" – I suspect it is because the years of British rule were remarkably short of scandals and violence and the Independence struggle was relatively peaceful and swift. The country does not fit either of the current stories about imperialism – there are too few atrocities and land grabs to satisfy the anti-colonialists and there is too little glory for the revisionist imperial historians. Another reason for Northern Rhodesia's relative obscurity is that it was largely a working class colony, heavily reliant on South African white labour – there were no glamorous aristocrats and none of the "society" goings-on of Kenya's Happy Valley.

Members of the Overseas Service Pensioners' Association are indignant about what they refer to as the "postcolonial cringe" and former officers have become defensive about their careers in the light of postcolonial critique. They are aware of the light that has been shone on the British handling of the Mau Mau uprising in Kenya, particularly the massacre at Hola Detention Camp (Elkins, 2005) and feel that the reputation of colonial services across the board has been tarnished. It does not help when a newspaper article revealing that colonial files were selectively destroyed before the handover of power is irrelevantly illustrated with a picture of police guarding Mau Mau suspects (Cobain, 2013).

John Orr-Ewing wrote:

Despite the talk you hear of repression etc. by the colonial system – I have absolutely no shame whatsoever about our time in NR – and I don't recognise that sort of a description at all.

At a joint seminar of The Overseas Services Pensioners' Association and

The Institute of Commonwealth Studies of the University of London, Jonathan Lawley commented:

'Colonialism' became a dirty word and we did not get the recognition for the immense achievement of bringing these countries into the modern world, into the Commonwealth. That is one of the great preoccupations of many of the people here in this room today. (OSPA, 2013 p.73)

As I said in the Introduction, I maintain that imperialism was an inevitable historical stage and do not believe it displays any different mixture of goodness and evil from preceding or succeeding eras. I also believe that the people living in the colonies were no more implicated in the system than those staying at home – imperialism was one continuous system that unfolded according to historical principles. As to whether the empire was "a good thing", well, the balance sheet certainly lists benefits as well as costs to colonised peoples, but it could never be a sustainable system. How could a population be expected to accept second class status in its own country? How could people not desire autonomy or equality of opportunity? Recently, when talking to the widow of a Provincial Commissioner I remarked that I felt that, "On balance, we probably did more good than harm in Northern Rhodesia" – she rounded on me indignantly, "What an incredible thing to say! Of course we did!" I'm less sure than she is of that "of course", but I'm willing to concede it might have balanced out in the long run.

The British were in the country for the purpose of mineral extraction, rather than for any generous project of road and rail construction, health and literacy, but it is undeniable that they were the agents of change and benefits did accrue, though we should never forget the huge local labour input at low wages. I am neither a historian nor a political scientist – my interest is in social structures and cultural formations and this research has aimed to discover how the legacy of empire plays out for its agents. When Northern Rhodesia came into existence as a protectorate in 1924, India was already well ahead in mobilising for Independence – colonialism was always going to be a short-lived enterprise in Northern Rhodesia and, as the empire dismantled, the expressed task of the administration was to prepare the country for Independence. This message was not, however, transmitted to those Europeans recruited to perform more mundane functions who, thanks largely to Roy Welensky, gained the impression that Northern Rhodesia could become a stable settler colony. We need to wonder what interests benefitted from perpetuating this delusion.

There is an elephant in the room, the matter of race and empire. Those of us who were white in Northern Rhodesia know that we were in the front line of British imperialism and, embarrassing though it may be, we cannot pretend any longer that we are unaware of the presence of the elephant. We have to acknowledge that, as in all colonial territories, there was a terrible indifference to the routine racial indignities.

Throughout my research, people have expressed love of the Northern Rhodesian bush and its animals. Their concern for the current deforestation and depleted wildlife echoes their sadness at separation from the country of their youth and from youth itself. Several people have written to me admiringly about *Operation Noah*, recalling how as children they had donated their pocket money or people they knew had volunteered to save animals threatened by the rising Zambezi waters when the Kariba Dam was build; but no one expressed concern for the people whose homes were flooded. "The fate of the fifty thousand Tonga had hardly caused a ripple in the world's newspapers" (Howarth, 1961 p.162).

Thayer Scudder studied the impact on Gwembe Tonga people at the time of their removal and, decades later, wrote, "In spite of a commendable effort made by resettlement officials, the time available before the dam wall was sealed was inadequate… people too often were moved to ill-prepared sites at which they became dependent on food relief." (Scudder, 2005 p. 37) Prior to the move, there was a stand-off with the Northern Rhodesian Police Mobile Unit, resulting in eight Gwembe deaths and many more injuries; there were epidemics and deaths, particularly of children, in the resettlement villages to which people were transported. People who wrote enthusiastically about *Operation Noah* seemed not to know about this – as schoolchildren we were taken to wonder at the engineering miracle of the dam, but we were never asked to consider the plight of the people who were moved. There was terrible callousness.

No one can remain oblivious to the fact that Northern Rhodesia's was a racially divided society and though this division was not as fully institutionalised in law as in either South Africa or Southern Rhodesia, in daily life there was not only a *de facto* segregation for most people, there was also constant sanctioning of any transgression of the "colour bar". Macmillan & Shapiro (1999 p.167) quote Stanley Fischer (now Vice-Chairman of the US Federal Reserve System) as saying of his Mazabuka childhood, "Racism was rife, there was no social mixing, and the school was of course segregated". He continued, "I remember once organising a cricket game with some African children and being reprimanded by a passerby." Routine segregation was doubly institutionalised when Federation came into being – its first Prime Minister, Godfrey Huggins, defended segregation in Post Offices thus: "You cannot expect the European to form up in a queue with dirty people, possibly an old *mfazi* with an infant on her back, mewling and puking and making a mess" (Rotberg, 1965 p. 255). Concepts of pollution and purity underwrote the system and where there are concepts of inherent impurity, moral panics about sexual transgression are never far behind. Barbara Carr wrote of her revulsion for European men in relationships with African women, but it was European women she feared for; John Gornall (2008) devotes a whole chapter of his autobiography to the fate awaiting European women marrying African men, taking the example of one unhappy marriage to prove that such liaisons were inevitably doomed.

An important way of hardening out the racial divide was in the generation of a rich vocabulary of contempt – terms that were extended to stigmatise transgressive whites by association, "*kaffirs*" and "*kaffir boeties*". There were two contradictory systems and there was no middle way for most people. As former Vice-President, Grey Zulu says in his memoirs:

Many of the Europeans who were sympathetic to the African cause were deported by the colonialists. Those who remained in the country were isolated, despised, watched and followed by the Special Branch .... In spite of this cordon, some of our friends used to visit me. It was these people who inspired me to continue fighting for our freedom. These white friends were prepared to suffer deportation and loss of jobs because of their beliefs in oneness, and that human beings were the same, regardless of colour or race. (Zulu, 2007 p. 53)

Zulu is not exaggerating – one of the two friends he names is my father.

Equal contact across the racial divide was almost impossible and where it did exist it was predominantly elite, highly educated or independently employed Europeans who participated in multiracial initiatives. Richard and Barbara Hall of *The African Mail* were outstanding in giving an effective voice to the Independence movement, as were the pioneering broadcasters, Harry Franklin and Peter Fraenkel. Many members of the Jewish community were avowedly anti-racist, one thinks of Agnes and Raymond Radunski, Joe Behrens, Hanania Elkaim and, of course Simon Zukas, who was deported for his work in resistance to Federation. Some missionaries and priests were sympathetic to the nationalist cause, famously Colin Morris and Merfyn Temple also several Jesuits and White Fathers (Pére Claude Galmiche told me about hiding UNIP men in the dairy when the Mobile Unit came looking for them, plying the police with the famous White Fathers' hospitality), but many churchmen were firmly on the side of the *status quo*. Most critics of the regime found it wise to keep their heads down; I was surprised to learn from Neville Isdell that at Gilbert Rennie School there were radicals, including himself and Morris Szeftel and a few teachers.

Several officers of the Provincial Administration and the Ministry of Education, and even the police, worked quietly against white hegemony. There was a Liberal Party, headed by Sir John Moffat, the last European leader of LegCo. Additionally, the Governor nominated liberals as European "unoffical" members of LegCo and the Federal Assembly to serve "for African Interests" (there were also African "unofficals for African interests"). Sir Stuart Gore-Brown was a long-standing Northern Rhodesia nominee and Robert Moffat, a Mkushi farmer and descendant of the early missionary of the same name, was the member in the Federal house. The very notion of separate "African interests" is telling.

Readjusting Attitude

Grace Keith's (1966) book *The Fading Colour Bar* demonstrates the ways in which many European people started to adjust their views around the time of Independence (though many didn't) and Barbara Hall told me with amusement about acquaintances who had formerly been heartily opposed to Independence approaching her for introductions to African politicians and others of influence. When I was in Australia, Ian Bruggemann commented that it was interesting how many people now claimed to have been "liberals", when they seemed so thin on the ground then. Many former Northern Rhodesians changed their ideas when they were exposed to a wider world, expressing shame at the thoughtless racism infusing their youthful outlook on life. Ian Scott, who became a professor of Political Science in Australia and Hong Kong wrote that:

I don't think that my values were shaped by Northern Rhodesia – at least I hope not. I think that I was much more influenced by my time at UCRN and post-graduate work in Canada and I rejected the notions of racial superiority, gender inequalities and all the colonial nonsense that made up my childhood.

David Gray now living in Cape Town commented:

I can only conclude that I was incredibly ill informed and naïve. I had been brought up to believe that White rule would go on for ever, that the Native population were happy with their lot and had never had it better, that things were just fine for everyone and that common sense would prevent Britain 'giving away' the colonies. Gradually the awful truth dawned on me. World Politics did not have a place for elitist societies where colour determined position. I did not believe the stories of atrocities in South Africa and was brainwashed with the propaganda.

But one needs to consider how Europeans' belief in their own intellectual and cultural superiority was almost universal. James Scott, contemplating resistance to regimes in which large sections of the community are powerless, lists what he calls the "weapons of the weak"; these are, "Foot dragging, false compliance, flight, feigned ignorance, sabotage, theft and, not least, cultural resistance." (Scott,1987 p. 34) Those who still expound upon their first-hand knowledge of the "stupidity" of African people might pause to think that a subordinate who professed not to know how to do the simplest of tasks might well have been performing the politics of resistance. But the "weapons of the weak" can be two-edged swords. Elite Europeans who met educated Africans as equals did not experience the tactics of feigned incompetence, but many mineworkers and railwaymen who depended on their race for their supervisory roles experienced little else on a daily basis – their "knowledge" of the backwardness of Africans deepened.

The NRG publication *A Brief Guide to Northern Rhodesia* for 1960 contains accounts of initiatives emanating from the Legislative Council to address the question of race discrimination – it is paltry stuff about bringing in the Women's Institute and the like for consultations. LegCo set up a Central Race Relations Advisory and Conciliation Committee which, in September 1960, was responsible for a law banning exclusion from tea rooms etc. on grounds of race but, "Accommodation, bars and cocktail bars do not fall within the list of premises scheduled in the ordinance, and clubs are not affected." (p.112) This, just two years before African majority Government! The same publication reports that,

"Various measures to promote better race relations were considered ... these included the teaching of African languages in European secondary schools" (p.111) but nothing came of that. Nothing could come of it, the European schools were run by the Federal Government and the Northern Rhodesia Government had no influence over the curriculum – language teaching could have made such a difference; European schools taught nothing about African society at all.

In July 1963, when everyone knew the end of Federation was coming, Harry Franklin (then Director of Information and Broadcasting Services for Northern Rhodesia) wrote in the *Spectator*:

The Colonial Office regime was admittedly paternalistic and slow to move with the times, but it was well-meaning and would have moved much faster in the emancipation of Africans under the stimulus, both internal and external, of the new thinking of the last decade, had it not had the opposition of Sir Roy Welensky's United Federal Party in considerable power in the territories, and in complete power in the Federal Government. The white men's agitation for Federation and the British Government's imposition of it set the Africans into one black camp and the whites in another. That is the pattern now. It may change in time, but it need never have appeared.

Geraldine Mackey wrote:

Their lives ran parallel to ours, never touching, and once I went to boarding school we had very little contact with Africans. At age 18 I left Africa, without having had more than a simple conversation with an African, and with no knowledge of their languages. When we emigrated to Australia I spent 6 years working in an Introductory English Centre in Canberra. Having lived in Zambia, I could really enjoy interacting with lots of different nationalities. However, I was once asked to speak a little of the native language of Zambia, and I hardly knew a single word!

Racism in Northern Rhodesia was a vicious circle. Without Federation, whereby African and European affairs were so effectively separated, there might have been a different outcome; there might not have been a European exodus. But that is daydreaming.

Ian Mackenzie wrote from Zimbabwe, but he was referring to Zambia as well:

It is such a shame that so many clever and talented people have left Africa.

Had they all stayed and made their own contributions instead of taking their skills away it would have not suffered many of the hardships that came after independence.

Many people who have written to me have said that the "of course" racial attitudes that prevailed in Northern Rhodesia are now a great embarrassment to them. Ron Sayer, said that he wished there were some way he could apologise to people he had been so unthinkingly unkind to as a boy. A great many others, however, have no such compunction, sometimes they have transferred their blame for the ills of the world onto some other category of people, but often they continue to circulate pseudo-science, pictures, stories and "jokes" that perpetuate their ideology of white supremacy.

Writing the book

I wrote this book out of my sense of ambivalence about my colonial heritage and I decided that it really was time that I examined the colonial remnants. I was interested in the outcome of European people's separation from an imperial past, but I was a little surprised that they mentioned African people so very rarely; the more I read, the more I realised that social life was so segregated that, all these years later, many people wrote as if there were no Africans in Africa.

Research monographs usually have a chapter near the beginning dealing with "methodology" – a "how I did it and why I did it that way" chapter. I am not sure that what I have written is a research monograph, I have used rather a lot of the techniques of journalism – that is, I've grabbed whatever facts and opinions I could without being too fussy about standardisation and comparability. I do, however, believe that I have remained constant to the anthropological method of participant observation, albeit in a form appropriate to a dispersed population. The anthropologists who trained me all went to live in African villages (as I did myself) and, as well as collecting genealogies and mapping dwellings, they believed that one should absorb what it was to be a member of the community. Subjectivity is not a dirty word in anthropology – one strives to experience things like the people one is living with and to lay oneself open to their interests and emotions. It makes anthropologists want to understand why people think and act the way they do, with the basic assumption that most people act fairly rationally.

The European former residents of Northern Rhodesia, however, do not all live in one village so I couldn't go to live with them and keep my eyes and ears open, but it is possible to discover what people themselves think matters by writing to people, going to talk to as many as possible, joining their Facebook groups and reading the books they recommend. I have agued throughout that there was a wide range of different European people in Northern Rhodesia and that to generalise is to do violence to that diversity; "the whites" did not think in concert – culture is a range of possibilities, not uniformity. People in anthropology are using terms like "multimodal research" and "multi-site ethnography", I'm just saying I did a lot of things as best I could.

I intended to start by finding people I had once known but lost touch with, asking them to refer me to others and on *ad infinitum.* In the event, I did not. Searching for former acquaintances using *Google,* I stumbled on a site called *The Great North Road* that existed to reunite old Northern Rhodesians. At first I used it to contact a few people whose names I recognised and to follow contributions to the bulletin board, but it became obvious that I could contact everyone in the group, so I posted on the bulletin board saying what I was interested in and asking people to contact me – precisely one person did, and I'd known him from school. Some of the comments being posted on the site suggested that the administrator might fulfill his threat to close it down as it was becoming acrimonious; I realized that if I were not to lose this precious resource I had better act fast. The site did shut down.

As the site enabled me to send emails to named people, I sent out 1,056 individual emails, in November 2007 explaining that I wanted to gather people's experiences and feelings about living in and leaving Northern Rhodesia/Zambia. I'd pruned the total list of 4,333 to exclude those who were under the age of 10 at Independence and those who arrived after Independence. Replies started flowing in, some with masses of information but also many that just said that they were interested, they'd loved the country, yes, I could use their data and they'd get back to me. Everyone who wrote received an immediate reply and those who said they'd write later got another prompt five months later, then another if necessary. Initially 378 people replied, but more trickled in over the years. This was a good response – given that the site had started in 1995, it was likely that several members would have died and more would have changed their email addresses. People sent my message on – I received a deluge of writing about the country, some anecdotal, some in note form, some beautifully written. I received unpublished novels and memoirs, scanned articles and photographs; some long correspondences developed.

If I were sensible I would have said I had masses of "raw material", started doing content analysis and published then and there, however, I'd become so enthusiastic about the diversity of the people writing to me that a sort of megalomania set in. How would it be if I could contact more than just the people who joined a reunion site? It would be wonderful to get the impressions of the full range of society – there were no members of the prestigious PA so far and I was a bit thin on other professionals, too.

In March 2009 I took the opportunity to call on Bob Huntley in Carmell and Liz and John Price in Connecticut for informal interviews while in America for a conference. In May I went to Australia to meet a number of people from the GNR who had corresponded, then in October I went to Johannesburg and Cape Town to meet others. I wanted to see people who had moved to Australia and South Africa in their new context. (I would like to dispel any assumption that I had a research grant for all this travelling – I used temporary lecturing appointments at the National University of Singapore to fund the research and think with amusement of the man who wrote to say he would not give me any information about himself unless I shared the publication profits!)

I was told a new site, *Northern Rhodesians and Zambians Worldwide,* had been set up by Hartley Heaton to replace the dormant *Great North Road*, but decided against trying to blitz the entire membership, though I have used it to make contacts. In 2011 it carried a notice about the Salisbury reunion lunch, which had not hitherto advertised itself. I signed up for lunch and met more District Commissioners in one day than I'd encountered in my years in Africa. Ann Bailey, the new organiser, gave me her address list, and I sent out letters this time. The PA were wonderful in their response and their enthusiasm for the country was undimmed. Many wrote, some asked me to come to visit them so I went to talk with as many as I could. That year my husband and I combined our holiday with contacting more former Northern Rhodesians, going to Natal and Cape Town – Natal, particularly around Pietermaritzburg, was such an important destination that it could not be neglected. We stayed as often as possible in guest houses run by former Northern Rhodesians as we drove down to the Cape.

I kept a running database of respondents, with country of current residence, year (or sometimes just decade) of birth, year of arrival in Northern Rhodesia or born there, year of departure from the country. I joined Northern Rhodesian Facebook groups, which were valuable for revealing current attitudes. I carried out the usual bibliographic searches on Northern Rhodesia and people I had contacted often referred me to self-published works that would not otherwise have surfaced.

Finally, I used various British and Zambian government sources. The Zambian Central Statistical Office dug out their rarely consulted, encyclostyled copy of the 1961 Census of the "non-African" population – someone scanned it and sent it to me as an email attachment and it has proved invaluable. There are going to be gaps and mistakes, but the idea has been to catch as many facets as possible of this diminishing population. I have not quoted every one, that would be impossible, but I have absorbed everything. I have tried to suppress my opinions until this Conclusion, but inevitably my view prevails in the construction of an argument – I do not agree with everything people have said or written, but these are the people I grew up amongst and I think I understand where they are coming from. There is a poem called *Homeland* by Michelle Frost that many former Northern Rhodesians sent to me, it contains these lines: "An immigrant? A pioneer?/ You are no longer welcome here," and it concludes, "Never complete. Never whole. /White Skin and an African soul." But souls are not standardised.

Doris Lessing, a woman who understood the contradictions of Central Africa better than many wrote, *An African once said to me that, beyond all the white man's more obvious crimes in Africa, there was the unforgivable one that, 'Even the best of you use Africa as a peg to hang your egos on.'* (Lessing, 1982) Guilty as charged!

ABREVIATIONS AND LOCAL TERMS

AK2/AK3	Model of NRG housing.
ANC	African National Congress
AAC or Anglo	Anglo-American Corporation (a mining company)
BSAC	British South Africa Company
Cambridge	Cambridge University Ordinary-Level School Certificate
CUKC	Citizen of the United Kingdom and Colonies
DC	District Commissioner
DO	District Officer
Highers	Cambridge University Higher-Level School Certificate
HMOCS	Her Majesty's Overseas Civil Service
KK	Kenneth Kaunda
LDA	Learner District Assistant
LegCo	Legislative Council
LM	Lourenço Marques
M-Levels	South African Matriculation, introduced in Federal Govt Schools 1962
MLA	Member of the Legislative Assembly
NRG	Northern Rhodesia Government
NRP	Northern Rhodesia Police
NRPA	Northern Rhodesia Police Association
NR/Z	Northern Rhodesia through into Zambia
ORB	Overseas Resettlement Board
OSPA	Overseas Service Pensioners Association
PA	Provincial Administration
PC	Provincial Commissioner
PK	*Picannin Kia* (small house – i.e. latrine)
PWD	Public Works Department
RST	Rhodesian Selection Trust (later Roan) (a mining company)
TT	Tanganyika Territory
UDI	Unilateral Declaration of Independence (Rhodesia)
UFP	United Federal Party

UNIP	United National Independence Party
ZANC	Zambia African National Congress
Bioscope	Cinema
Boer	Afrikaner Farmer (extended to Afrikaners in general)
Boma	District Government Office (Swahili. Literally, a stockaded space)
Braai	Barbeque (From Afrikaans, *braaivleis* = grilled flesh)
Bwana	Sir (Swahili, from Arabic *abuna* = *father*)
Chachacha	Civil disorder & violence in Independence struggle (from the dance)
Chambusi	Latrine
Dagga	Cannabis
Dambo	Low lying marshy land that dries out in the winter months
Dona	Madam (from Portuguese)
Ghoghos	Insects
Jol	Party
Kapasu	District Messenger (Aid to DO or Chief, also a sort of rural policeman)
Katundu	Baggage, stuff
Kia	Dwelling
Kist	Chest (Afrikaans, particularly for a trousseau)
Koppie/kopje	Hill
Lumpers	Lump Sum – compensation, paid on termination of NRG employment
Makoro	Dug-out canoe
Miombo	Swahili for Brachystegia, a genus of trees common throughout Central Africa
Mobile Unit	Riot police
Muzungu	White person (from Swahili = aimless wanderer. Slightly derogatory)
Ndalama	Money
Nyama	Meat
Nyoko	Snake

Ouma	Grandmother (Afrikaans)
Oupa	Grandfather (Afrikaans)
Rondavel	Round hut, often made of clay or unburned brick
Sadza	Stiff maize "porridge" (similar to *polenta*)
Situpa (or Citupa)	Identity pass-book
Special Branch	Police Intelligence Unit
Stenographer	Shorthand-Typist
Swart gevaar	Black peril

ACNOWLEDGEMENTS

The biggest debt is to my husband Louis. People conventionally thank their spouses, but not only did Louis encourage me to begin this project, he kept encouraging me to carry on with it. The research has been time-consuming and could never have been completed without his understanding and unwavering support, including acceptance of my mounting travel expenses, long absences and diminishing standards of housekeeping. Louis came with me on my first return trip to Zambia, when I was so unjustifiably apprehensive, and learned then why the country matters so much. He has read several iterations of this text and listened to more stories about Zambia than it is reasonable to expect of any man. My son John Louis (better known to many as the musician and writer, Louis Barabbas) and I have always enjoyed arguing about style and content, so I was delighted when he offered to copy-edit this work, then proofread it. (Any remaining errors are my responsibility, as I went on changing things.)

Royal Holloway, University of London made me an Honorary Research Fellow for five years, granting me valuable access to an academic library. The National University of Singapore appointed me three times as Visiting Teaching Fellow; there I enjoyed a stimulating and supportive academic environment and began the research for this book.

I have listed the former Northern Rhodesians who expressed support for this project by responding to my overtures. I have not been able to mention all of them in the text itself but a great many sent me valuable accounts that I hope to make available via a dedicated website. Ann Baily provided an address list of people who attended the Salisbury reunion lunches, introducing me to a section of the Northern Rhodesian population that doesn't use social media. Not a few people offered open-handed hospitality to me as a complete stranger. Elise and Ron de Kock in Johannesburg, Julie and Norman Swenson in Perth, De'Ann and Ronnie Brooks in KwaZulu/Natal, Tommy Tomkins in Devon, Marion and John Fuller-Sessions in Derbyshire all had me to stay and I cannot begin to list the lunches I have been given. Linda Chonya of the Central Statistical Office in Lusaka provided a scanned copy of the otherwise unobtainable 1961 Northern Rhodesia Census. Alistair Smart lent me his precious copy of the Northern Rhodesia Government Staff List and a run of back numbers of the NR reunion group newsletter. Chris Lyon circulated the membership of the NRPA and sent copies of *Nkhwazi,* their journal. I have re-discovered many long-lost old friends spread around the globe – I hope all these people think that it was worthwhile.

RESPONDENTS

Abrams Geoffrey
Acheson Denis
Alexander Cathy
Alexander Raine
Anderson Eve
Anderson David
Anderson Ray
Andrew Jon
Andrews Carol
Andrews Fred
Angus Andrew
Angus Barbara
Anton-Smith John
Archibald Norman
Armstrong Trevor
Arnot Nick
Arnot Richard
Ashley Robert
Askew, Brenda
Atcheson Jill
Atkiss David
Attersoll Butch
Autef Sheelagh
Bailey Anne
Baker Norman
Balloch Anona
Barbor Gaye
Barr Caroline
Barr Gavin
Bayldon Roger
Beckford Ian
Behrens Joe

Bence Robin
Bennet Frank
Beveridge Keith
Birchall Stepanie
Birnie Christine
Blackstock Lorraine
Blunden John
Bobolski Judy
Bolton Raymond
Bond Mick
Bond Wendy
Booth George
Bourne P
Boutwood Jenny
Boutwood Robert
Bowcock P
Bowler Tony
Bown Hugh
Boyd Pat
Boyle Graham
Bragg Stewart
Brennan, Dale
Brentnall Faith
Bromwich Eric
Bromwich Peter
Brooklyn Richard
Brooks Deann
Brooks Ronnie
Broughton Hilary
Broughton Jamie
Brown Dudley
Brown Mary

Browning David
Browning Rae
Bruce Deborah
Bruce Don
Bruce Tony
Bruggeman Eunice
Bruggemann Ian
Brummer Jenny
Budkowski Jan
Burnie Jack
Burns Stewart
Burns Wendy
Butterworth Eilony
Butterworth Robert
Butterworth Brenda
Byrne Brian
Cairns Dr James
Cairns Mrs Faith
Cangley Sheilagh
Carlin Colin
Carlin Marion
Cartmell Ivor
Castle Jo
Cazalet Dave
Cera Eileen
Chattaway Alan
Clay Robin
Clegg-Butt Tony
Clemence Jo
Clibborn-Dyer Ron
Clibborn-Dyer
Veronica

259

Cluer Barry

Cochrane Geoffrey

Coetzee Collette

Coetzee Michael

Coffin Rex

Collinson Jill

Cooper Anthony

Cooper Dave

Cooper Julian

Cooper Mark

Cooper Richard

Copeland Chris

Copeland John

Coppard Roy

Costopoulos John

Cotton Chris

Cowie Paul

Craft Ian

Crawford Ron

Cray Paul

Cribb John

Cribb Marion

Critchell Raymond

Cross Hugh

Crowle John

Crowther Charley

Cummings Harvey

d'Avray David

d'Elbee Priscilla

Dacre Philip

Dalton Lesley

Daly Patrick

Daniels David

Davies Barry

Davies Tom

De Backer Pamela

De Haas Piet

De Jager Rose

De Kock Elise

De Kock Ron

De Lange Margaret

De Lange Steven

De Navarro Jill

De Swardt Clarence

Dielissen Hans

Diellessen Peter

Diesel VernieY

Dillon Christina

Dorey Anne

Dowling Keiron

Doyle-Davidson Malcolm

Drew Judy

Dublon George

Duckham Alison

Dunbar Lesley

Dunn Liz

Dunning Amelia

Dunning Jim

Durrbaum Cathy

Dutton Derek

Dye Mary

Eastman Muriel

Eglington Bob

Eltze Denis

Emslie Noreen

Engelbrecht Martin

Englert Tricia

Espey Don

Evans Edgar

Everest Roger

Fann Sandra

Fernie Ken

Ferrett Peter

Field Julia

Field Martin

Fillery Paul

Fineron Tim

Finlayson Gerry

Fisher Greg

Fisher Sheine

Fitzpatrick Arthur

Flower-Smith M

Flower-Smith Priscilla

Forrest Adrian

Foster Val

Fourie Skatie

Fraser Kim

Freed Neil

Freeman Sydney

Frowd Joan

Frowd John

Frowd Tony

Fuchiareli Dominic

Fuller S

Fuller-Sessions M

Galaun Jack

Galloway Jane

Galmiche Claude

Game Ian

Gandar Doug

Gersh Bernard

Gilbert Otto	Hanford Francis	Holroyd Jess
Gillies Bob	Hannah J	Hooper Linda
Gird Christine	Harbott Maureen	Hopkins Margaret
Giorgio Penny	Harbott Michael	Horley Jon
Glendening David	Hart Stephen	Horn Karen
Glynn Terry	Harwood Maxie	Hounsell David
Godfrey Joanna	Haslam Stephen	Hovelmeir Errol
Goodfellow John	Hassall Ian	Howard Philip
Goodwin Stuart	Hawkey Malcolm	Hoyte Hal
Gornall John	Hawkins Jeremy	Hunt Heather
Gornall Liz	Hawkins Elizabeth	Huntley Robert
Gotting Fay	Hayes Linda	Hyde John
Gray David	Hayward Jenny	Immelman Caroline
Grebert Yves	Heape Colin	Isaacs Frances
Greenall Cyril	Heape Jane	Isdell Pamela
Greening Sarah	Heathcote Alan	Isdell Neville
Gretton Heather	Heathcote Brian	Jackson Moira
Grewar Donald	Heaton Harley	Jackson Nigel
Grewar Doug	Heron Marjorie	Jacobs Barbara
Greyvenstein Diana	Hesom Rose	James Ronald
Grieve Jerry	Hey Chris	Jenkins, Lynn
Griffiths Hywel	Heydenrych Maggie	Jennings Colin
Groenewald Rod	Heyes Ronald	Jewsbury Carol
Groth P	Hicks Barry	Johnson Barrie
Guest Veronica	Higgs John	Johnson Jean
Guthrie Tom	Hill Christopher	Johnson Mike
Guy Judith	Hill Roland	Johnson Martin
Haddow John	Hills Peter	Johnson Tony
Hall Barbara	Hoar Paul	Johnston Richard
Hall Douglas	Hoar Sue	Joseph Nevill
Hambley John	Hodgeson Derek	Kallman George
Hambley Janice	Hodkinson George	Kellett Maddy
Hamilton Eileen	Holden Jim	Kellett Peter
Hampson Roger	Holmes Carole	Kenning Val

Kerr Coleen

Kilner Russell

King Rita

Kloppers Rosemary

Klyberg Rev CJ

Knott Bill

Knott Jan

Korunich Frank

Krause Gaynor

Kriel Eve

Lallemand R

Lamb Elsabe

Lambert John

Lambert Michael

Lambley Phil

Landsberg Glen

Lantzendorffer-Jones
Charmian

Lawley Jonathan

Lazarevic George

Leach Jane

Leach Jonathan

Leach Neal

Lee Ann

Lee Kevin

Lee Mary

Lee Phillip

Legg Christopher

Lindenberg Paul

Linette Martin

Ling Colin

Lloyd Espeth

Lombard Ray

Long Irene

Long Tricia

Lonsdale Gillian

Luscombe Geraldine

Luff Peter

Lyon Chris

Lyons Trevor

MacDonald Alistair

MacDonald Lynette

Mackenzie Ian

Mackenzie Noreen

Mackey Geraldine

Mackinson Barbara

Mackinson Ian

MacLeod Ken

Madocks Rod

Maitland Elaine

Maltby Chris

Marcus Shaun

Markotter Keith

Marston Roger

Martin Marianne

Mavronicolas Theo

Maxwell Mary

May Helen

Maybank John

McChesney, Connie

McChesney R

McDonald Ian

McGovern Frank

McGregor Janice

McIntosh George

McKenzie John M

McLaren Ian

McLean Don

McLean Stuart

McMahon Michael

McMullen James

McMullen Lorna

Merry Gail

Metcalf Margot

Miles William

Miller Cynthia

Miller Jasmine

Mills Ted

Minne Michael

Minnear Brian

Moffat David

Moorcroft Rosemary

Moreland Linda

Morris Colin

Morris Kate

Morris P

Morrish Judy

Morrison Alex

Morze-Langan Lynne

Mossop Geoff

Muir, G

Mulholand Joseph

Murray Danielle

Murray Patrick

Nadauld Lynthia

Nelson Cathrine

Newton Denise

Nicholas I

Nicholas Mike

Nightingale Jacqueline

Nissen Jerry

Nixon Bruce

Noak Michael

Noall Marilyn

Noel A

North P

Nortje John

O'Connell-Jones Basil

O'Connell-Jones Betty

O'Hara Jane

O'Hara Tim

Oakes Lynette

Olive Robert

Ormrod Sue

Orr-Ewing John

Ouzman Lee

Overton Sybil

Paans Audrey

Page Michael

Paget Ian

Pain Maggie

Pain Philip

Pakeman Elise

Pamphilon Philippa

Parkyn Amanda

Pascore Danuta

Paterson Lynne

Paterson R

Patterson Sharon

Payne John

Payne Mike

Peacock M

Peacock Maude

Pearson Tony

Pedler Flora

Pedler R

Penstone Martin

Perks Frances

Perry Philippa

Petrie Noreen

Phipps Penny

Pigg Gerald

Pigg Denise

Pigrum Dennis

Pinsent Ewan

Pitchford John

Plain Robert

Plimmer John

Pocock Mucchi

Pollock Brenda

Pollock Duncan

Price John

Price Liz

Price Neville

Prince Betsy

Quick Tim

Quirk Tim

Radunski Saul

Rawlins Patsy

Rawlins Susan

Rawlinson Judy

Redden Jean

Redman Lindsay

Reid Fulton

Reid R

Renaud Annemarie

Rendall David

Ridley Roger

Rigby Heather

Rigby Peter

Robbins Elizabeth

Roberts John

Robinson, Brian

Robinson Margaret

Robinson Pat

Robson Monica

Roczynski Ted

Ron Aviva

Rorison Jenny

Ross Roland

Rowles Hugh

Rusbridger Alan

Russell Elaine

Russell Lindsay

Russell Paul

Ryan Paddy

Rynn Renee

Saffery David

Salmon D

Sampson Richard

Sandiford Sheelagh

Sayer Ron

Schillig Jane

Schmal Leslie

Schmal Lisalotte

Schofield Shirley

Schofield Victor

Schonland Michael

Schultz Vince

Scott Ian

Scott-Williams Lynden

Seaton Norman

Setterfield Peter

Sheehy-Williams Katherine

Sher Ellis

Shewmaker Sherman

Simmonds David

Simpson Gillian

Slade Jackie

Sleigh Findlay (James)

Small Anne

Small David

Smart Alastair

Smart Jann

Smith Don

Smith Joanna

Smith Kathy (Kate)

Smith Linda

Smith Petronella

Smith Rosemary

Snow Graham

Snyman Trevor

Solomon Joseph

Sparks Tony

Spindler Ruth

Stapleburg (Fred) Rudolph

Steers John

Stern Eddy

Stevens C

Stracey Richard

Strang Catherine

Sunlay Rae

Swenson Julie

Sydenham Heather

Szeftel Morris

Tanner Mark

Taylor June

Theron Hugo

Thom Andrew

Thomas Arthur

Thomas Derek

Thomas Gwyneth

Thomas Joan

Thomas Owen

Thomas Ron

Thomas Sue

Thompson David

Thompson Jimmie

Thompson John

Thornicroft Humphrey

Thrall Roy

Tibbit Roy

Tibbit Rosemary

Tilney Oonagh

Tokarczyk George

Tompkins Tommy

Topping Paul

Townsend Brian

Townsend Moira

Trail Robert

Trevor Mark (Buz)

Trott Donna

Turnbull-Jackson Trevor

Tyler Nick

Tyne John

Tyrer Henry

van den Brink Leslie

Vaughan-Johnston Robin

Viljoen Ben

Visser Marianne

Wade Aileen

Wade Bill

Wagner Michael

Walden Brian

Walden Liz

Walker Lyn

Wallace Tom

Waller Chris

Walters Angela

Ward Mark

Wardrop Richard

Watson Alister

Watt Alastair

Wawn Ian

Weatherall Sydney

Webster Robert

Wheeler Paul

Weston Nora

Weston Roy

Whitaker John

White Patrick

White Philippa

Whittome, Elizabeth

Wild Sarah

Wilken Ronald

Wilkinson Margaret

Williams David

Williams Harold

Williams Hilton

Williams Norman

Williams Ray

Wilson Ann

Wilson Mike

Wilson Rob

Winstanley Heather

Winton Chris

Witt Peter

Witt Rosemary

Wood Dave

Wood Tony

Woodhams Barry

Woods John

Worrill Robert

Wright Anthea

Wright David

Wright Lindy

Wright Mik

Wright Noel

Wright Tim

Wylie Karl

Yodaiken Martin

Young Allan

Young Mac

Young Patsy

Zonkie Kate

BIBLIOGRAPHY

Adichie, C. (2009) The Danger of a Single Story. TED Talks. Transcript: http://ssw.unc.edu/files/TheDangerofaSingleStoryTranscript.pdf

Allen, C. (ed) (1979) *Tales from the Dark Continent: Images of British Colonial Africa in the Twentieth Century.* London: Futura.

Appelbaummarch, B. (2014) "Stanley Fischer, Fed Nominee, has Long History of Policy Leadership." *New York Times* 12/03/2014.

Ardener, S. (ed) (1984) *Incorporated Wife.* London: Croom Helm.

Arrigoni, H. (1998) *British Colonialism: Thirty Years Serving Democracy or Hypocrisy?* Bideford, Devon: Edward Gaskell Publishers.

Baena, R. (2008) "Of Missess and Tuan Kechils: Colonial Childhood Memoirs as Cultural Mediation in British Malaya." ARIEL: *A Review of International English Literature,* 39: 89-112.

Baena, R. (2009) "Not Home but Here: Rewriting Englishness in Colonial Childhood Memoirs." *English Studies*, 90: 435-459.

Baines, G. (2008) "Blame, Shame or Reaffirmation? White conscripts reassess the meaning of the 'Border War' in post-apartheid South Africa." *Interculture*, 5(3): 214-227.

Baldwin, R. (1966) *Economic Development and Export Growth: A study of Northern Rhodesia, 1920-1960.* Berkeley: University of California Press.

Bate, H. (1953) *Report from the Rhodesias.* London: Melrose.

Baucom, I. (2005) *Spectres of the Atlantic: Finance capital, slavery and the philosophy of history.* Durham NC: Duke University Press.

Belich, J. (2005) "The Rise of the Anglo-World: Settlement in North America and Australia, 1784-57" in P.Buchner & D.Francis (eds) *Rediscovering the British World.* Calgary: University of Calgary Press.

Belich, J. (2011) *Replenishing the Earth: The settler revolution and the rise of the Anglo-World, 1783-1939.* Oxford: Oxford University Press.

Bendien, E. (2012) "Remembering (in) the past perfect: Ethical shifts in times." *Memory* Studies 5(4): 445-461.

Benjamin, W. (ed. H. Arendt, tr. H. Zorn) (1999) (original French 1940) "Theses on the Philosophy of History" in *Illuminations.* London: Pimlico.

Bergson, H. (tr. N. Paul, & S. Palmer,) (2004) (Original French 1912) *Matter and Memory.* New York: Dover Publications.

Bewes, T. (2011) *The Event of Postcolonial Shame*. Princeton, New Jersey: Princeton University Press.

Bickers, R. (ed.) (2010) *Settlers and Expatriates: Britons over the seas*. Oxford: Oxford University Press.

Birmingham, D. & Martin, P. (1983) *History of Central Africa. Volume Two*. London: Longman.

Blacksmith Institute (2013) *The World's Worst 2013: The top ten toxic threats*. New York http://www.worstpolluted.org/docs/TopTenThreats2013.pdf

Blixen, K. (1937) *Out of Africa*. Harmondsworth; Penguin.

Bloom, K. (2010) *Ways of Staying*. London: Portobello Books.

Bolze, L. & Martin, R. (1978) The *Whenwes of Rhodesia*. Bulawayo: Books of Rhodesia.

Bonnett, A. (1999) *Anti-Racism*. London: Routledge.

Boyer, P. & Wertsch, J. (eds) (2009) *Memory in Mind and Culture*. New York : Cambridge University Press.

Bradley, E. (1950) *Dearest Priscilla: Letters to the wife of a colonial civil servant*. London: Max Parish.

Bradley, K. (1950) *The colonial service as a career.* London: HMSO.

Bradley, K. (1952) *Copper Venture: The discovery and development of Roan Antelope and Mufulira*. London: Mufulira Copper Mines Ltd & Roan Antelope Copper Mines Ltd.

Brelsford, W. (1954) *The story of the Northern Rhodesia Regiment*. Southampton: L Galago.

Brelsford, W. (1960) *Handbook to the Federation of Rhodesia & Nyasaland*. London: Cassell.

Brelsford, W. (1965) *Generation of Men: The European pioneers of Northern Rhodesia*. Salisbury: Stuart Manning for the Rhodesia Society.

British South Africa Company (1902) *The Rhodesia Civil Service List*. Salisbury, Rhodesia: Argoas Printing & Publishing. (re-published in facsimile 2012 London: Jeppestown Press.)

Brown, R. (1973) "Anthropology and Colonial Rule: Godfrey Wilson and the Rhodes-Livingstone Institute, Northern Rhodesia" in. T. Asad (ed) *Anthropology and the Colonial Encounter*. London: Ithaca.

Burawoy, M. (1972) T*he Colour of Class on the Copper Mines: From African advancement to Zambianization*. Lusaka: Institute for African Studies, University of Zambia.

Butler, L. (2007) *Copper Empire: Mining and the Colonial State in Northern Rhodesia*, 1930-64. London: Palgrave Macmillan.

Camus, A. (ed. P. Thody. tr. E. Kennedy) (1970) *Lyrical and Critical Essays*. New York: Vintage Books.

Camus, A. (tr. D. Hapgood) (1995) *The First Man*. London: Hamish Hamilton.

Chongo, C. (2009) "The Impact of Rhodesia's Unilateral Declaration of Independence on Zambia's Economic and Socio-political Developments, 1965-1979." M.A. Thesis University of Zambia, Lusaka.

Cobain, I (2013) "Revealed: The Bonfire of Papers at the End of Empire." *The Guardian* 29th November 2013 http://www.theguardian.com/uk-news/2013/nov/29/revealed-bonfire-papers-empire

Coleman, F. (1971) *The Northern Rhodesian Copperbelt 1899-1962: Technological Development up to the end of the Central African Federation.* Manchester: Manchester University Press.

Colson, E. (1971) "Heroism, Martyrdom and Courage: An essay on Tonga ethics" in T.Beidelman (ed.) *The Translation of Culture: Essays to E.E.Evans-Pritchard.* London: Tavistock Press.

Connerton, P. (1989) *How Societies Remember*. Cambridge: Cambridge University Press.

Connerton, P. (2006) *How Modernity Forgets*. Cambridge: Cambridge University Press.

Connerton, P. (2008) "Seven Types of Forgetting." *Memory Studies 1* (1): 59-71

Conway, M. (1996) "Autobiographical Knowledge and Autobiographical Memories" In D. Rubin (ed) *Remembering our Past: Studies in autobiographical memory*. pp 67-93 Cambridge: Cambridge University Press.

Conway, M. (2005) "Memory and the Self." *Journal of Memory and Language.* 53: 594-628.

Counsell, C. and Mock, R. (eds) (2009) *Performance, Embodiment and Cultural Memory*. Newcastle: Cambridge Scholars.

Critchley, R. (1960) "Operation Noah." *Oryx: The International Journal of Conservation.* 5 (3):100-107.

Crowther, M. (ed) (1984) *The Cambridge History of Africa. Vol* 8. 1940-1975. Cambridge: Cambridge University Press,

Crush, J. & Tevera, D. (eds) (2010) *Zimbabwe's Exodus: Crisis, migration, survival*. Cape Town: Southern Africa Migration Programme.

Darwin, J. (2010) "Orphans of Empire" in R. Bickers (ed.) *Settlers and Expatriates: Britons over the seas*. Oxford: Oxford University Press.

Deleuze, G. (tr. P. Patton) (1994) *Difference and Repetition*. London: Athone Press.

Deleuze, G. (tr. R. Howard) (2000) *Proust and Signs*. Minneapolis: University of Minnesota Press.

Draaisma, D. (tr. Pomerans, A & E) (2004) *Why Life Speeds Up as you get Older: How memory shapes our past*. Cambridge: Cambridge University Press.

Draaisma, D. (tr. Waters, L) (2013) *The Nostalgia Factory: Memory, time and ageing*. New Haven: Yale University Press

Dunn, C. (1959) *Central African Witness*. London: Victor Gollancz.

Eaton, W. (1996) *A Chronicle of Modern Sunlight: The story of what happened to the Rhodesians*. Rohnert Park CA: Inno Vision.

Edemariam, A. "The Cost of Survival" The Guardian 5th March 2005 http://www.theguardian.com/world/2004/mar/05/southafrica.books accessed 26/02/2014

Edmonds, D. (2013) "Should we Judge People of Past Eras for Moral Failings?" *BBC News Magazine* 13th August 2013 http://www.bbc.co.uk/news/magazine-23772194 accessed 24/03/2014

Fabian, J. (2001) "Remembering the Other: Knowledge and Recognition" in *Anthropology with an Attitude*. Stanford: Stanford University Press. 158-178.

Fernyhough, C. (2012) *Pieces of light: The new science of memory*. London: Profile Books.

Ferneyhough, C. (2014) "What novels can tell us about memory." *Huffington Post* http://www.huffingtonpost.com accessed 05/04/2014

Forster, E. (1924, 2005) *A Passage to India*. Harmondsworth: Penguin Books.

Franklin, H. (1963) "Dying at the Falls." *The Spectator* 4th July 1963.

Franklin, H. (1963) *Unholy Wedlock: The Failure of the Central African Federation*. London: George Allen & Unwin.

Fraser, A. & Larmer M. (2010) "Introduction" *Zambia, Mining and Neoliberalism: Boom and Bust*. London: Macmillan.

Frost, M. (undated) *Homeland* https://www.youtube.com/watch?v=eN8q3PNHTpo

Fuller, A. (2006) "A Conversation with Alexandra Fuller." *Boldtype* May www.randomhouse.com/boldtype/0303/fuller/interview.html (Accessed 07/10/13)

Gann, L. (1964) *A History of Northern Rhodesia: Early Days to 1953*. London: Chatto and Windus,

Gelfand, M. (1961) *Northern Rhodesia in the Days of the Charter*. Oxford: Blackwell.

Gewald, J-B, Hinfelaar, M. & Macola, G. (eds) (2008) *One Zambia, Many Histories: Towards a history of post-colonial Zambia*. Leiden: Brill.

Gewald, J-B, (2009) *"Rumours of Mau Mau in Northern Rhodesia*, 1950-1960." Afrika Focus 22(1): 37-56.

Gewald, J-B, Hinfelaar, M. & Macola, G. (eds) (2011) *Living the End of Empire: Politics and society in late colonial Zambia*. Leiden: Brill.

Gilroy, P. (2009) *Postcolonial Melancholia*. New York: University of Columbia Press.

Geurts, K. (2005) "Consciousness as 'Feeling in the Body': A West African Theory of Embodiment, Emotion and the Making of Mind" in D.Howes (ed) *Empire of the Senses: The Sensual Culture Reader*. Oxford: Berg.

Goanet (2013) "Banda expels Goans from Malawi." http://lists.goanet.org/pipermail/goanet-goanet.org/2013-April/230466.html

Golding, R. (2000) "Daily Thoughts for a Reluctant Capitalist." *The Observer* 29th October 2000
http://www.theguardian.com/money/2000/oct/29/observercashsection.theobserver8

Grayling, A.C. *The Science Studio Interview (with Roger Bingham)* Downloaded 23/04/2011 undated interview http://thesciencenetwork.org/media/videos/296/Transcript.pdf

Grayling, A.C.(2008) *Desert Island Disks* BBC Radio 4, 9:00AM Fri, 15 Aug 2008 http://www.bbc.co.uk/iplayer/episode/b00cx1ds/Desert_Island_Discs_AC_Grayling/

Gross, D. (2000) *Lost Time: On remembering & forgetting in late modern life*. Amhurst: University of Massachusetts Press.

Halbwachs, M. (ed. & tr. L. Coser) (1992) *On Collective Memory*. Chicago: University of Chicago Press.

Hall, B. (1964) *Tell Me, Josephine.* London: Pan.

Hall, R. (1965) *Zambia.* New York: Frederick A. Praeger.

Hall, R. (1969) *The High Price of Principles: Kaunda and the white south.* London: Hodder & Stoughton.

Hansen, K. (1989) *Distant Companions: Servants and employees in Zambia 1900-1985.* Ithaca & London: Cornell University Press.

Hansen, K. (1992) "White Women in a Changing World: Employment, voluntary work and sex in post-World War II Northern Rhodesia" In N. Chaudhuri & M. Strobel (eds) *Western Women and Imperialism: Complicity and Resistance.* Bloomington: Indiana University Press.

Hansen, R. (1999) "The Politics of Citizenship in 1940s Britain: The British Nationality Act." *Twentieth Century British History.* 10 (1):67-95.

Hobsbawm, E. & Ranger, T. (eds) (1983) *The Invention of Tradition.* Cambridge & New York: Cambridge University Press.

Hoelscher, S. & Alderman, D. (2004) "Memory and Place: geographies of a critical Relationship." *Social & Cultural Geography*, 5 (3): 347-355.

Howarth, D. (1961) *The Shadow of the Dam.* New York: Macmillan. http://archive. org/stream/shadowofthedam030815mbp/shadowofthedam030815mbp_djvuxt

Howe, S. (2013) "Crosswinds and Countercurrents: Macmillan's Africa in the 'Long View' of decolonization" in L. Butler & S. Stockwell (eds) *The wind of change: Harold Macmillan and British decolonization (Cambridge Imperial and Post-colonial Studies Series).* London: Palgrave Macmillan.

Hoy, D. (2009) *The Time of our Lives: A critical history of temporality.* Cambridge MA: MIT Press.

Hughey, M. (2012) *White Bound: Nationalists, antiracists and the shared meanings of race.* Redwood City CA: Stanford University Press.

Hyam, R. (2007) *Britain's Declining Empire: The road to decolonisation 1918-1968.* Cambridge: Cambridge University Press.

James, H. (1887) *The Diary of a Man of Fifty.* Gutenberg electronic version http://www.gutenberg.org/files/2426/2426-h/2426-h.htm

John, V. (2009) "Christian Cult Stole our Kids, Say Parents." *The Saturday Star*, SA 07th November 2009 http://www.highbeam.com/doc/1G1-211441114.html

John, V. (2012) "New Jo'burg Church has more than a Whiff of Cult." *Mail and Guardian* 21st December 2012 http://mg.co.za/article/2012-12-21-00-new-joburg-church-has-more-than-a-whiff-of-cult

Kalusa, W. (2011) "The Killing of Lillian Margaret Burton and Black and White Nationalisms in Northern Rhodesia (Zambia) in the 1960s." *Journal of Southern African Studies*. 37: 63-77.

Kangwa, J. (2004) "Having a Place of your own in Kitwe" in R. Home & H. Lim (eds) *Demystifying the Mystery of Capital: Land Tenure & Poverty in Africa & the Caribbean*. London: The Glass House Press.

Keith, G. (1966) The Fading Colour Bar. London: Robert Hale.

Kikamba, L. (2013) "White Women who Stepped out of Line." *The Bulletin & Record*, Zambia February, 2013. http://www.bulletinandrecord.com

Kirk-Green, A. (1999) *On Crown Service: A History of HM Colonial and Overseas Civil Services 1837-1997*. London. New York: I.B.Tauris.

Kirk-Green, A. (2006) *Symbol of Authority: The British District Officer in Africa*. London: IB Tauris.

Kirk-Green, A. (2012) *Aspects of Empire: A Second Corona Anthology*. London: I.B.Tauris.

Larmer, M. (2004) "If We are Still Here Next Year: Zambian Historical Research in the Context of Decline, 2002–2003." *History in Africa* 31: 215-229

Legg, S. (2007) "Reviewing Geographies of Memory/Forgetting." *Environment and Planning A* 39 (2): 456-466

Lessing, D. (1982) "Laurens van der Post" in J. Taylor (ed.) *Notebooks, memoirs, archives: Reading and re-reading Doris Lessing*. London: Routledge & Kegan Paul.

Lessing, D. (2004) "Writing Autobiography" in *Time Bites*. London: Harper Perennial.

Louw, E. & Mersham, G. (2001) "Packing for Perth: The growth of a Southern African Diaspora." *Asian & Pacific Migration Journal*. 10(2): 303-333

Macmillan, H. (1960) *The Wind of Change* http://www.africanrhetoric.org/pdf

Macmillan, H. & Shapiro, F. (1999) *Zion in Africa: The Jews of Zambia*. London: I.B.Tauris.

Mamdani, M. (2012) *Define and Rule: Native as Political Identity*. Cambridge MA: Harvard University press.

Martin, P. (1998) "Beyond Independence" in D. Birmingham & P. Martin (eds) *History of Central Africa: The contemporary years - since 1960*. London: Longman.

McCulloch, J. (2000) *Black Peril, White Virtue: Sexual Crime in Southern Rhodesia, 1902-1935*. Bloomington: Indiana University Press.

McNally, S. (undated) *Zimbabwe pensions petition report.* http:www. zimbabwesituation.com/pensionspetition.html

Milner-Thornton J.B, (2009) "Absent White Fathers: coloured identity in Zambia" in M. Adhikari (ed.) *Burdened By Race: Coloured Identities in southern Africa.* Cape Town: University of Cape Town Press.

Milner-Thornton, J. (2012) *The Long Shadow of the British Empire: The ongoing legacies of race and class in Zambia.* New York: Palgrave Macmillan.

Moore-Gilbert, B. (2009) *Postcolonial Life-writing: Culture, politics and self-representation.* London: Routledge.

Murphey, P. (ed) (2005) *British Documents on the End of Empire: Central Africa. Part One Closer Association* 1945-1958. London: Institute of Commonwealth Studies.

Newell, S. (2008) "Dirty Whites: 'Ruffian-Writing' in Colonial West Africa." *Research in African Literatures.* 39(4): 2-13

Ngugi Wa Thiong'o (1981) *Decolonizing the Mind.* London: James Currey.

O'Reilly (2010) "In South Africa, whites are becoming squatters." *Sunday Times.*http://www.sundaytimes.lk/100328/International/int_17.html

Overseas Service Pensioners' Association (2013) *Legacy of Empire: A Transcript of the Proceedings of the Seminar.* No. 8 Occasional Paper OSPA Research Project.

Paxman, J. (2011) *Empire: What Ruling the World Did to the British.* London: Viking.

Phimister, I. (2011a) "Proletarians in Paradise: The historiography and historical sociology of white miners on the Copperbelt" in J-B Gewald, et.al. (eds) *Living the end of Empire: Politics and society in late colonial Zambia.* Leiden: Brill.

Phimister, I. (2011b) "Workers in Wonderland? White miners and the Northern Rhodesian Copperbelt, 1946-1962." *South African Historical Journal.* 63(2): 183-233.

Phiri, B. (2006) *A Political History of Zambia: From the colonial period to the 3rd Republic.* Asmara, Eritrea: Africa World Press.

Powdermaker, H. (1962) *Copper Town: Changing Africa, the human situation on the Rhodesian Copperbelt.* New York: Harper and Row.

Radstone, S. & Schwarz, B. (eds) (2010) *Memory: Histories, theories, debates.* New York: Fordham University Press.

Ranger, T. (1980) "Making Northern Rhodesia Imperial: Variations on a royal theme, 1924-1938." *African Affairs*.79:349-373.

Rathbone, C. Moulin, C. & Conway, M. (2008) "Self-centred Memories: The reminiscence bump and the self." *Memory & Cognition* 36 (8): 1403-1414.

Rathbone, C, Conway, M. & Moulin, C. (2011) "Remembering and Imagining: The role of the self." *Consciousness and Cognition* 20 (4): 1175-1182.

Richman, T. (ed) (2010) *Should I Stay or Should I Go? To live in or leave South Africa*. Cape Town: Two Dogs Publications.

Ricoeur, P. (tr K. Blamey & D. Pellauer) (2004) *Memory, History, Forgetting*. Chicago: University of Chicago Press.

Roberts, A. 1976. *A History of Zambia*. New York: Africana.

Roberts, A. (1986) "The Imperial Mind" in A. Roberts (ed.) *The Colonial Moment in Africa: Essays on the movement of minds and materials* 1900-1940. Cambridge: Cambridge University Press.

Roberts, A. (2011) "Northern Rhodesia: The Post-war Background, 1945-53" in J-B. Gewald et al (eds) *Living the End of Empire: Politics and society in late colonial Zambia*. Leiden: Brill.

Rosenthal, E. (undated) R*hodesian Jewry and its Story. Part V*. Harare. Zimbabwe: Jewish Board of Deputies. (Available as a pdf)

Rotberg, R. (1965) *The Rise of Nationalism in Central Africa: The making of Malawi and Zambia 1873-1964*. Cambridge MA: Harvard University Press

Rotberg, R. (1977) *Black Heart: Gore-Brown and the Politics of Multiracial Zambia*. Berkeley LA: University of California Press.

Rotberg, R. (1992) Black Heart: Gore Brown and the Politics of Multiracial Zambia. Oakland CA: University of California Press.

Salmon, D. (2010) "The Creation of Zambia" Unpublished MA Thesis, University of Keele, Staffs.

Sampson, R. (1956) *They Came to Northern Rhodesia: Being a record of persons who had entered what is now the Territory of Northern Rhodesia by 31st December 1902*. Lusaka.

Schumaker, L. (1996) "A Tent with a View: Colonial officers, anthropologists and the making of the field in Northern Rhodesia, 1937-1960." *Science in the field*. OSIRIS 2nd Series. 11: 237-258.

Schwarz, B. (2011) *Memories of Empire, Volume 1: The white man's world*. Oxford: Oxford University Press.

Scott, G. (1959) "Colour Bar Cafés" *The Spectator* http://archive.spectator.co.uk/article/17th-july-1959/3/colour-bar-cafs

Scott, J. (1987) *Weapons of the Weak: Everyday forms of peasant resistance*. New Haven CT: Yale University Press.

Scudder, T. (2005) *The Kariba Case Study*. Working Paper 1227, California Institute of Technology. Pasadena CA.

Shapiro, F. (2002) *Haven in Africa*. Jerusalem: Gefen Publishing.

Simoes da Silva, T. (2008) "Narrating Redemption: Life writing and whiteness in the New South Africa: Gillian Slovo's 'Every Secret Thing'." *ARIEL. A Review of International English Literature*. 39: 91-107

Shipway, M. (2008) *Decolonization and its Impact: Comparative approach to the end of Colonial Empires*. Chichester: Wiley-Blackwell.

Shurmer-Smith, P. (2000) "Loving India" in *Losing my Innocence*. Portsmouth:University of Portsmouth Working Papers in Geography No 37: 7-13

Shurmer-Smith, P. (2002) "Postcolonial Geographies" in P. Shurmer-Smith (ed.) *Doing Cultural Geography*. London: Sage.

Shurmer-Smith, P. (2011) "Once the Dust of Africa is in your Blood: Tracking Northern Rhodesia's white diaspora." *Acme* 10 (1) 82-92.

Simpson, A. (1998) "Memory and Becoming Chosen Other: Fundamentalist Elite-Making in a Zambian Catholic Mission School" in R.Werbener (ed) *Memory and the Postcolony: African anthropology and the critique of power*. London: Zed Books: 209-228.

Smailes, D, Meins, E. and Fernyhough, C. (2014) 'The impact of negative affect on reality discrimination.' *Journal of behavior therapy and experimental psychiatry* 45 (3): 389-395.

Stonehouse, J. (1960) *Prohibited Immigrant*. London: Bodley Head.

Taylor, J. & Lehmann, D. (1961) *Christians of the Copperbelt: The growth of the Church in Northern Rhodesia*. London: SCM Press.

Titchener, E. (1895) "Affective Memory." *Philosophical Review*. 4 (1): 65-76.

Uusikakala, K. (2008) *Memory Meanders: Place, home and commemoration in an ex-Rhodesian diaspora community*. Helsinki: Helsinki University Press.

van Velsen, J. (1969) "Procedural Informality: reconciliations and false comparisons" in M.Gluckman (ed) *Ideas and procedures in African customary law*. Oxford: Oxford University press.

Veracini, L. (2010) *Settler Colonialism: A theoretical overview*. Basingstoke: Palgrave Macmillan.

Wainaina, N. (2005) "How to Write about Africa." *Granta*. 92.

Walder, D. (2009) "Writing, Representation and Postcolonial Nostalgia." *Textual Practice*, 23(6): 935-946.

Walder, D. (2011) *Postcolonial Nostalgias: Writing, representation and memory*. London: Routledge.

Ward, S. (2005) "Worlds Apart: Three "British" Prime Ministers at Empire's end" in P. Buchner & D. Francis (eds) *Rediscovering the British World*. Calgary: University of Calgary Press.

Webster, A. (2006) *The Debate on the Rise of the British Empire*. Manchester: Manchester University Press.

Welensky, R. (1964) *Welensky's 4000 Days: The Life and Death of the Federation of Rhodesia & Nyasaland*. London: Collins.

Werbener, R. (1998) "Beyond Oblivion: Confronting memory crisis" in R.Werbener (ed) *Memory and the postcolony: African anthropology and the critique of power*. London: Zed Books.

White, L. (2000) *Speaking with Vampires: Rumour and history in colonial Africa*. Berkeley: University of California Press.

Wright, T. (2001) *The History of the Northern Rhodesia Police*. Bristol: British Empire & Commonwealth Museum Press.

Young, R. (2008) *The Idea of English Ethnicity*. Oxford: Blackwell.

Young, R. (2009) "What is the Postcolonial?" *ARIEL. A Review of International English Literature*. 40: 13-25.

MEMOIRS, BIOGRAPHIES AND NOVELS

Barnes, S. (1986) *Phil Edmonds: A singular man*. London: The Kingswood Press.

Bennett, F. (2006) *Under an African Sun: Memoirs of a Colonial Officer in Northern Rhodesia*. London: The Radcliffe Press.

Bishop, D. *Goodbye Africa*. Eloquent Books. Kindle Edition.

Boyd, R. (1996) *A Colonial Odyssey*. Ringwood, Hants: Navigator Books.

Bradley, K. (1943) *The Diary of a District Officer*. London: Thomas Nelson & Son.

Bradley, K. (1966) *Once a District Officer*. New York: St Martin's Press.

Bruce, A. (2008) *The Consequence of Memory*. Salt Spring Island, BC: Glendambo Publishing.

Carr, B. (1963) *Not for me the Wilds*. London: Baily Bros & Swinfen.

Charlton, L. (1969) *Spark in the Stubble: Colin Morris of Zambia*. London: Epworth Press.

Coe, D. & Greenall, E. (2003) *Kaunda's Gaoler: the memoirs of a District Officer in Northern Rhodesia & Zambia*. London, New York: The Radcliffe Press.

Conrad, K. (2010) *In the Shadow of the Tokolosh*. Chelmsford, Essex: Silverling.

Courtenay, B. (1989) *The Power of One*. London: Penguin Books.

Dorman, T. (1993) *An African Experience: An education officer in Northern Rhodesia (Zambia)*. London: The Radcliffe press.

Evans, E. (2013) *An African Story.* Kindle. Independently published.

Fuller, A. (2003) *Don't Let's go to the Dogs Tonight: An African childhood*. London: Picador.

Fuller, A. (2012) *Cocktail Hour under the Tree of Forgetfulness*. London: Simon & Schuster.

Gardam, J. (2005) *Old Filth*. London: Abacus.

Godwin, P. (1997) *Mukiwa: A white boy in Africa*. London: Picador.

Godwin, P. (2007) *When a Crocodile Eats the Sun*. London: Picador.

Gornall, J. (2008) *No Better Life: The Experiences of a Police Officer in Central Africa*. Nelson, NZ: The Copy Press.

Harbott, M. & M. (2012) *Our Fine Romance: An autobiography*. Victoria BC: M&M Productions.

Hassell, I. (2013) *Hamba Gashle*. Ebookit.com Kindle Edition.

Herbert, E. (2002) *Twilight on the Zambezi: Late Colonialism in Central Africa*. New York: Palgrave Macmillan.

Hitchcock, B. (1974) *Bwana – Go Home*. London: Robert Hale.

Hudson, J. (1999) *A Time to Mourn: A personal account of the 1964 Lumpa Church Revolt in Zambia*. Lusaka: Bookworld Publishers.

Isdell, N. & Beasley, D. (2011) *Inside Coca-Cola: A CEO's life story of building the world's most popular brand*. New York: St Martin's Press.

Lamb, C. (1999) *The Africa House*. London: Viking, Penguin Books.

Lawley, J. (2010) *Beyond the Malachite Hills: A Life of Colonial Service and Business in the New Africa*. London: I.B.Tauris.

Lloyd, J. (2013) *The Bundu, the Beat and Beyond*. Bloomington, IN: AuthorHouse.

Mackinson, I. (2003) *Footsteps in the Dust*. Nursling, Hampshire. Privately published

Mayoss, R. (1995) *A Taste for Dust*. London: Minerva Press.

Maxwell, M. (2000) *Land of the Long Grass*. Weltevredenpark SA: Covos Day Books.

Morris, C. (1961) *The Hour after Midnight: A missionary's experiences of the racial and political struggle in Northern Rhodesia*. London: Longman.

Morris, C. (1969) *Unyoung, Uncoloured, Unpoor*. London: Epworth Press.

Morris, K. (2000) *A Zambian Odyssey 1958-1998*. UK. Privately Published.

Morrish, J. (2011) *A Decade in Africa*. Eastbourne, UK: Pearl Press.

O'Connell-Jones, B. (2008) A*mazing Grace*. Hillcrest SA: Grace Gospel Church.

Parkyn, A. (2012) *Roses under the Miombo Trees: An English girl in Rhodesia*. Beauchamp, Leicestershire: Matador.

Pitchford, J. (2013) *The Last District Officer*. Kinloss, Moray: Librario Publishing. Kindle Edition.

Prain, R. (1981) *Reflections on an Era: Fifty Years of Mining in Changing Africa. The Autobiography of Sir Ronald Prain*. Letchworth, Surrey: Metal Bulletin Books.

Rukavina, K. (1951) *Jungle Pathfinder: The Biography of Chirupula Stephenson*. London: Hutchinson.

Sadler, E. (2013) *My Life: A story of my life in letters*. CreateSpace Independent Publishing Platform. Kindle Edition.

Salmon, D. (2009) *Letters from Africa*. Privately published, no publication place given.

Salmon, D. (2012) *Letters from Africa. Volume 2*. Privately published, no publication place given.

Salmon, D (2014)) *Letters from Africa. Volume 3*. Privately published, no publication place given.

Sampson, R. (2002) *With Sword and Chain in Lusaka: A Londoner's life in Zambia 1948-1972*.Victoria BC: Trafford.

Sardanis, A. (2003) *Africa, Another Side of the Coin: Northern Rhodesia's final years and Zambia's nationhood.* London: I.B. Tauris.

Schofield, S. (ed.) (1993) *The Donas Remember.* Privately Published. Kindle Edition.

Short, R. (1973) *African Sunset.* London: Johnson.

Smith, L. (2009) *Returning to Myself.* Durban, KwaZulu: Fish Eagle Books.

Snelson, P. (1992) *To Independence and Beyond: Memoirs of a Colonial and Commonwealth Civil Servant.* London: The Radcliffe Press

Stevens, P. (2012) *White Bird Under the Sun.* Privately Published.

Taylor, S. (2000) *Livingstone's Tribe: A journey from Zanzibar to the Cape.* London: Flamingo.

Temple, M. (1991) *New hope for Africa: With a bicycle from Nairobi to Kariba.* Reading, UK: Taurus.

Temple, M. (eds R. Quine & R. Lubett) (2010) *Zambia Stole my Heart.* London: Millipede Books.

Zukas, S. (2002) *Into Exile and Back.* Lusaka: Bookworld Publishers.

Zulu, A. (2007) *Memoirs of Alexander Grey Zulu.* Lusaka: Times of Zambia Publishing.

OFFICIAL PUBLICATIONS

Central Statistical Office, Zambia (1965) *Final Report of the September 1961 Census of Non-Africans.* Lusaka: Government of the Republic of Zambia.

Hansard *Debate on Northern Rhodesia (African Development)* HC Deb 1st June 1956 vol. 553 cc656-80

HMG (1926) *Colonial Report Northern Rhodesia, 1924-25.* London: HMSO.

HMG Colonial Office (1933) *Annual Report on the social and economic progress of the people of Northern Rhodesia.* London: HMSO.

HMG Colonial Office (1938) Report on the social and economic progress of the people of Northern Rhodesia - 1937. Annual Colonial Reports No 1868. London: HMSO (available online: http://libsysdigi.library.illinois.edu/ilharvest/Africana/Books2011-05/3064635/3064635_1937/3064635_1937_opt.pdf

HMG Colonial Office (1956) *Colonial Reports – Northern Rhodesia, 1955.* London: HMSO

HMG Colonial Office(1962) *Report on Northern Rhodesia*. London: HMSO.

Northern Rhodesia Government (1963) *Staff List*. The Government Printer: Lusaka.

Northern Rhodesian Information Office (1953) *The Northern Rhodesia Handbook*. The Government Printer: Lusaka.

The Rhodes-Livingstone Museum (1955-64) *Northern Rhodesia Journal* Vol I-V. Lusaka. The Government Printer available online at http://www.nrzam. org.uk

BLOGS & WEBSITES

Robin Clay: http://www.spanglefish.com/RobinClay/index.asp

Northern Rhodesians and Zambians Worldwide: http://www.zambiaworldwide. org

Northern Rhodesia and Zambia: http://www.nrzam.org.uk

The Great North Road http://www.greatnorthroad.org (dormant, but can still be searched)

Lightning Source UK Ltd.
Milton Keynes UK
UKOW06f1922190315

248195UK00014B/292/P